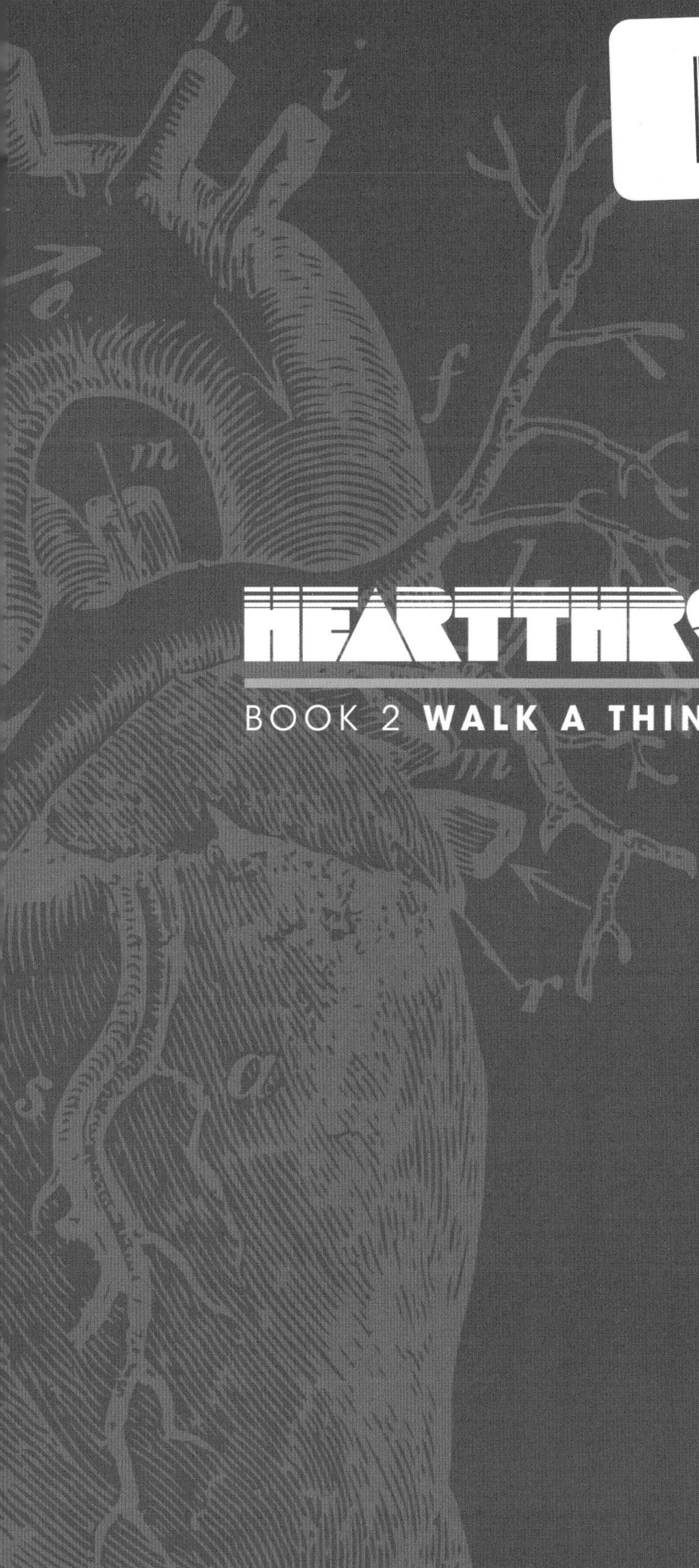

HEARTTHROB

BOOK 2 **WALK A THIN LINE**

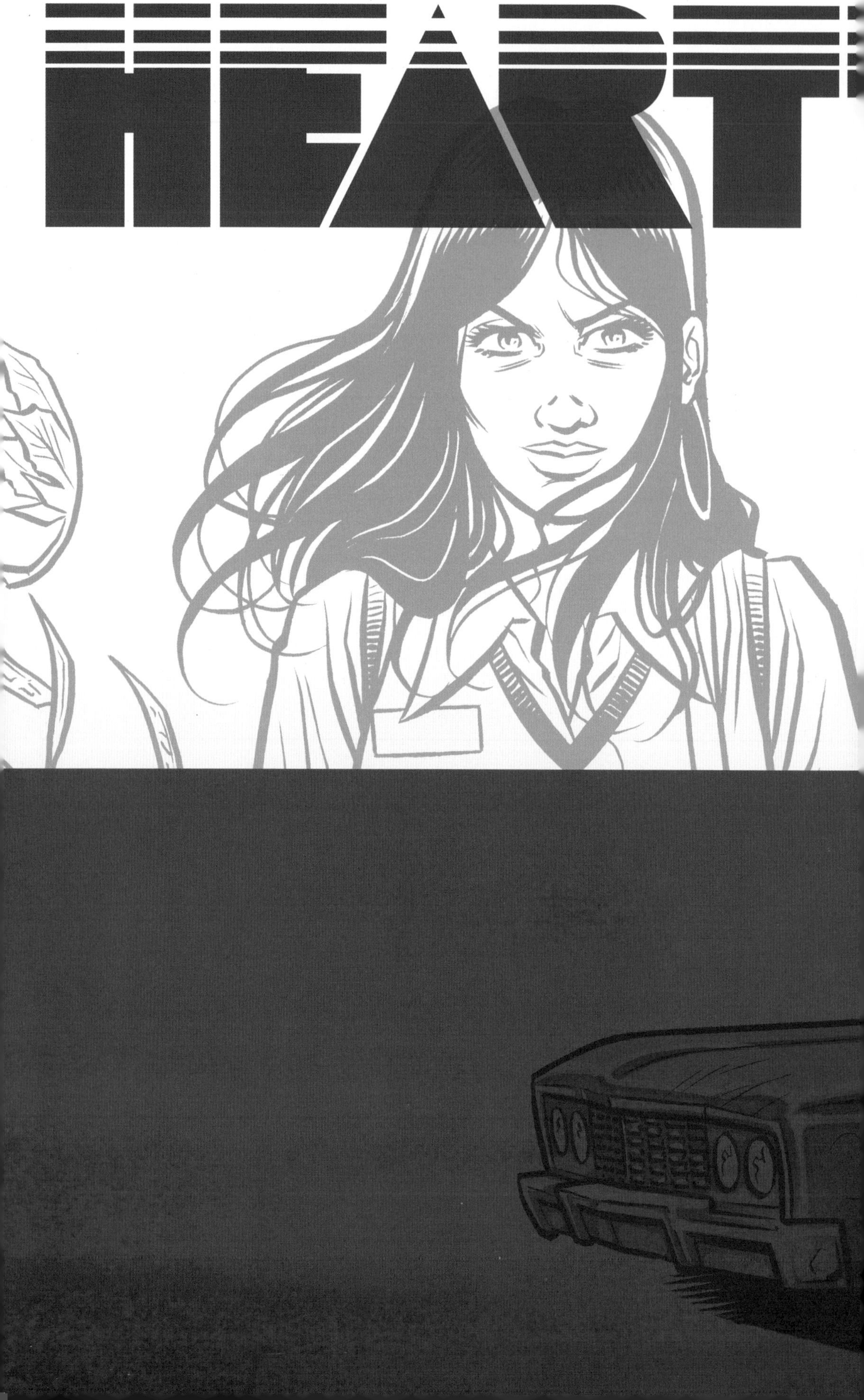
HEART

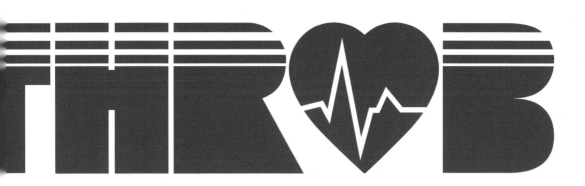

BOOK 2 WALK A THIN LINE

WRITTEN BY
CHRISTOPHER SEBELA

ILLUSTRATED BY
ROBERT WILSON IV

COLORED BY
NICK FILARDI

LETTERED BY **CRANK!**

DESIGNED BY **DYLAN TODD**

EDITED BY **DESIREE WILSON**

AN ONI PRESS PUBLICATION

CHAPTER 1

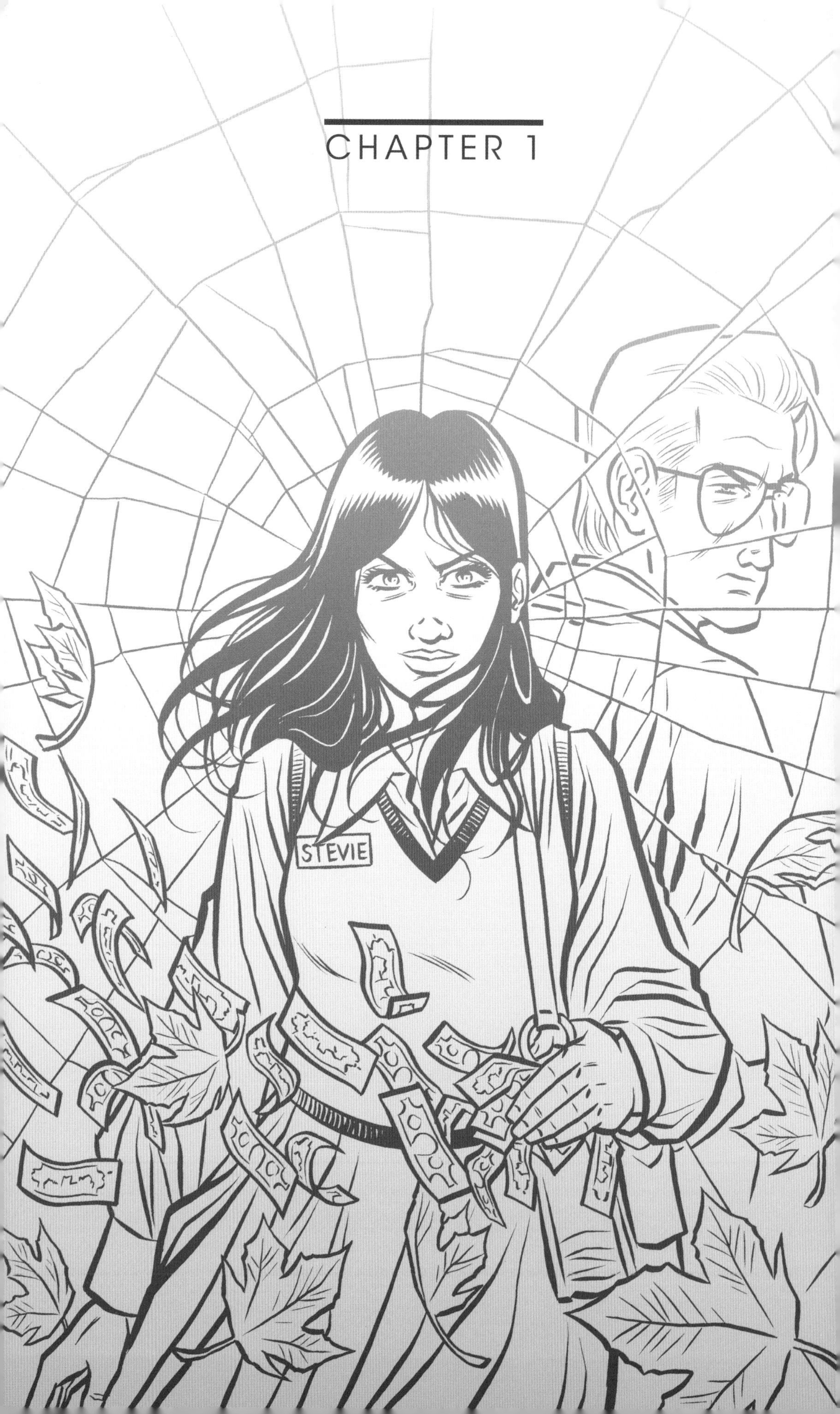
STEVIE

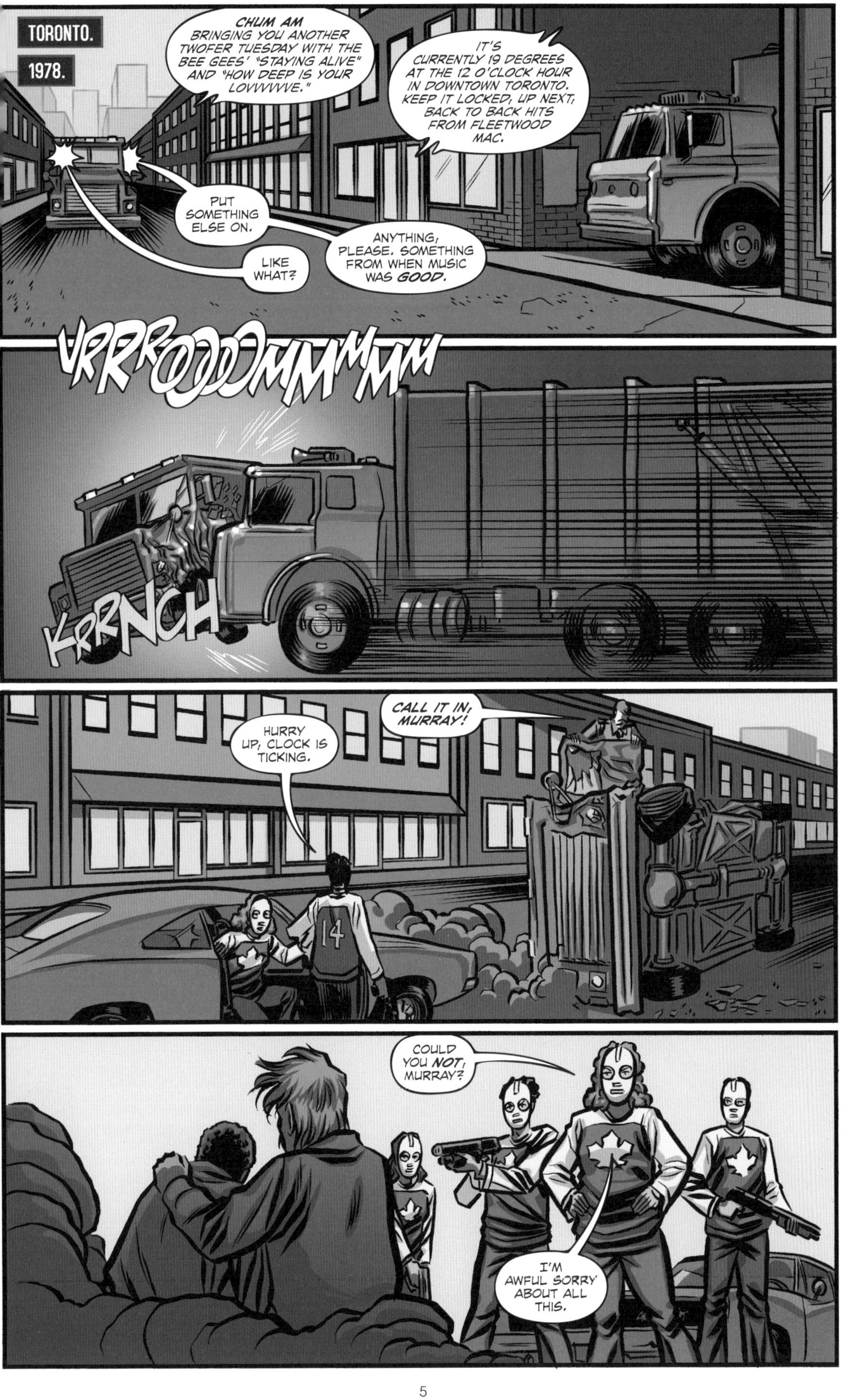
TORONTO.
1978.
CHUM AM BRINGING YOU ANOTHER TWOFER TUESDAY WITH THE BEE GEES' "STAYING ALIVE" AND "HOW DEEP IS YOUR LOVVVVVVE."
IT'S CURRENTLY 19 DEGREES AT THE 12 O'CLOCK HOUR IN DOWNTOWN TORONTO. KEEP IT LOCKED, UP NEXT, BACK TO BACK HITS FROM FLEETWOOD MAC.
PUT SOMETHING ELSE ON.
LIKE WHAT?
ANYTHING, PLEASE. SOMETHING FROM WHEN MUSIC WAS GOOD.
VRRROOOOMMMMM
KRRNCH
HURRY UP, CLOCK IS TICKING.
CALL IT IN, MURRAY!
COULD YOU NOT, MURRAY?
I'M AWFUL SORRY ABOUT ALL THIS.

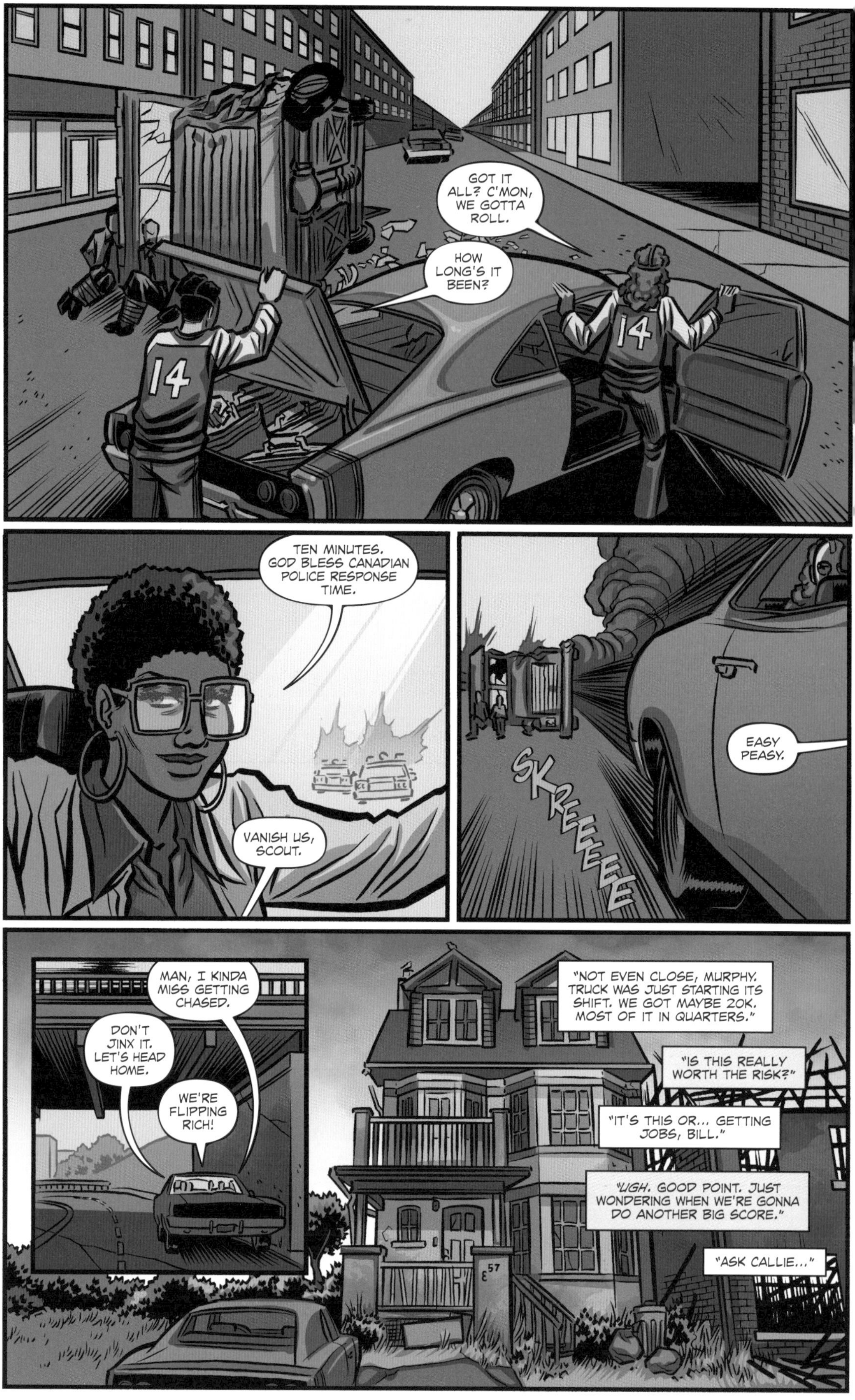
GOT IT ALL? C'MON, WE GOTTA ROLL.
HOW LONG'S IT BEEN?
TEN MINUTES. GOD BLESS CANADIAN POLICE RESPONSE TIME.
VANISH US, SCOUT.
EASY PEASY.
SKREEEEEE
MAN, I KINDA MISS GETTING CHASED.
DON'T JINX IT. LET'S HEAD HOME.
WE'RE FLIPPING RICH!
"NOT EVEN CLOSE, MURPHY. TRUCK WAS JUST STARTING ITS SHIFT. WE GOT MAYBE 20K. MOST OF IT IN QUARTERS."
"IS THIS REALLY WORTH THE RISK?"
"IT'S THIS OR... GETTING JOBS, BILL."
"UGH. GOOD POINT. JUST WONDERING WHEN WE'RE GONNA DO ANOTHER BIG SCORE."
"ASK CALLIE..."

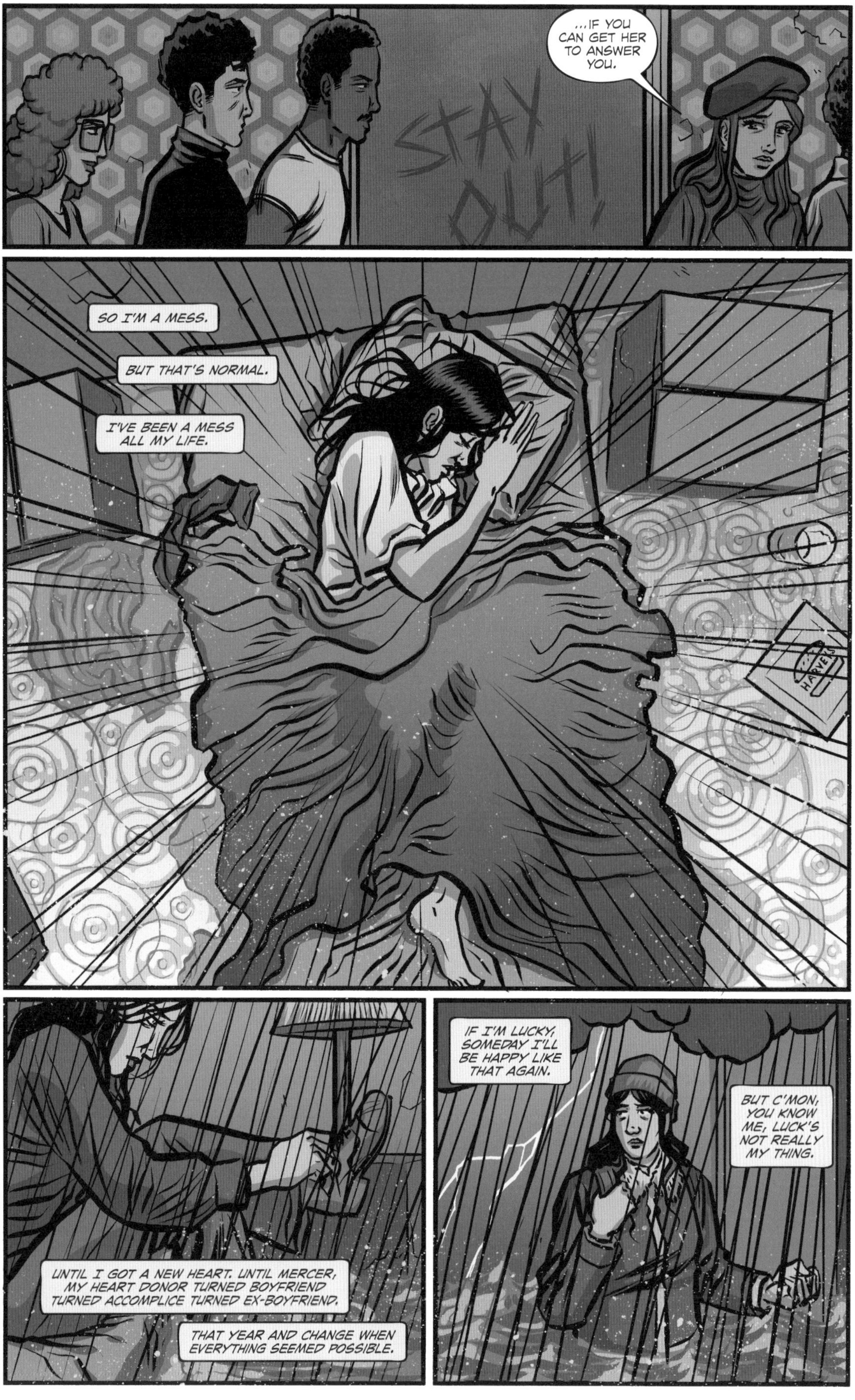
STAY OUT!
...IF YOU CAN GET HER TO ANSWER YOU.
SO I'M A MESS.
BUT THAT'S NORMAL.
I'VE BEEN A MESS ALL MY LIFE.
HARVEYS
UNTIL I GOT A NEW HEART. UNTIL MERCER, MY HEART DONOR TURNED BOYFRIEND TURNED ACCOMPLICE TURNED EX-BOYFRIEND.
THAT YEAR AND CHANGE WHEN EVERYTHING SEEMED POSSIBLE.
IF I'M LUCKY, SOMEDAY I'LL BE HAPPY LIKE THAT AGAIN.
BUT C'MON, YOU KNOW ME, LUCK'S NOT REALLY MY THING.

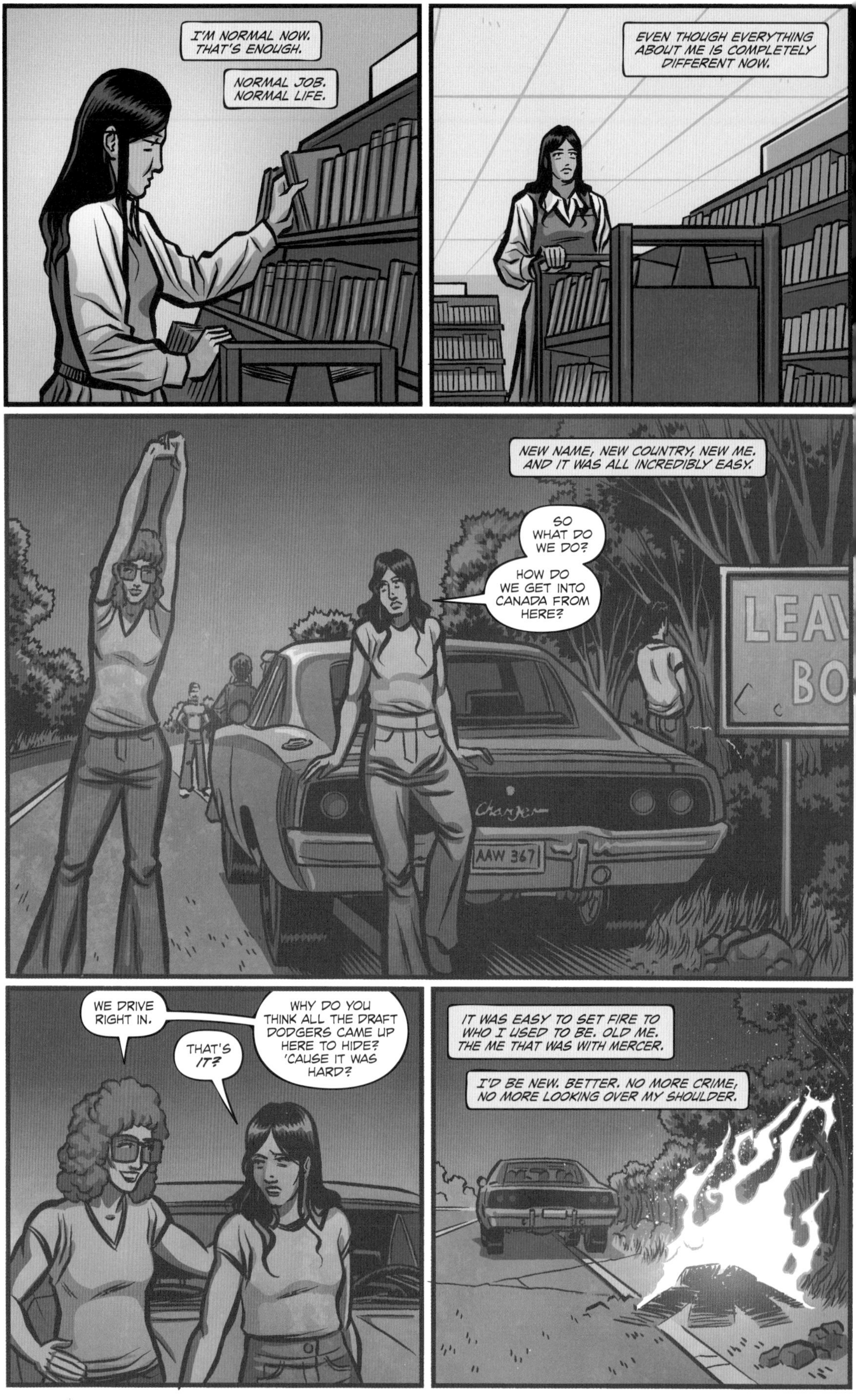
I'M NORMAL NOW. THAT'S ENOUGH.
NORMAL JOB. NORMAL LIFE.
EVEN THOUGH EVERYTHING ABOUT ME IS COMPLETELY DIFFERENT NOW.
NEW NAME, NEW COUNTRY, NEW ME. AND IT WAS ALL INCREDIBLY EASY.
SO WHAT DO WE DO?
HOW DO WE GET INTO CANADA FROM HERE?
LEAV
BO
Charger
AAW 367
WE DRIVE RIGHT IN.
THAT'S IT?
WHY DO YOU THINK ALL THE DRAFT DODGERS CAME UP HERE TO HIDE? 'CAUSE IT WAS HARD?
IT WAS EASY TO SET FIRE TO WHO I USED TO BE. OLD ME. THE ME THAT WAS WITH MERCER.
I'D BE NEW. BETTER. NO MORE CRIME, NO MORE LOOKING OVER MY SHOULDER.

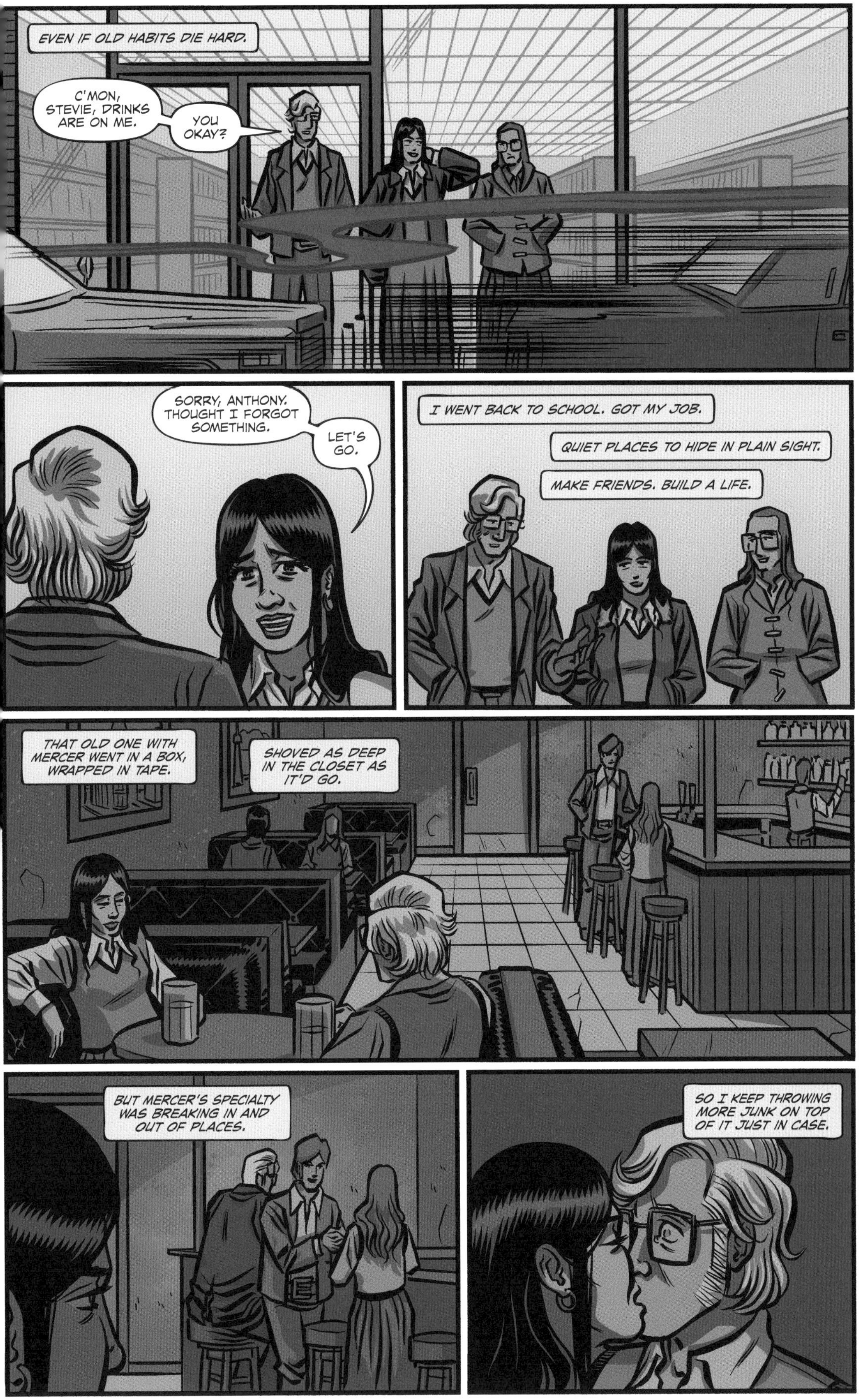
EVEN IF OLD HABITS DIE HARD.
C'MON, STEVIE, DRINKS ARE ON ME.
YOU OKAY?
SORRY, ANTHONY. THOUGHT I FORGOT SOMETHING.
LET'S GO.
I WENT BACK TO SCHOOL. GOT MY JOB.
QUIET PLACES TO HIDE IN PLAIN SIGHT.
MAKE FRIENDS. BUILD A LIFE.
THAT OLD ONE WITH MERCER WENT IN A BOX, WRAPPED IN TAPE.
SHOVED AS DEEP IN THE CLOSET AS IT'D GO.
BUT MERCER'S SPECIALTY WAS BREAKING IN AND OUT OF PLACES.
SO I KEEP THROWING MORE JUNK ON TOP OF IT JUST IN CASE.

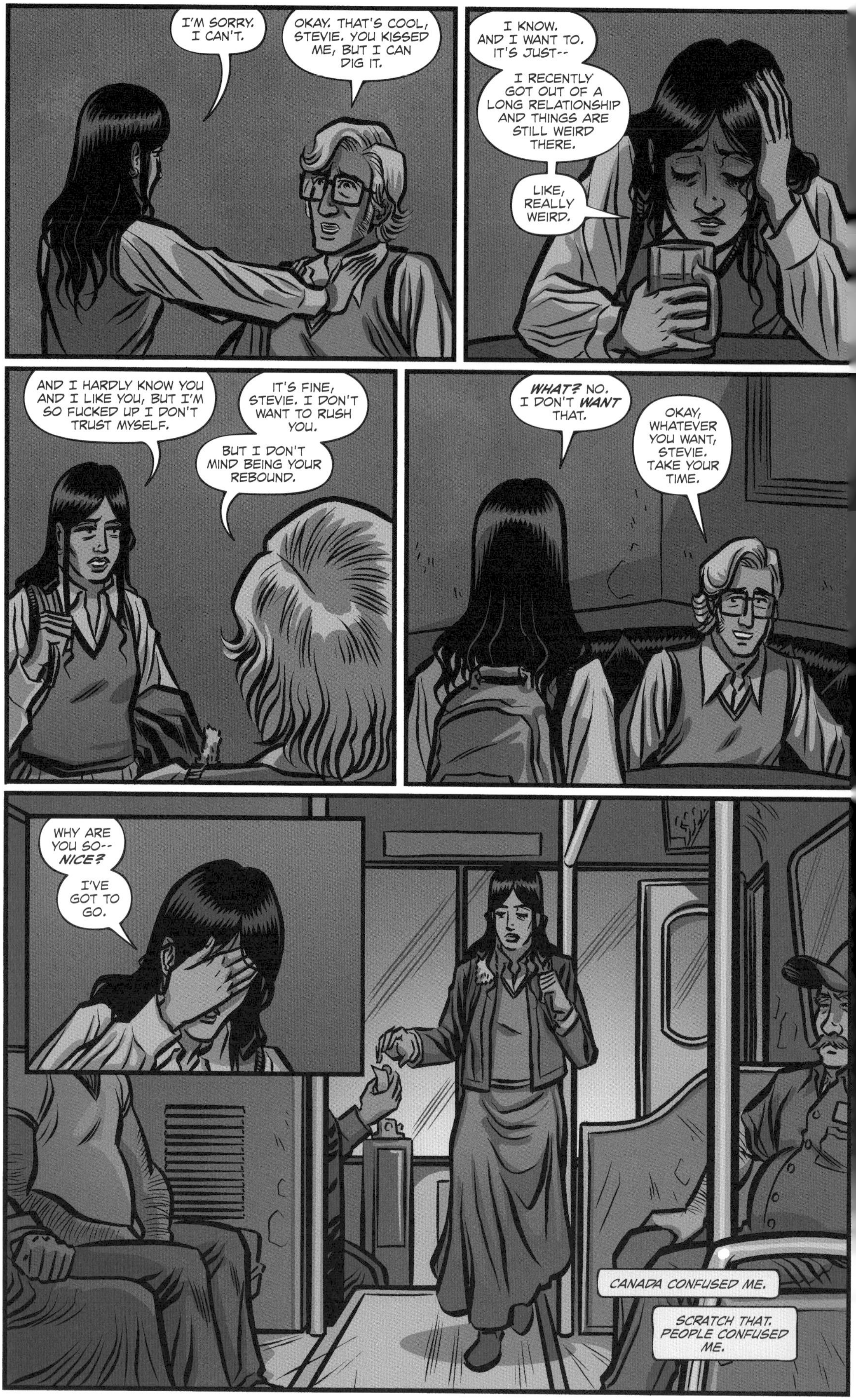
I'M SORRY. I CAN'T.
OKAY. THAT'S COOL, STEVIE. YOU KISSED ME, BUT I CAN DIG IT.
I KNOW. AND I WANT TO. IT'S JUST--
I RECENTLY GOT OUT OF A LONG RELATIONSHIP AND THINGS ARE STILL WEIRD THERE.
LIKE, REALLY WEIRD.
AND I HARDLY KNOW YOU AND I LIKE YOU, BUT I'M SO FUCKED UP I DON'T TRUST MYSELF.
IT'S FINE, STEVIE. I DON'T WANT TO RUSH YOU.
BUT I DON'T MIND BEING YOUR REBOUND.
WHAT? NO. I DON'T WANT THAT.
OKAY, WHATEVER YOU WANT, STEVIE. TAKE YOUR TIME.
WHY ARE YOU SO-- NICE?
I'VE GOT TO GO.
CANADA CONFUSED ME.
SCRATCH THAT. PEOPLE CONFUSED ME.

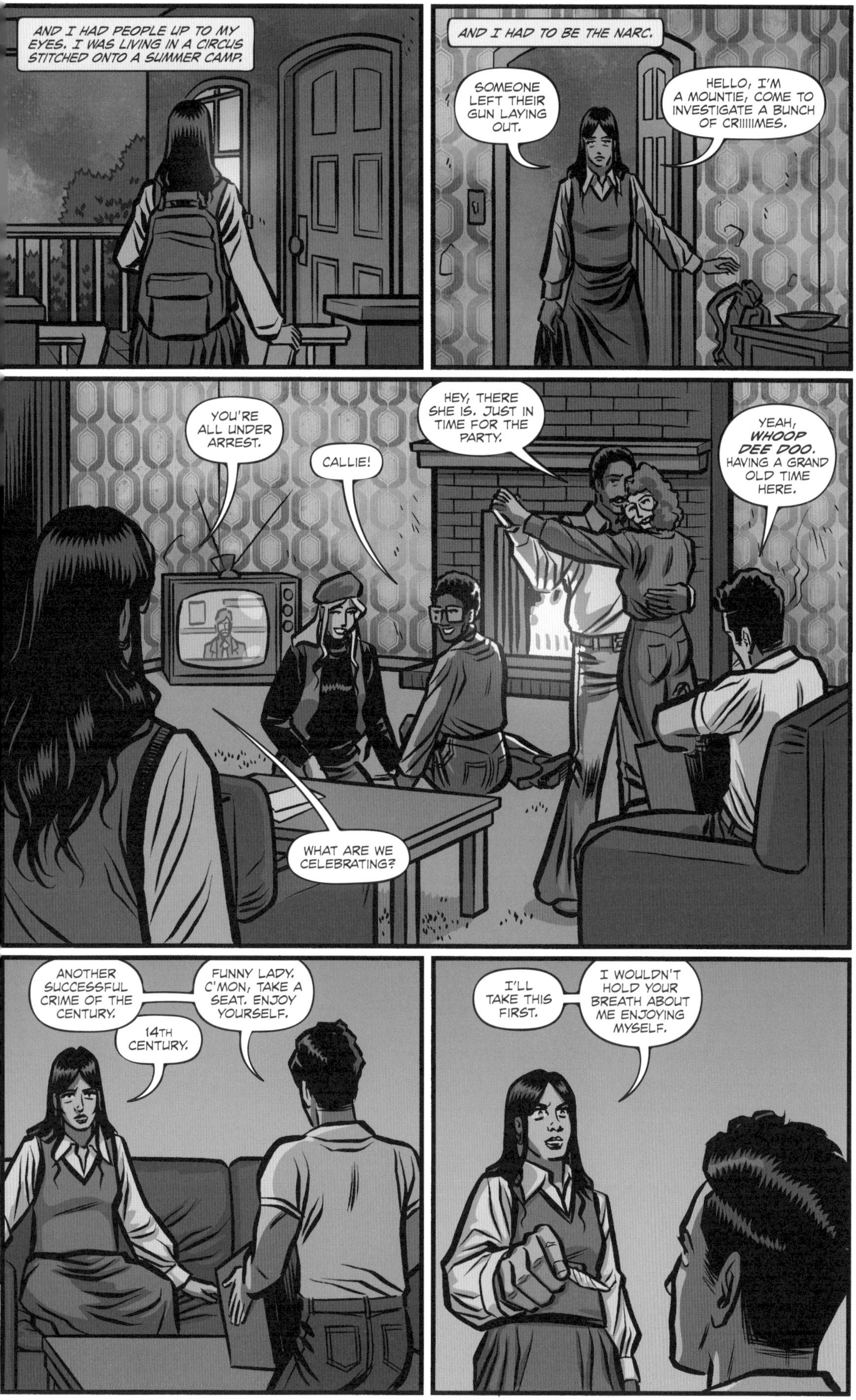
AND I HAD PEOPLE UP TO MY EYES. I WAS LIVING IN A CIRCUS STITCHED ONTO A SUMMER CAMP.
AND I HAD TO BE THE NARC.
SOMEONE LEFT THEIR GUN LAYING OUT.
HELLO, I'M A MOUNTIE, COME TO INVESTIGATE A BUNCH OF CRIIIIIMES.
YOU'RE ALL UNDER ARREST.
CALLIE!
HEY, THERE SHE IS. JUST IN TIME FOR THE PARTY.
YEAH, WHOOP DEE DOO. HAVING A GRAND OLD TIME HERE.
WHAT ARE WE CELEBRATING?
ANOTHER SUCCESSFUL CRIME OF THE CENTURY.
14TH CENTURY.
FUNNY LADY. C'MON, TAKE A SEAT. ENJOY YOURSELF.
I'LL TAKE THIS FIRST.
I WOULDN'T HOLD YOUR BREATH ABOUT ME ENJOYING MYSELF.

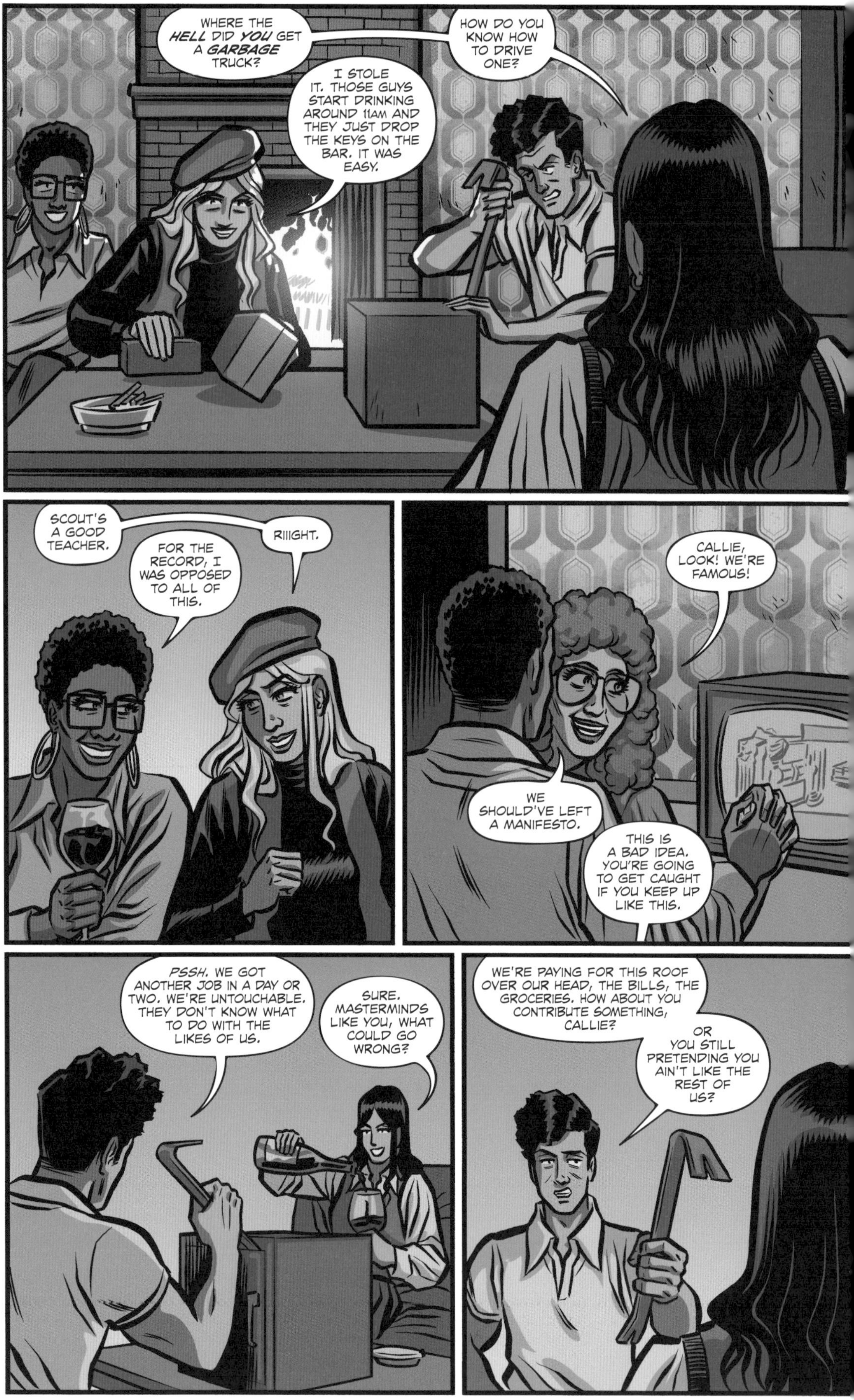
WHERE THE *HELL* DID *YOU* GET A *GARBAGE* TRUCK?
HOW DO YOU KNOW HOW TO DRIVE ONE?
I STOLE IT. THOSE GUYS START DRINKING AROUND 11AM AND THEY JUST DROP THE KEYS ON THE BAR. IT WAS EASY.
SCOUT'S A GOOD TEACHER.
RIIIGHT.
FOR THE RECORD, I WAS OPPOSED TO ALL OF THIS.
CALLIE, LOOK! WE'RE FAMOUS!
WE SHOULD'VE LEFT A MANIFESTO.
THIS IS A BAD IDEA. YOU'RE GOING TO GET CAUGHT IF YOU KEEP UP LIKE THIS.
PSSH. WE GOT ANOTHER JOB IN A DAY OR TWO. WE'RE UNTOUCHABLE. THEY DON'T KNOW WHAT TO DO WITH THE LIKES OF US.
SURE. MASTERMINDS LIKE YOU, WHAT COULD GO WRONG?
WE'RE PAYING FOR THIS ROOF OVER OUR HEAD, THE BILLS, THE GROCERIES. HOW ABOUT YOU CONTRIBUTE SOMETHING, CALLIE?
OR YOU STILL PRETENDING YOU AIN'T LIKE THE REST OF US?

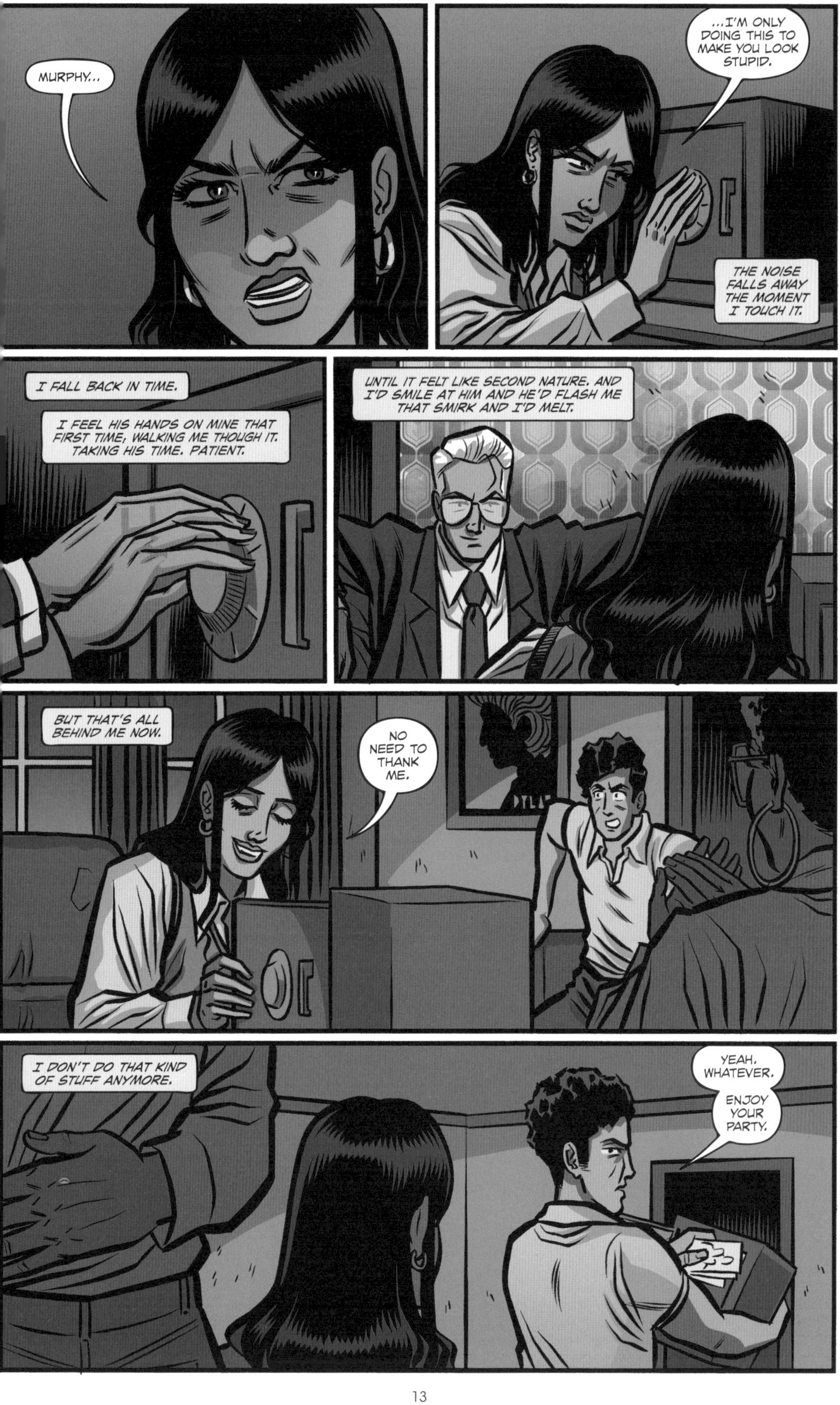

MURPHY...
...I'M ONLY DOING THIS TO MAKE YOU LOOK STUPID.
THE NOISE FALLS AWAY THE MOMENT I TOUCH IT.
I FALL BACK IN TIME.
I FEEL HIS HANDS ON MINE THAT FIRST TIME, WALKING ME THOUGH IT. TAKING HIS TIME. PATIENT.
UNTIL IT FELT LIKE SECOND NATURE. AND I'D SMILE AT HIM AND HE'D FLASH ME THAT SMIRK AND I'D MELT.
BUT THAT'S ALL BEHIND ME NOW.
NO NEED TO THANK ME.
I DON'T DO THAT KIND OF STUFF ANYMORE.
YEAH. WHATEVER.
ENJOY YOUR PARTY.

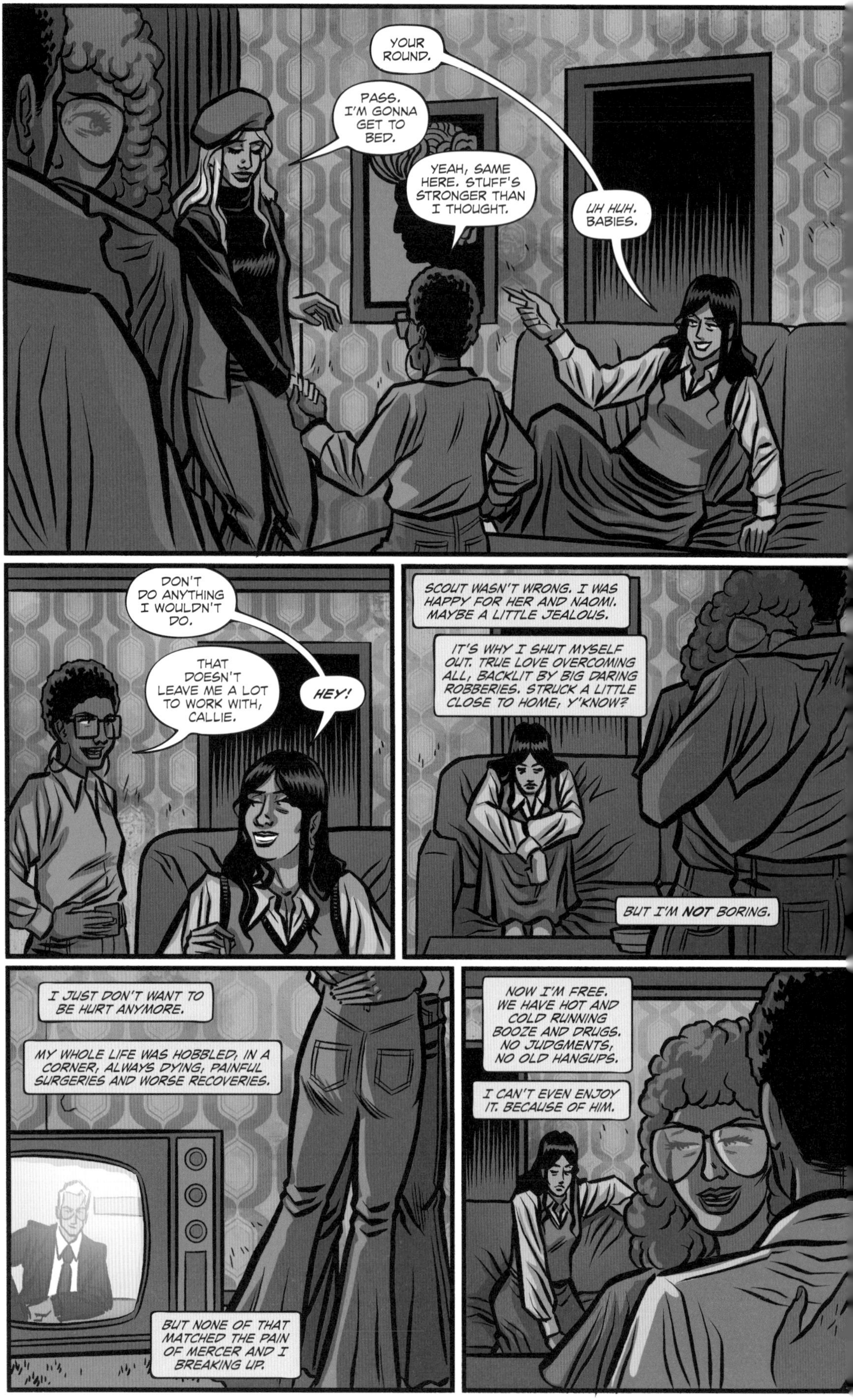
YOUR ROUND.
PASS. I'M GONNA GET TO BED.
YEAH, SAME HERE. STUFF'S STRONGER THAN I THOUGHT.
UH HUH. BABIES.
DON'T DO ANYTHING I WOULDN'T DO.
THAT DOESN'T LEAVE ME A LOT TO WORK WITH, CALLIE.
HEY!
SCOUT WASN'T WRONG. I WAS HAPPY FOR HER AND NAOMI. MAYBE A LITTLE JEALOUS.
IT'S WHY I SHUT MYSELF OUT. TRUE LOVE OVERCOMING ALL, BACKLIT BY BIG DARING ROBBERIES. STRUCK A LITTLE CLOSE TO HOME, Y'KNOW?
BUT I'M **NOT** BORING.
I JUST DON'T WANT TO BE HURT ANYMORE.
MY WHOLE LIFE WAS HOBBLED, IN A CORNER, ALWAYS DYING, PAINFUL SURGERIES AND WORSE RECOVERIES.
BUT NONE OF THAT MATCHED THE PAIN OF MERCER AND I BREAKING UP.
NOW I'M FREE. WE HAVE HOT AND COLD RUNNING BOOZE AND DRUGS. NO JUDGMENTS, NO OLD HANGUPS.
I CAN'T EVEN ENJOY IT. BECAUSE OF HIM.

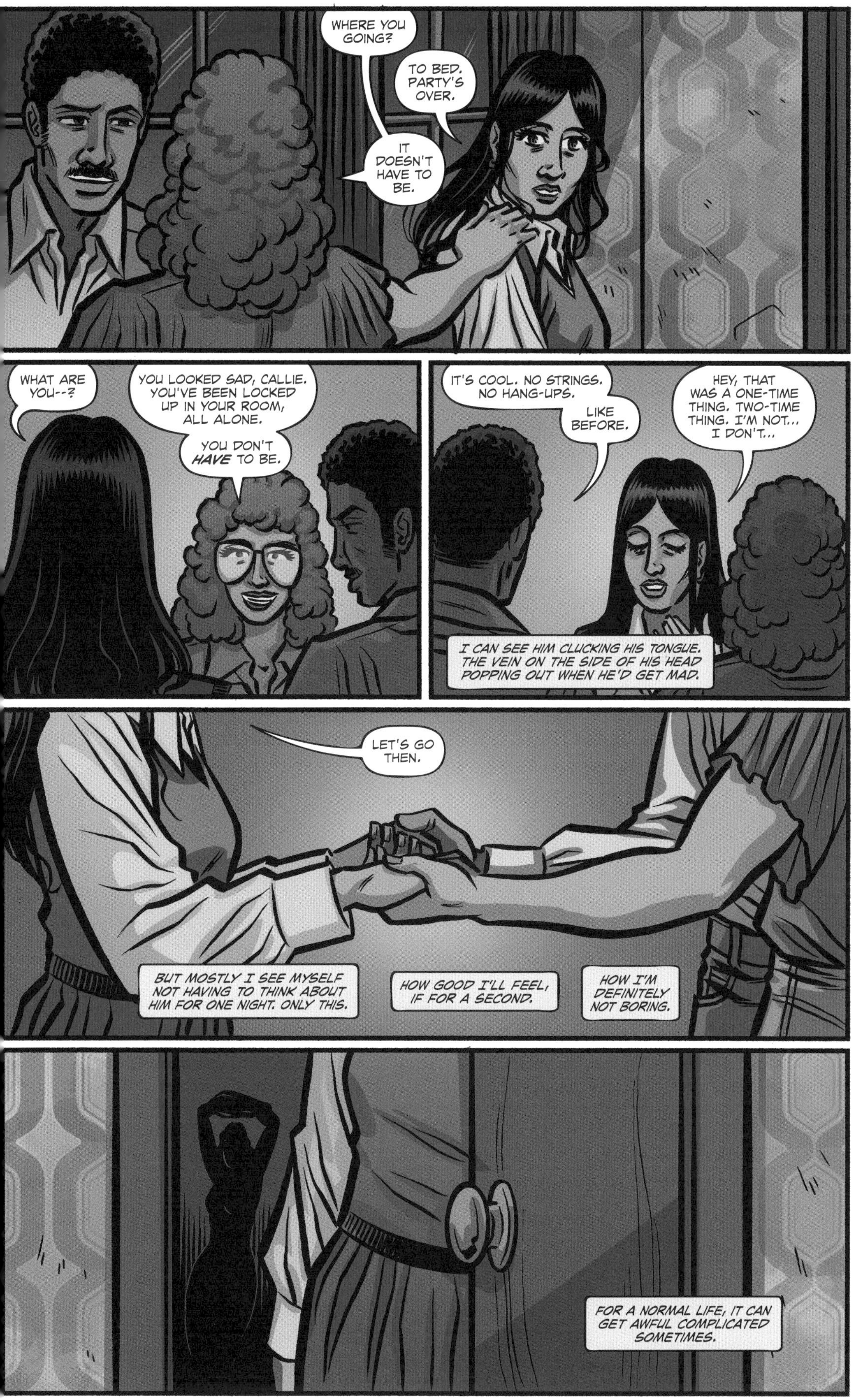
WHERE YOU GOING?
TO BED. PARTY'S OVER.
IT DOESN'T HAVE TO BE.
WHAT ARE YOU--?
YOU LOOKED SAD, CALLIE. YOU'VE BEEN LOCKED UP IN YOUR ROOM, ALL ALONE.
YOU DON'T *HAVE* TO BE.
IT'S COOL. NO STRINGS. NO HANG-UPS.
LIKE BEFORE.
HEY, THAT WAS A ONE-TIME THING. TWO-TIME THING. I'M NOT... I DON'T...
I CAN SEE HIM CLUCKING HIS TONGUE. THE VEIN ON THE SIDE OF HIS HEAD POPPING OUT WHEN HE'D GET MAD.
LET'S GO THEN.
BUT MOSTLY I SEE MYSELF NOT HAVING TO THINK ABOUT HIM FOR ONE NIGHT. ONLY THIS.
HOW GOOD I'LL FEEL, IF FOR A SECOND.
HOW I'M DEFINITELY NOT BORING.
FOR A NORMAL LIFE, IT CAN GET AWFUL COMPLICATED SOMETIMES.

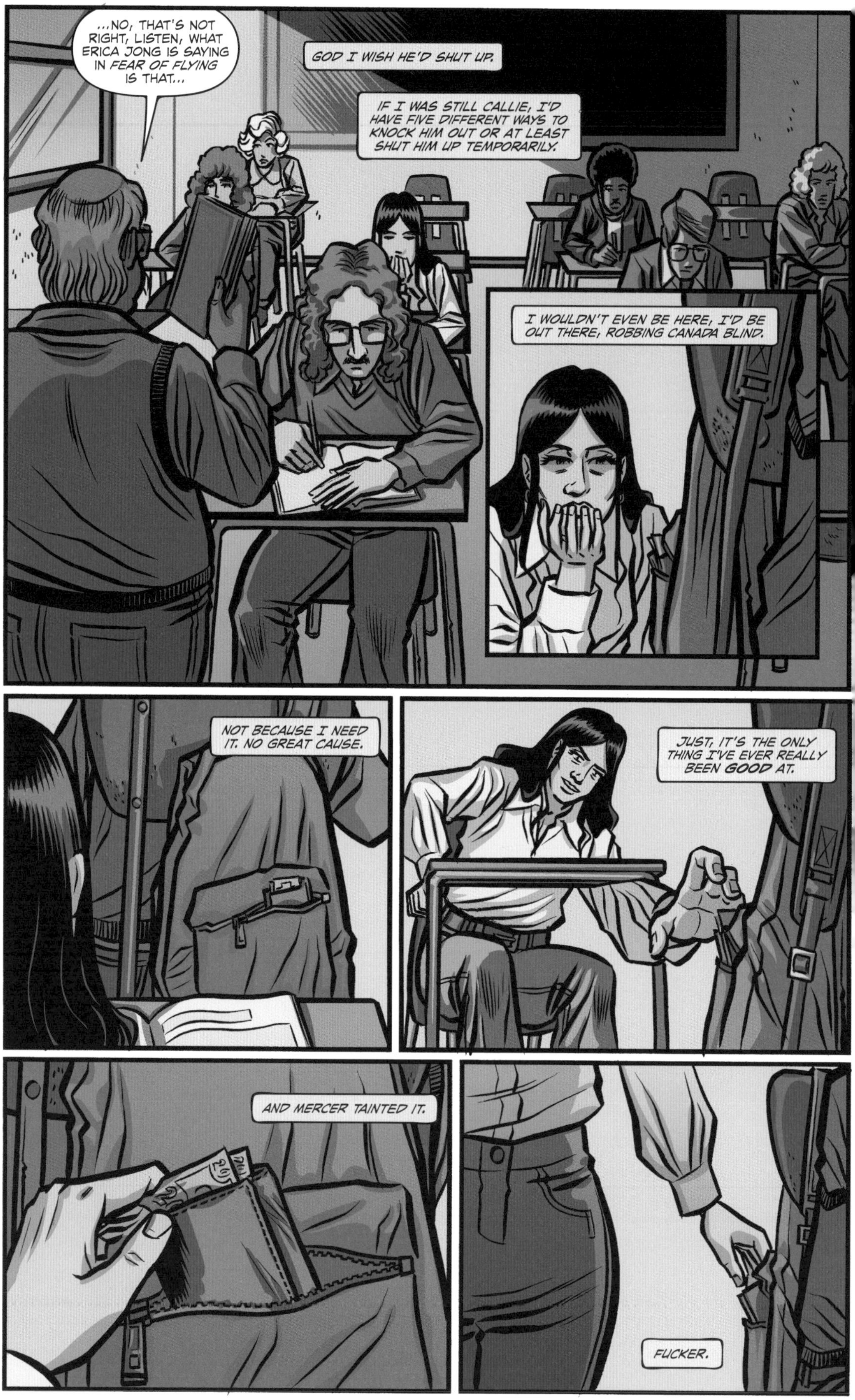
...NO, THAT'S NOT RIGHT, LISTEN, WHAT ERICA JONG IS SAYING IN FEAR OF FLYING IS THAT...
GOD I WISH HE'D SHUT UP.
IF I WAS STILL CALLIE, I'D HAVE FIVE DIFFERENT WAYS TO KNOCK HIM OUT OR AT LEAST SHUT HIM UP TEMPORARILY.
I WOULDN'T EVEN BE HERE; I'D BE OUT THERE, ROBBING CANADA BLIND.
NOT BECAUSE I NEED IT. NO GREAT CAUSE.
JUST, IT'S THE ONLY THING I'VE EVER REALLY BEEN GOOD AT.
AND MERCER TAINTED IT.
FUCKER.

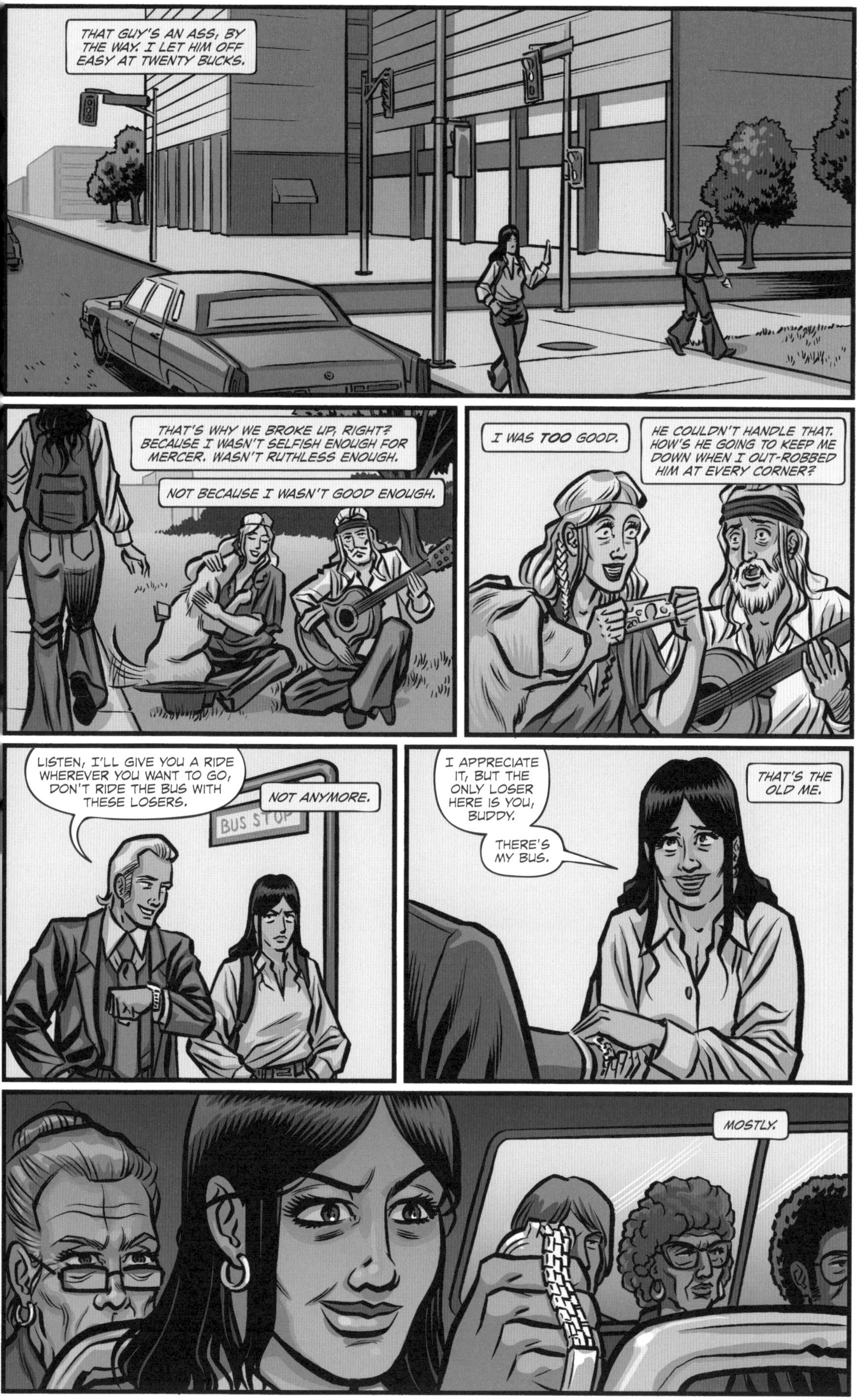
THAT GUY'S AN ASS, BY THE WAY. I LET HIM OFF EASY AT TWENTY BUCKS.
THAT'S WHY WE BROKE UP, RIGHT? BECAUSE I WASN'T SELFISH ENOUGH FOR MERCER. WASN'T RUTHLESS ENOUGH.
NOT BECAUSE I WASN'T GOOD ENOUGH.
I WAS TOO GOOD.
HE COULDN'T HANDLE THAT. HOW'S HE GOING TO KEEP ME DOWN WHEN I OUT-ROBBED HIM AT EVERY CORNER?
LISTEN, I'LL GIVE YOU A RIDE WHEREVER YOU WANT TO GO, DON'T RIDE THE BUS WITH THESE LOSERS.
BUS STOP
NOT ANYMORE.
I APPRECIATE IT, BUT THE ONLY LOSER HERE IS YOU, BUDDY.
THERE'S MY BUS.
THAT'S THE OLD ME.
MOSTLY.

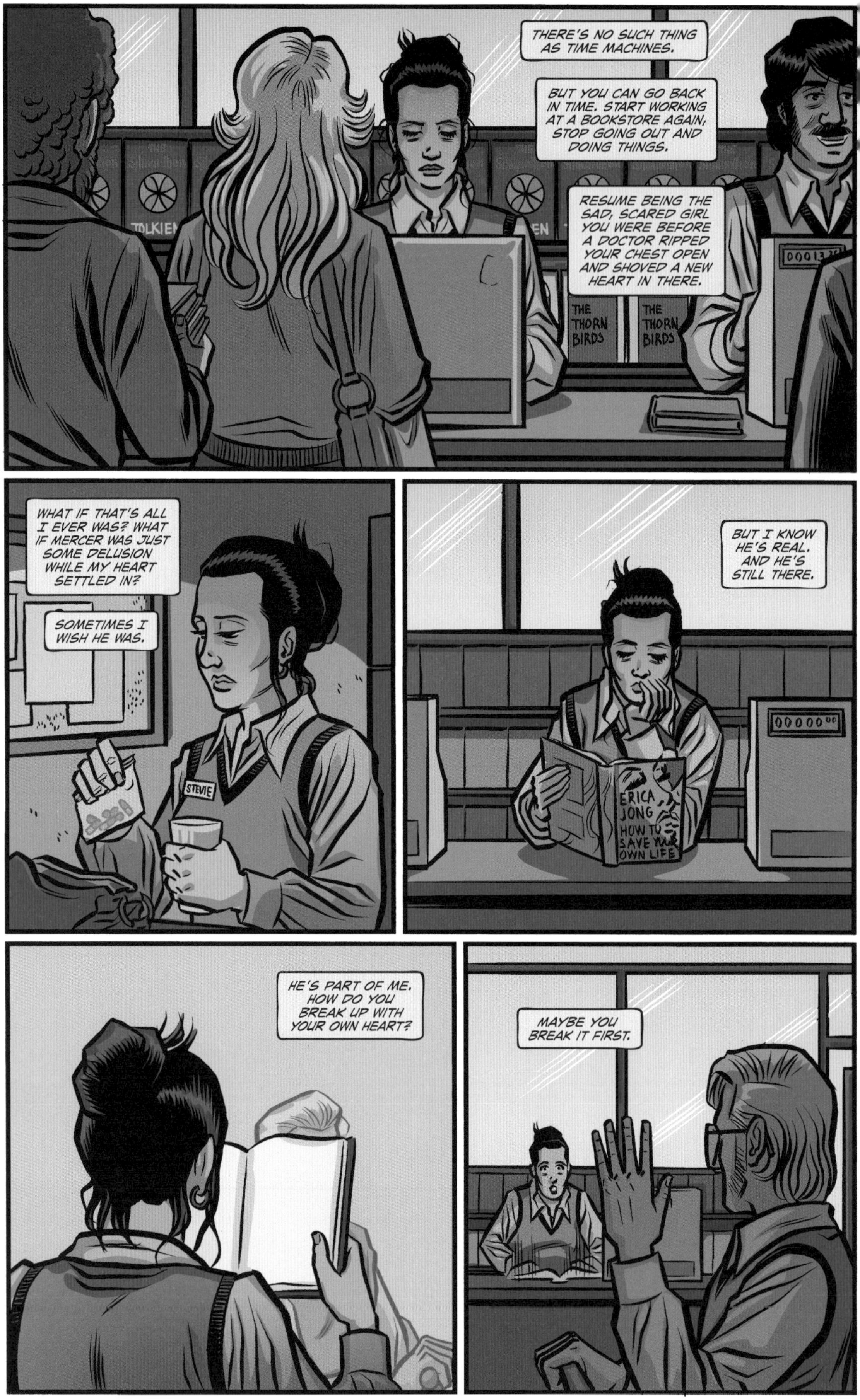

TOLKIEN
THERE'S NO SUCH THING AS TIME MACHINES.
BUT YOU CAN GO BACK IN TIME. START WORKING AT A BOOKSTORE AGAIN, STOP GOING OUT AND DOING THINGS.
RESUME BEING THE SAD, SCARED GIRL YOU WERE BEFORE A DOCTOR RIPPED YOUR CHEST OPEN AND SHOVED A NEW HEART IN THERE.
THE THORN BIRDS
THE THORN BIRDS
WHAT IF THAT'S ALL I EVER WAS? WHAT IF MERCER WAS JUST SOME DELUSION WHILE MY HEART SETTLED IN?
SOMETIMES I WISH HE WAS.
STEVIE
BUT I KNOW HE'S REAL. AND HE'S STILL THERE.
ERICA JONG
HOW TO SAVE YOUR OWN LIFE
HE'S PART OF ME. HOW DO YOU BREAK UP WITH YOUR OWN HEART?
MAYBE YOU BREAK IT FIRST.

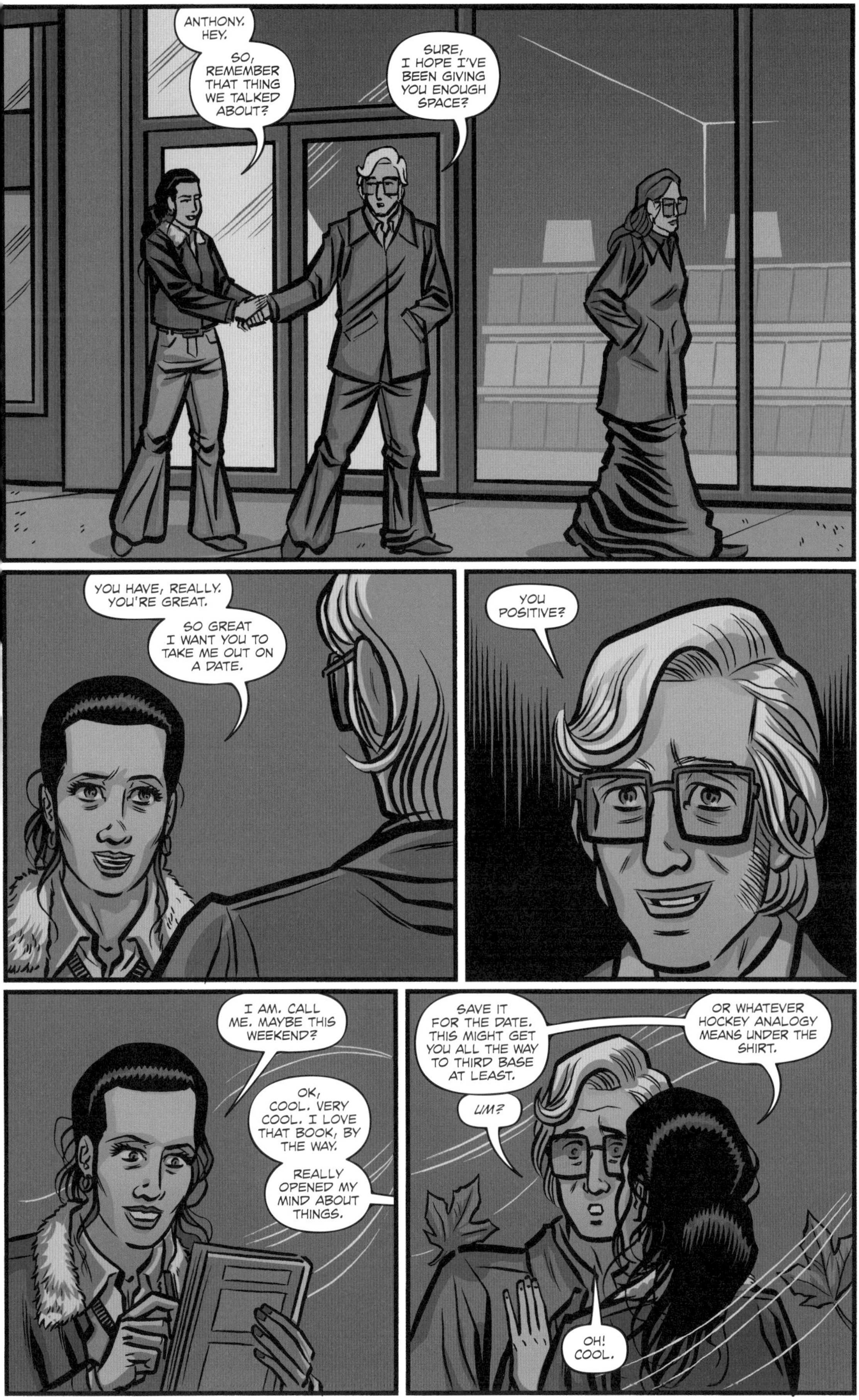
ANTHONY. HEY.
SO, REMEMBER THAT THING WE TALKED ABOUT?
SURE, I HOPE I'VE BEEN GIVING YOU ENOUGH SPACE?
YOU HAVE, REALLY. YOU'RE GREAT.
SO GREAT I WANT YOU TO TAKE ME OUT ON A DATE.
YOU POSITIVE?
I AM. CALL ME. MAYBE THIS WEEKEND?
OK, COOL. VERY COOL. I LOVE THAT BOOK, BY THE WAY.
REALLY OPENED MY MIND ABOUT THINGS.
SAVE IT FOR THE DATE. THIS MIGHT GET YOU ALL THE WAY TO THIRD BASE AT LEAST.
OR WHATEVER HOCKEY ANALOGY MEANS UNDER THE SHIRT.
UM?
OH! COOL.

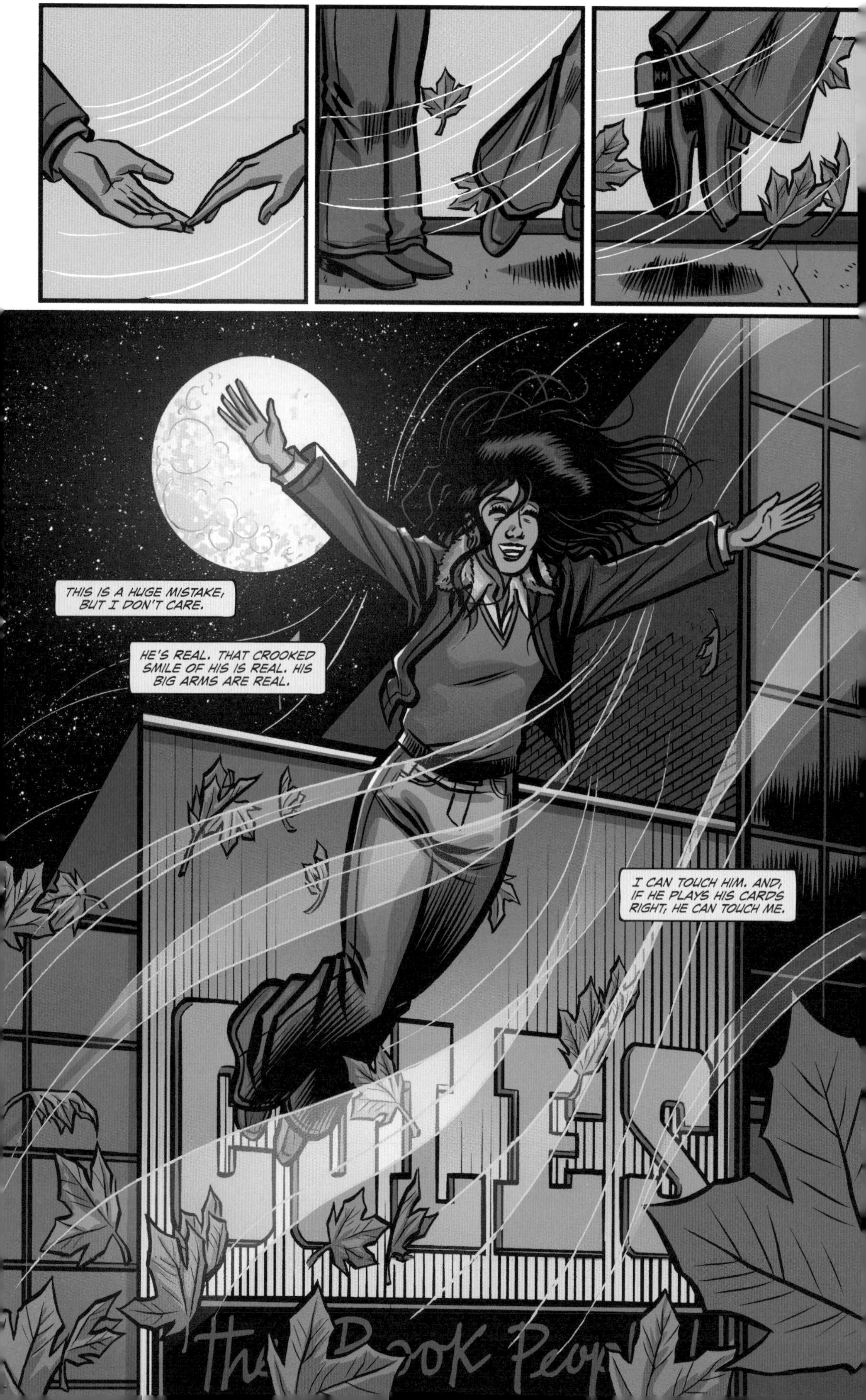
THIS IS A HUGE MISTAKE, BUT I DON'T CARE.
HE'S REAL. THAT CROOKED SMILE OF HIS IS REAL. HIS BIG ARMS ARE REAL.
I CAN TOUCH HIM. AND, IF HE PLAYS HIS CARDS RIGHT, HE CAN TOUCH ME.

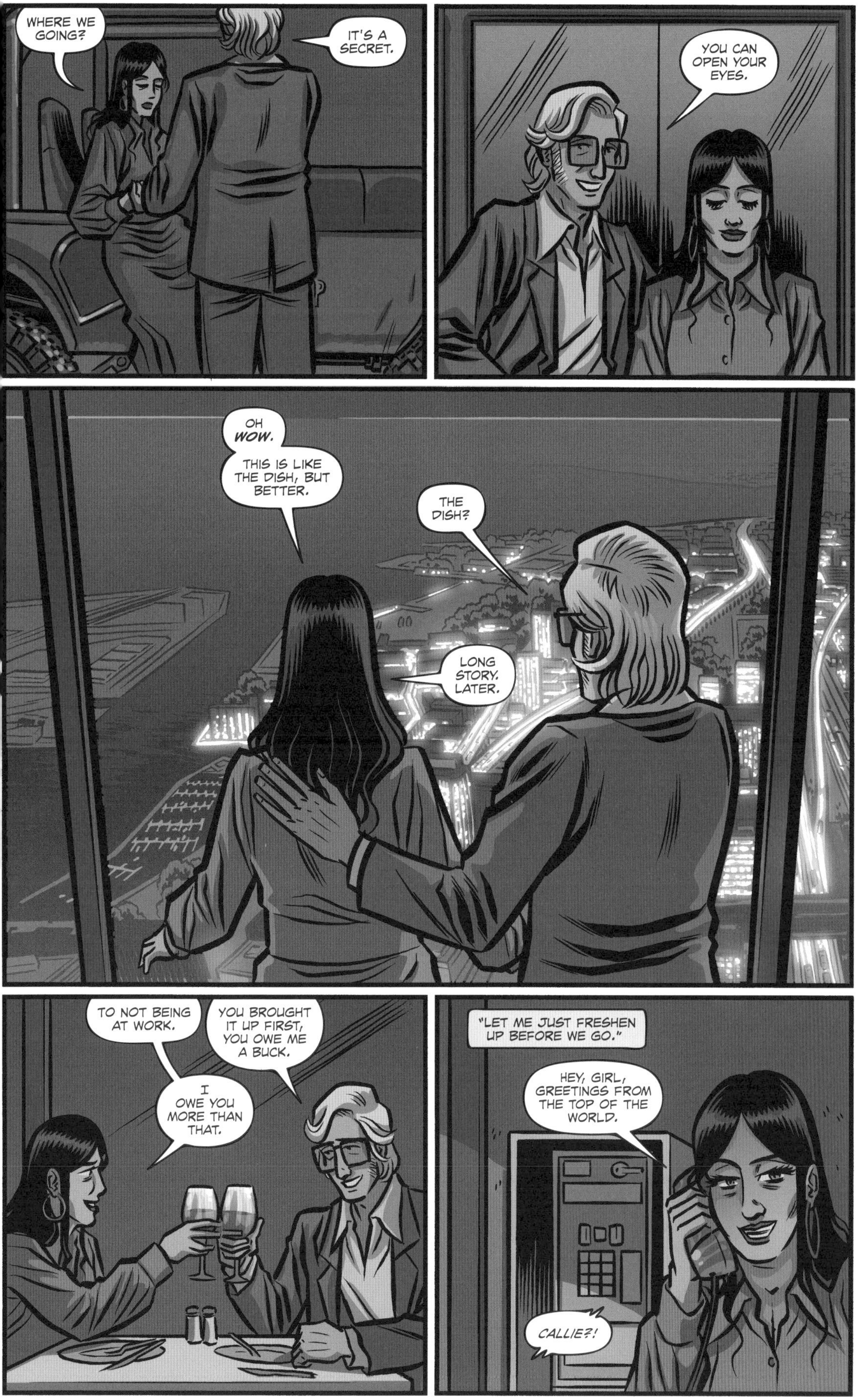
WHERE WE GOING?
IT'S A SECRET.
YOU CAN OPEN YOUR EYES.
OH *WOW*.
THIS IS LIKE THE DISH, BUT BETTER.
THE DISH?
LONG STORY. LATER.
TO NOT BEING AT WORK.
YOU BROUGHT IT UP FIRST, YOU OWE ME A BUCK.
I OWE YOU MORE THAN THAT.
"LET ME JUST FRESHEN UP BEFORE WE GO."
HEY, GIRL, GREETINGS FROM THE TOP OF THE WORLD.
CALLIE?!

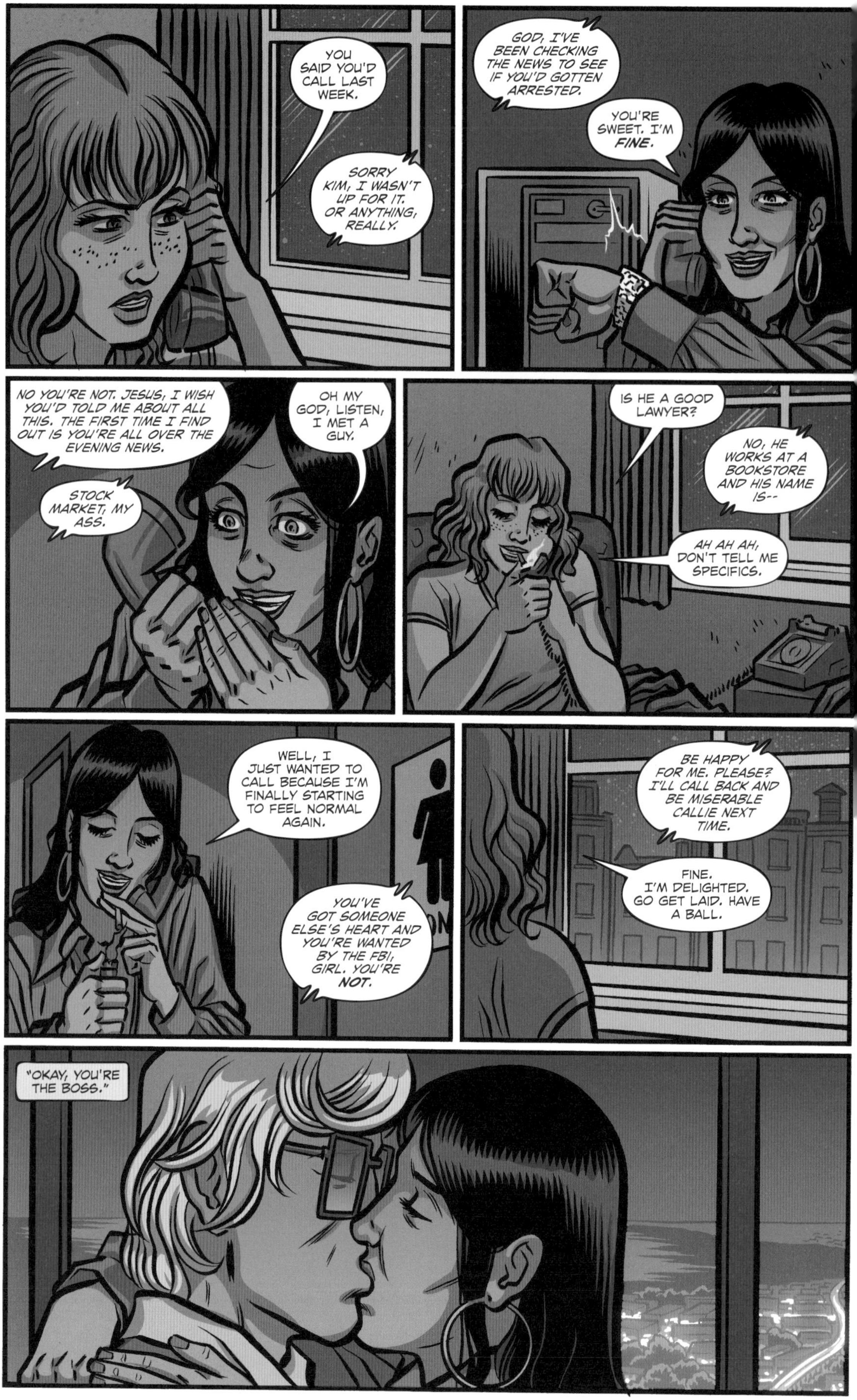
YOU SAID YOU'D CALL LAST WEEK.
SORRY KIM, I WASN'T UP FOR IT. OR ANYTHING, REALLY.
GOD, I'VE BEEN CHECKING THE NEWS TO SEE IF YOU'D GOTTEN ARRESTED.
YOU'RE SWEET. I'M FINE.
NO YOU'RE NOT. JESUS, I WISH YOU'D TOLD ME ABOUT ALL THIS. THE FIRST TIME I FIND OUT IS YOU'RE ALL OVER THE EVENING NEWS.
STOCK MARKET, MY ASS.
OH MY GOD, LISTEN, I MET A GUY.
IS HE A GOOD LAWYER?
NO, HE WORKS AT A BOOKSTORE AND HIS NAME IS--
AH AH AH, DON'T TELL ME SPECIFICS.
WELL, I JUST WANTED TO CALL BECAUSE I'M FINALLY STARTING TO FEEL NORMAL AGAIN.
YOU'VE GOT SOMEONE ELSE'S HEART AND YOU'RE WANTED BY THE FBI, GIRL. YOU'RE NOT.
BE HAPPY FOR ME. PLEASE? I'LL CALL BACK AND BE MISERABLE CALLIE NEXT TIME.
FINE. I'M DELIGHTED. GO GET LAID. HAVE A BALL.
"OKAY, YOU'RE THE BOSS."

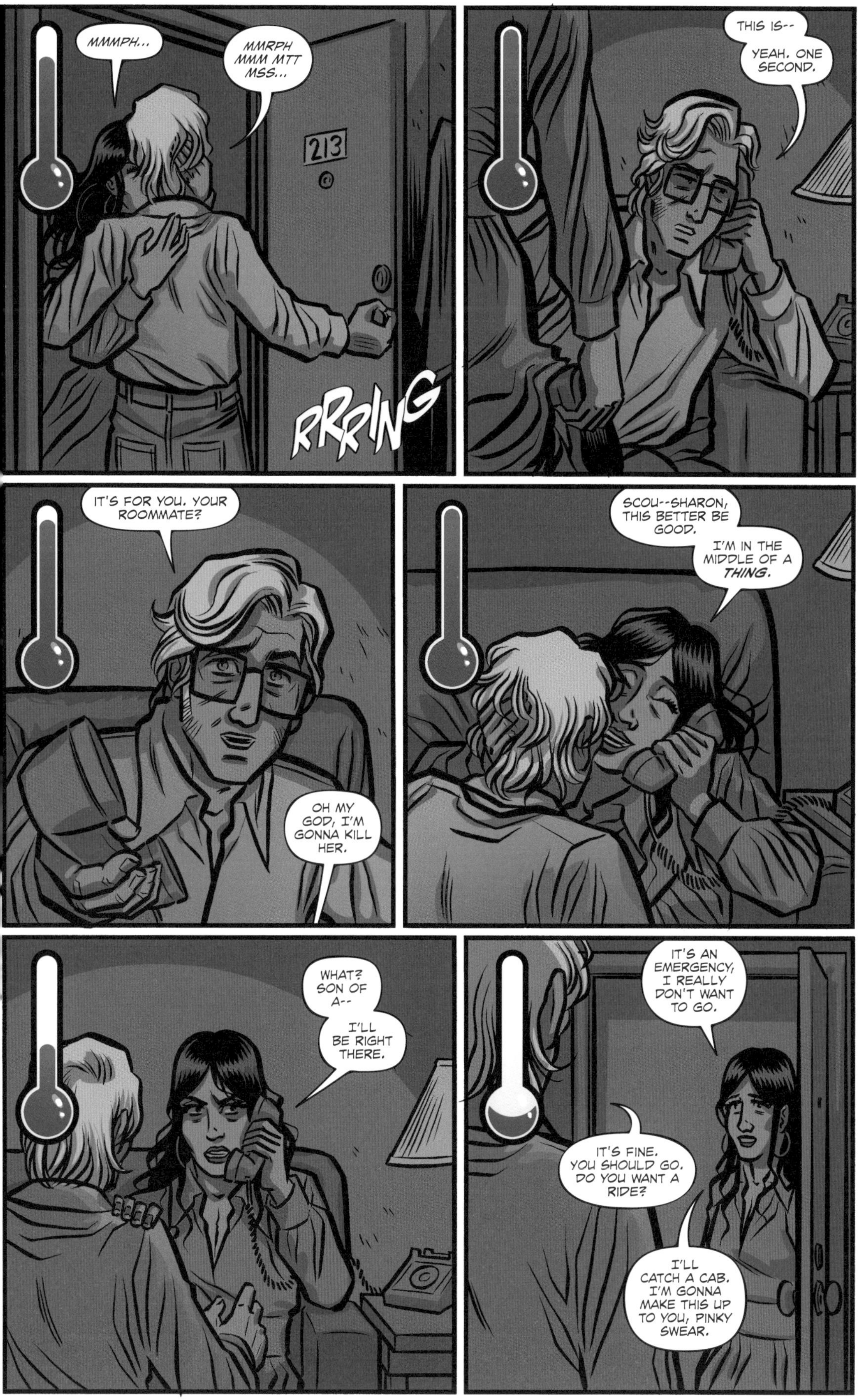
MMMPH...
MMRPH MMM MTT MSS...
213
RRRING
THIS IS--
YEAH. ONE SECOND.
IT'S FOR YOU. YOUR ROOMMATE?
OH MY GOD, I'M GONNA KILL HER.
SCOU--SHARON, THIS BETTER BE GOOD.
I'M IN THE MIDDLE OF A *THING.*
WHAT? SON OF A--
I'LL BE RIGHT THERE.
IT'S AN EMERGENCY, I REALLY DON'T WANT TO GO.
IT'S FINE. YOU SHOULD GO. DO YOU WANT A RIDE?
I'LL CATCH A CAB. I'M GONNA MAKE THIS UP TO YOU, PINKY SWEAR.

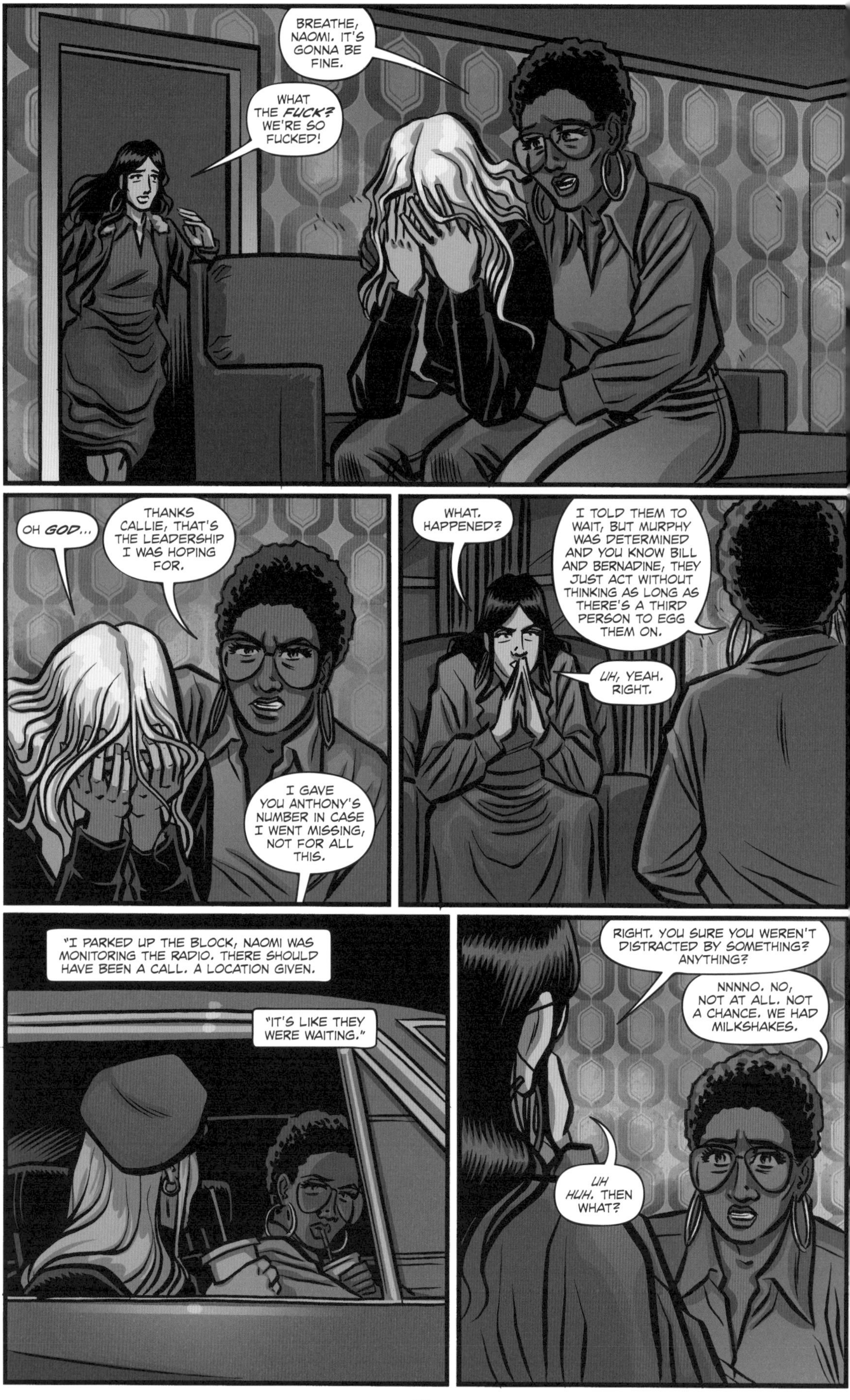
BREATHE, NAOMI. IT'S GONNA BE FINE.
WHAT THE *FUCK?* WE'RE SO FUCKED!
OH *GOD*...
THANKS CALLIE, THAT'S THE LEADERSHIP I WAS HOPING FOR.
I GAVE YOU ANTHONY'S NUMBER IN CASE I WENT MISSING, NOT FOR ALL THIS.
WHAT. HAPPENED?
I TOLD THEM TO WAIT, BUT MURPHY WAS DETERMINED AND YOU KNOW BILL AND BERNADINE, THEY JUST ACT WITHOUT THINKING AS LONG AS THERE'S A THIRD PERSON TO EGG THEM ON.
UH, YEAH. RIGHT.
"I PARKED UP THE BLOCK, NAOMI WAS MONITORING THE RADIO. THERE SHOULD HAVE BEEN A CALL. A LOCATION GIVEN.
"IT'S LIKE THEY WERE WAITING."
RIGHT. YOU SURE YOU WEREN'T DISTRACTED BY SOMETHING? ANYTHING?
NNNNO. NO, NOT AT ALL. NOT A CHANCE. WE HAD MILKSHAKES.
UH HUH. THEN WHAT?

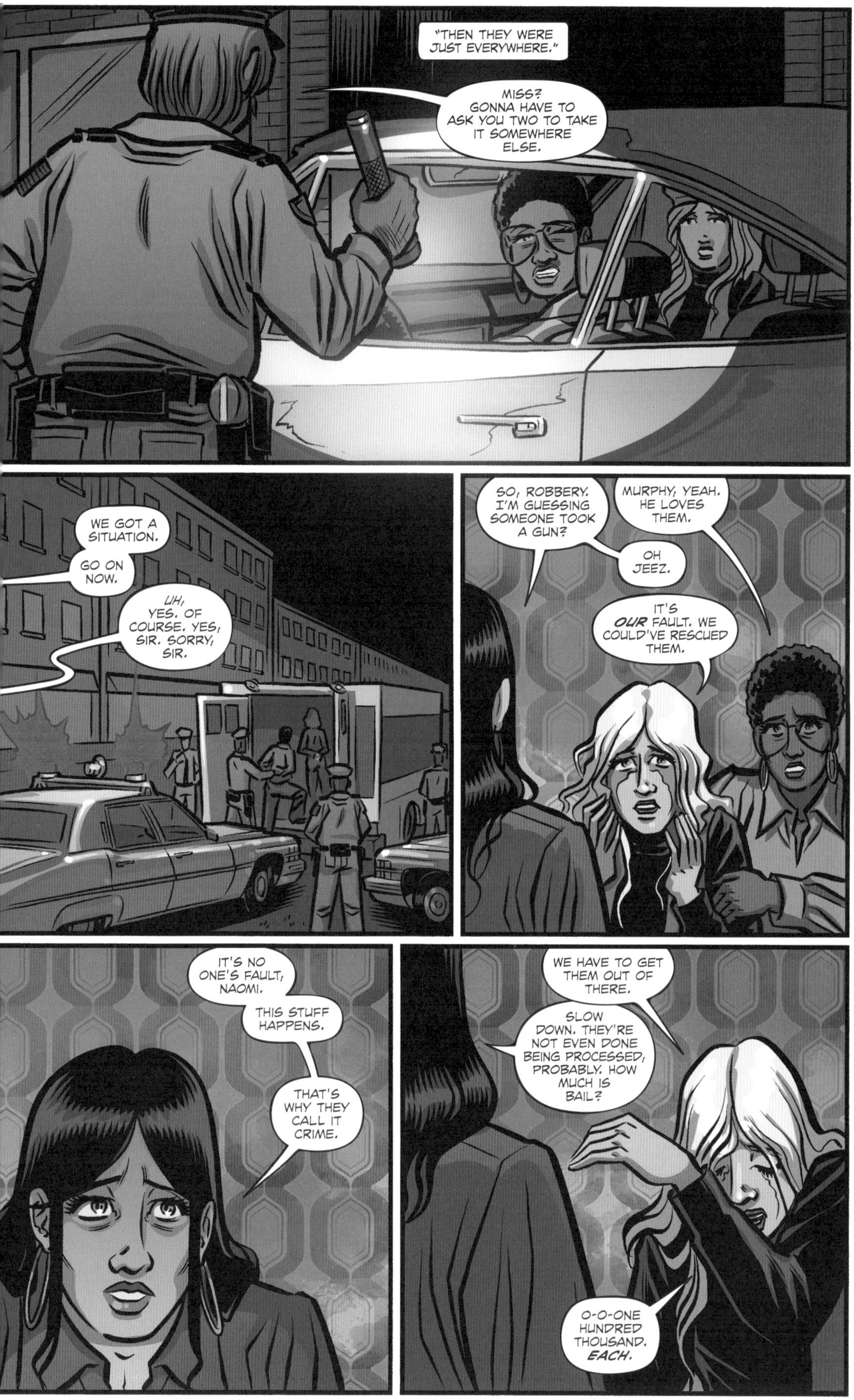
"THEN THEY WERE JUST EVERYWHERE."
MISS? GONNA HAVE TO ASK YOU TWO TO TAKE IT SOMEWHERE ELSE.
WE GOT A SITUATION.
GO ON NOW.
UH, YES. OF COURSE. YES, SIR. SORRY, SIR.
SO, ROBBERY. I'M GUESSING SOMEONE TOOK A GUN?
MURPHY, YEAH. HE LOVES THEM.
OH JEEZ.
IT'S OUR FAULT. WE COULD'VE RESCUED THEM.
IT'S NO ONE'S FAULT, NAOMI.
THIS STUFF HAPPENS.
THAT'S WHY THEY CALL IT CRIME.
WE HAVE TO GET THEM OUT OF THERE.
SLOW DOWN. THEY'RE NOT EVEN DONE BEING PROCESSED, PROBABLY. HOW MUCH IS BAIL?
O-O-ONE HUNDRED THOUSAND. EACH.

WAIT HERE, I'LL TALK TO HER.

WE'LL FIGURE SOMETHING OUT.

THIS CAT? ALL SHE HAS TO WORRY ABOUT IS BEING FED AND SCRATCHED BEHIND THE EARS. I'M KIND OF JEALOUS.

CALLIE, I'M SORRY. I KNOW YOU DON'T DO THIS KIND OF STUFF ANYMORE.

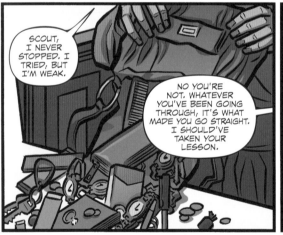

SCOUT, I NEVER STOPPED. I TRIED, BUT I'M WEAK.

NO YOU'RE NOT. WHATEVER YOU'VE BEEN GOING THROUGH, IT'S WHAT MADE YOU GO STRAIGHT. I SHOULD'VE TAKEN YOUR LESSON.

INSTEAD OF... LISTEN, NAOMI'S BEEN WITH THEM FOR ALMOST FIVE YEARS. THEY'RE HER *FAMILY*. WE'VE GOT TO DO SOMETHING.

I KNOW. THEY KNOW WHERE WE LIVE, THAT THERE'S AT LEAST ONE INTERNATIONAL FUGITIVE HERE.

I DON'T THINK THEY WOULD CRACK, BUT THEY'RE ONLY HUMAN. *I'D* CRACK.

I KNOW WHAT WE HAVE TO DO.

GET THE BEST LAWYERS OR BARRISTERS OR WHATEVER THIS COUNTRY HAS.

NO, SCOUT. THERE'S A BAG UNDER THE SINK. GET IT FOR ME.

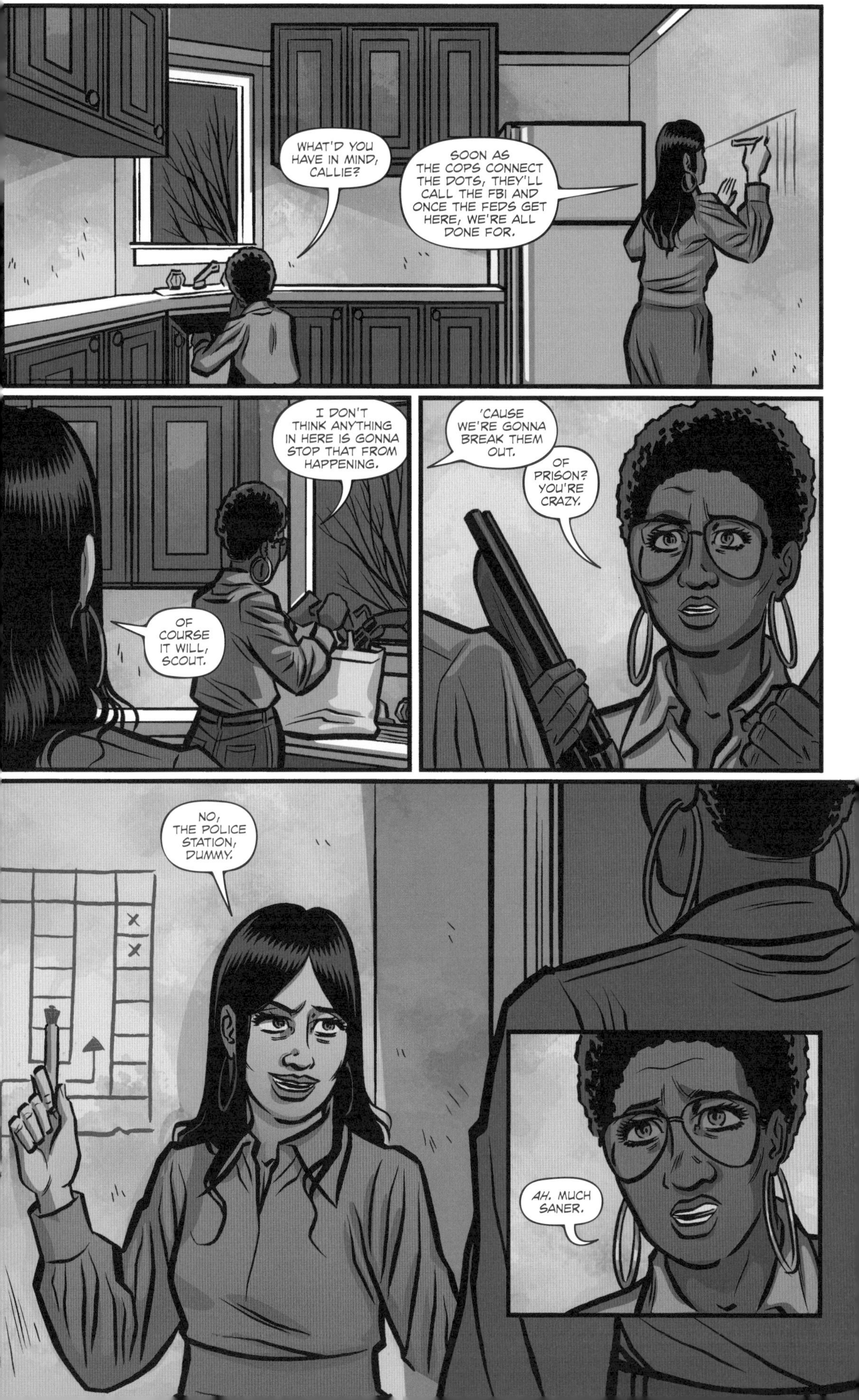
WHAT'D YOU HAVE IN MIND, CALLIE?
SOON AS THE COPS CONNECT THE DOTS, THEY'LL CALL THE FBI AND ONCE THE FEDS GET HERE, WE'RE ALL DONE FOR.
I DON'T THINK ANYTHING IN HERE IS GONNA STOP THAT FROM HAPPENING.
OF COURSE IT WILL, SCOUT.
'CAUSE WE'RE GONNA BREAK THEM OUT.
OF PRISON? YOU'RE CRAZY.
NO, THE POLICE STATION, DUMMY.
AH. MUCH SANER.

CHAPTER 2

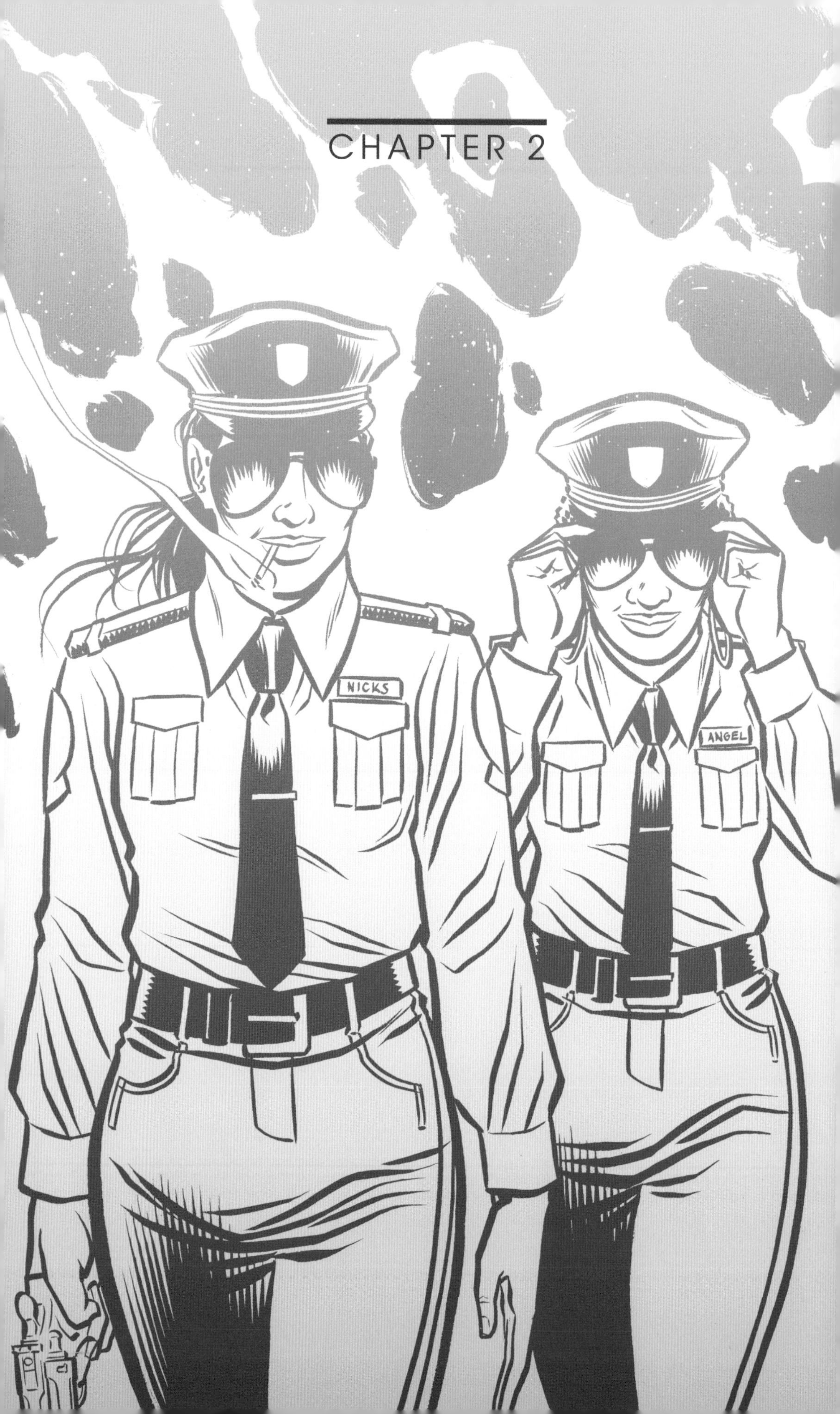
NICKS
ANGEL

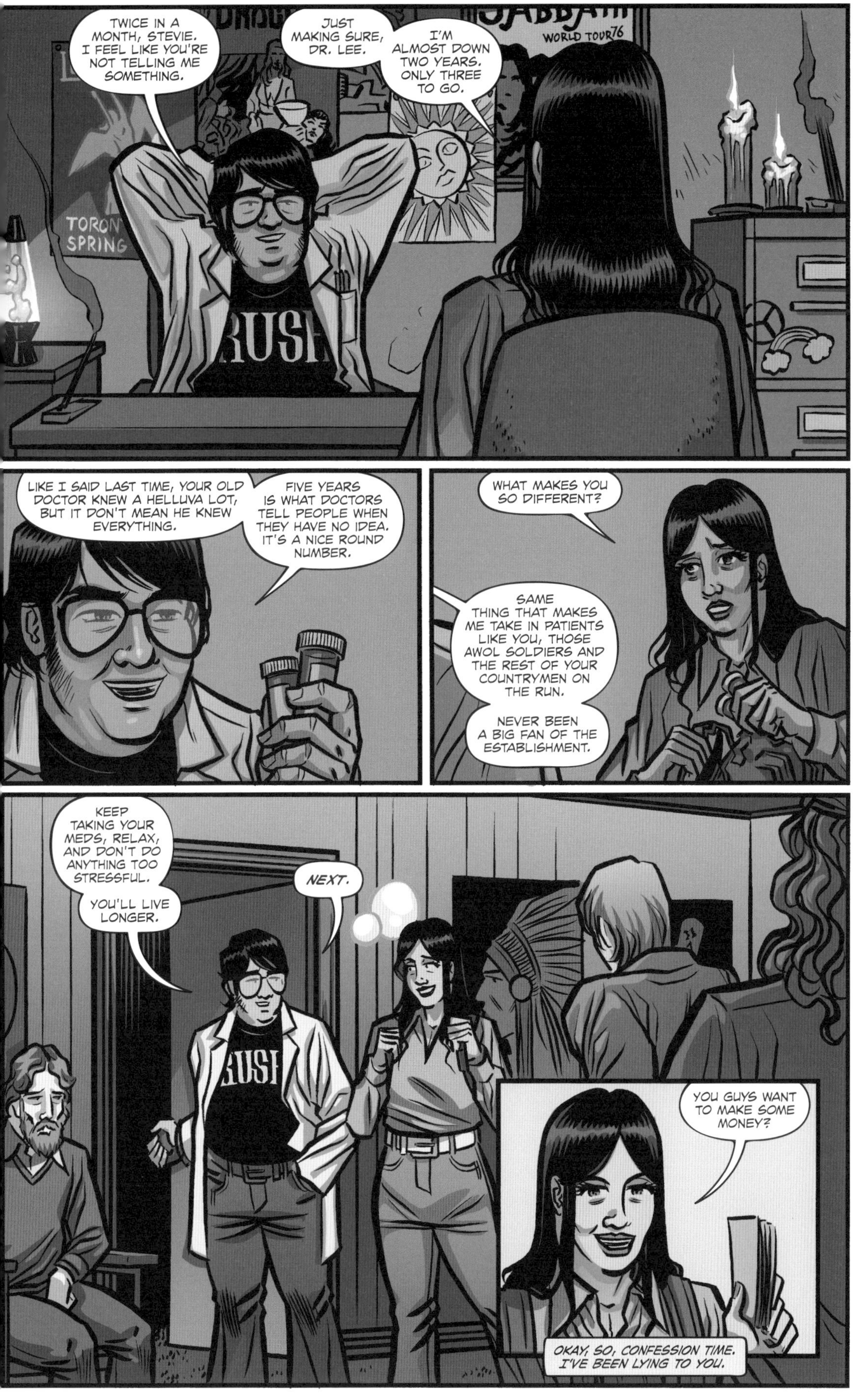

TWICE IN A MONTH, STEVIE. I FEEL LIKE YOU'RE NOT TELLING ME SOMETHING.
JUST MAKING SURE, DR. LEE.
I'M ALMOST DOWN TWO YEARS. ONLY THREE TO GO.
WORLD TOUR 76
TORON
SPRING
RUSH
LIKE I SAID LAST TIME, YOUR OLD DOCTOR KNEW A HELLUVA LOT, BUT IT DON'T MEAN HE KNEW EVERYTHING.
FIVE YEARS IS WHAT DOCTORS TELL PEOPLE WHEN THEY HAVE NO IDEA. IT'S A NICE ROUND NUMBER.
WHAT MAKES YOU SO DIFFERENT?
SAME THING THAT MAKES ME TAKE IN PATIENTS LIKE YOU, THOSE AWOL SOLDIERS AND THE REST OF YOUR COUNTRYMEN ON THE RUN.
NEVER BEEN A BIG FAN OF THE ESTABLISHMENT.
KEEP TAKING YOUR MEDS, RELAX, AND DON'T DO ANYTHING TOO STRESSFUL.
YOU'LL LIVE LONGER.
NEXT.
RUSH
YOU GUYS WANT TO MAKE SOME MONEY?
OKAY, SO, CONFESSION TIME. I'VE BEEN LYING TO YOU.

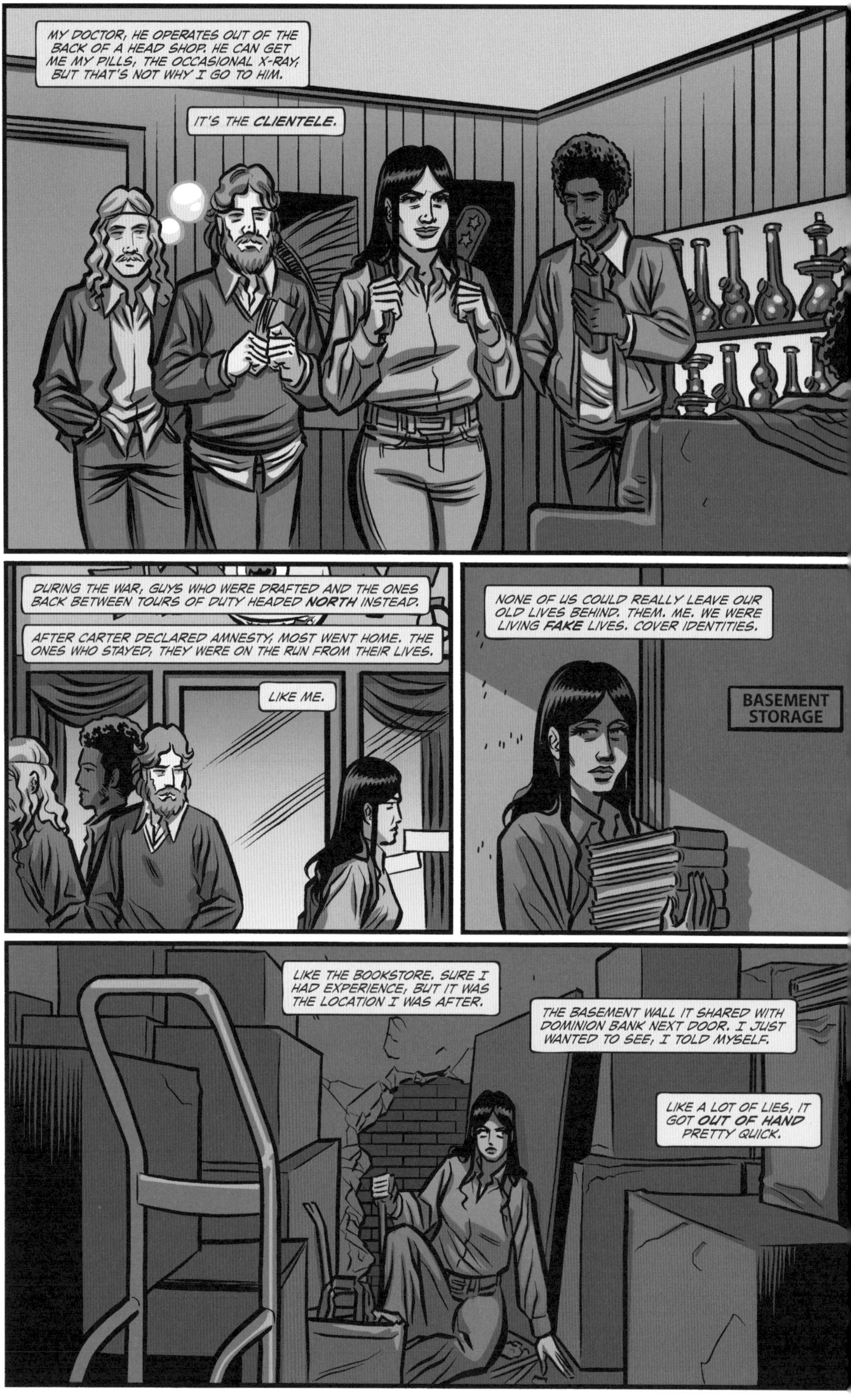
MY DOCTOR, HE OPERATES OUT OF THE BACK OF A HEAD SHOP. HE CAN GET ME MY PILLS, THE OCCASIONAL X-RAY, BUT THAT'S NOT WHY I GO TO HIM.
IT'S THE CLIENTELE.
DURING THE WAR, GUYS WHO WERE DRAFTED AND THE ONES BACK BETWEEN TOURS OF DUTY HEADED NORTH INSTEAD.
AFTER CARTER DECLARED AMNESTY, MOST WENT HOME. THE ONES WHO STAYED, THEY WERE ON THE RUN FROM THEIR LIVES.
LIKE ME.
NONE OF US COULD REALLY LEAVE OUR OLD LIVES BEHIND. THEM. ME. WE WERE LIVING FAKE LIVES. COVER IDENTITIES.
BASEMENT STORAGE
LIKE THE BOOKSTORE. SURE I HAD EXPERIENCE, BUT IT WAS THE LOCATION I WAS AFTER.
THE BASEMENT WALL IT SHARED WITH DOMINION BANK NEXT DOOR. I JUST WANTED TO SEE, I TOLD MYSELF.
LIKE A LOT OF LIES, IT GOT OUT OF HAND PRETTY QUICK.

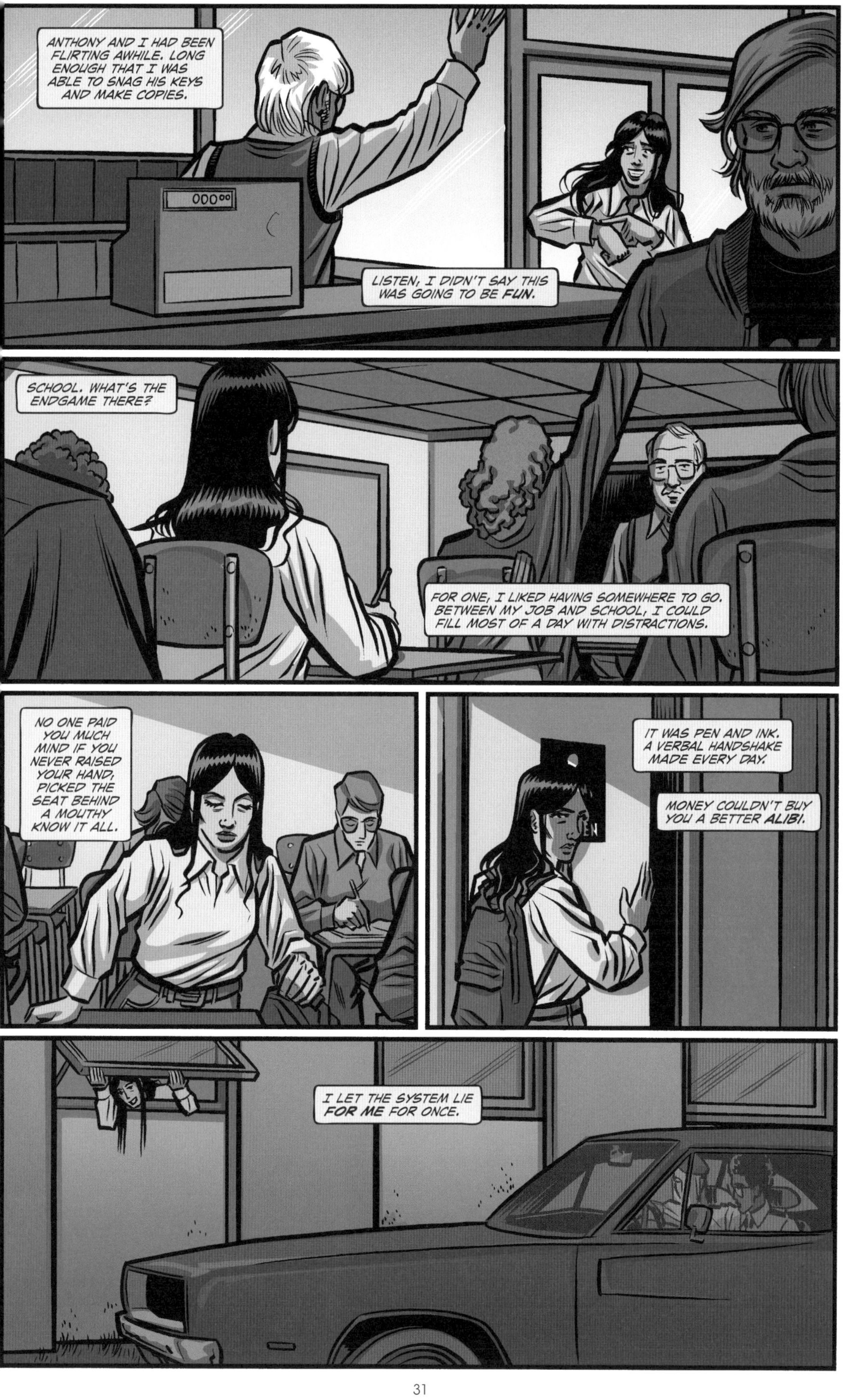
ANTHONY AND I HAD BEEN FLIRTING AWHILE. LONG ENOUGH THAT I WAS ABLE TO SNAG HIS KEYS AND MAKE COPIES.
LISTEN, I DIDN'T SAY THIS WAS GOING TO BE FUN.
SCHOOL. WHAT'S THE ENDGAME THERE?
FOR ONE, I LIKED HAVING SOMEWHERE TO GO. BETWEEN MY JOB AND SCHOOL, I COULD FILL MOST OF A DAY WITH DISTRACTIONS.
NO ONE PAID YOU MUCH MIND IF YOU NEVER RAISED YOUR HAND, PICKED THE SEAT BEHIND A MOUTHY KNOW IT ALL.
IT WAS PEN AND INK. A VERBAL HANDSHAKE MADE EVERY DAY.
MONEY COULDN'T BUY YOU A BETTER ALIBI.
I LET THE SYSTEM LIE FOR ME FOR ONCE.

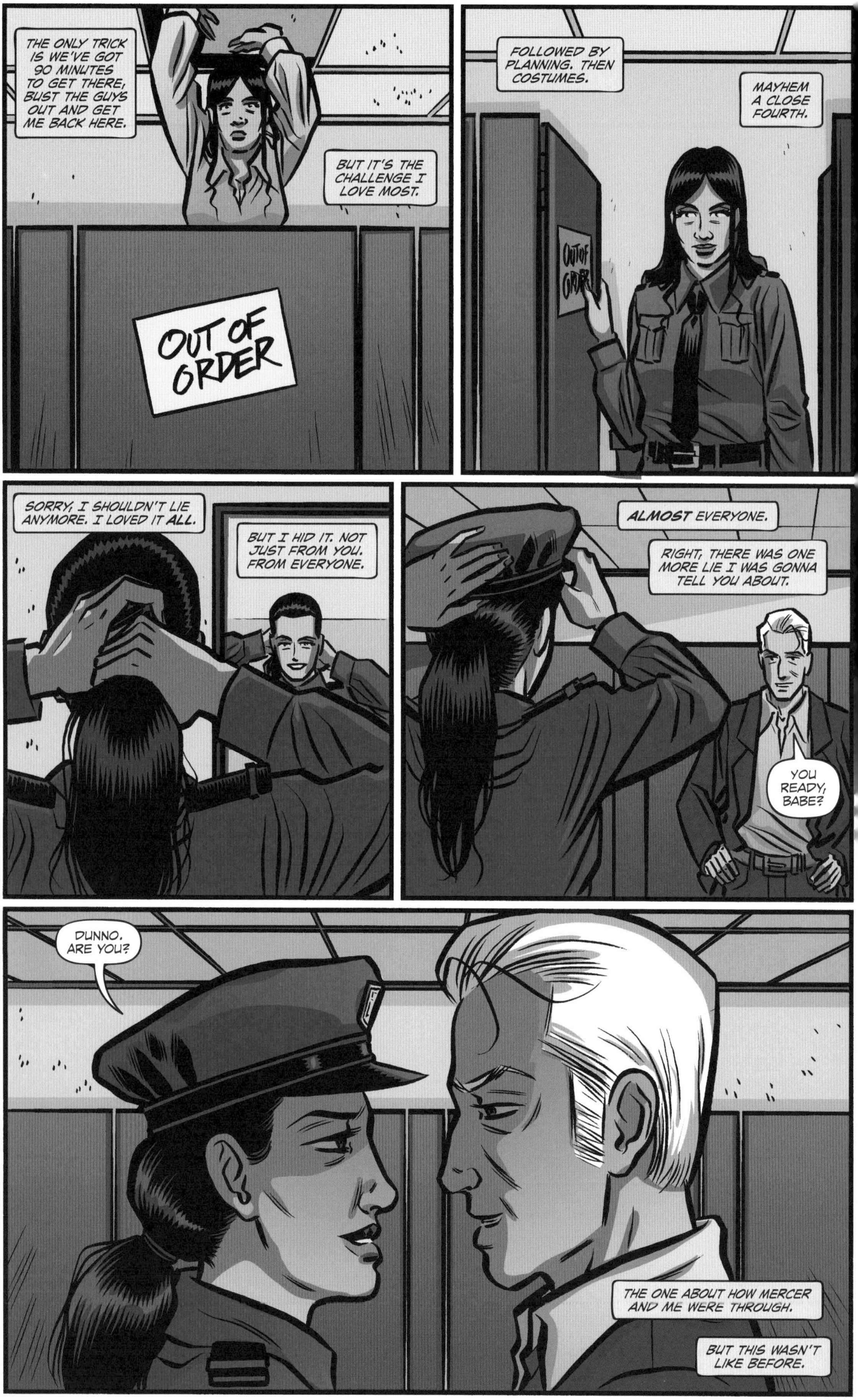
THE ONLY TRICK IS WE'VE GOT 90 MINUTES TO GET THERE, BUST THE GUYS OUT AND GET ME BACK HERE.
BUT IT'S THE CHALLENGE I LOVE MOST.
OUT OF ORDER
FOLLOWED BY PLANNING. THEN COSTUMES.
MAYHEM A CLOSE FOURTH.
OUT OF ORDER
SORRY, I SHOULDN'T LIE ANYMORE. I LOVED IT ALL.
BUT I HID IT. NOT JUST FROM YOU. FROM EVERYONE.
ALMOST EVERYONE.
RIGHT, THERE WAS ONE MORE LIE I WAS GONNA TELL YOU ABOUT.
YOU READY, BABE?
DUNNO. ARE YOU?
THE ONE ABOUT HOW MERCER AND ME WERE THROUGH.
BUT THIS WASN'T LIKE BEFORE.

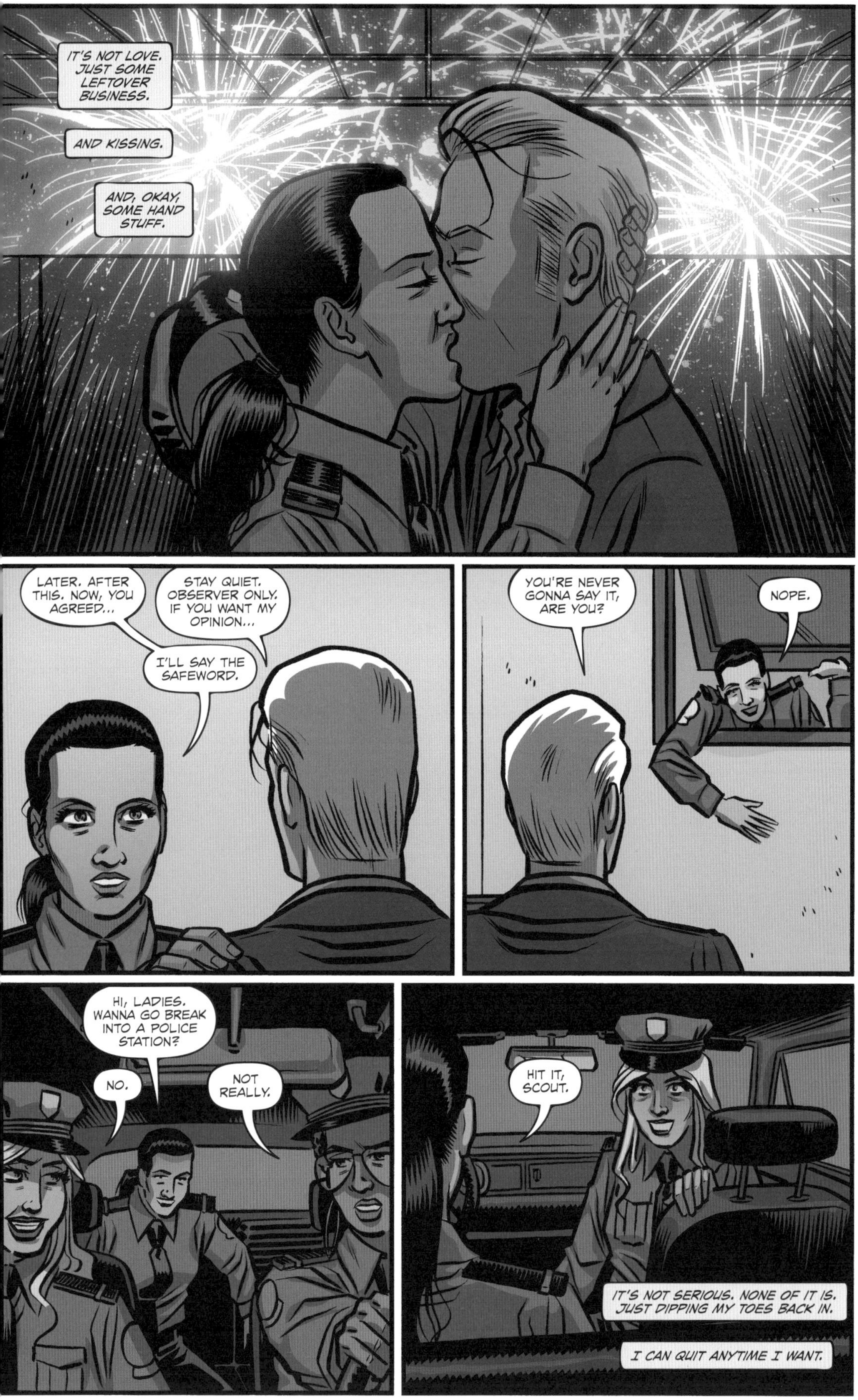
IT'S NOT LOVE. JUST SOME LEFTOVER BUSINESS.
AND KISSING.
AND, OKAY, SOME HAND STUFF.
LATER. AFTER THIS. NOW, YOU AGREED...
STAY QUIET. OBSERVER ONLY. IF YOU WANT MY OPINION...
I'LL SAY THE SAFEWORD.
YOU'RE NEVER GONNA SAY IT, ARE YOU?
NOPE.
HI, LADIES. WANNA GO BREAK INTO A POLICE STATION?
NO.
NOT REALLY.
HIT IT, SCOUT.
IT'S NOT SERIOUS. NONE OF IT IS. JUST DIPPING MY TOES BACK IN.
I CAN QUIT ANYTIME I WANT.

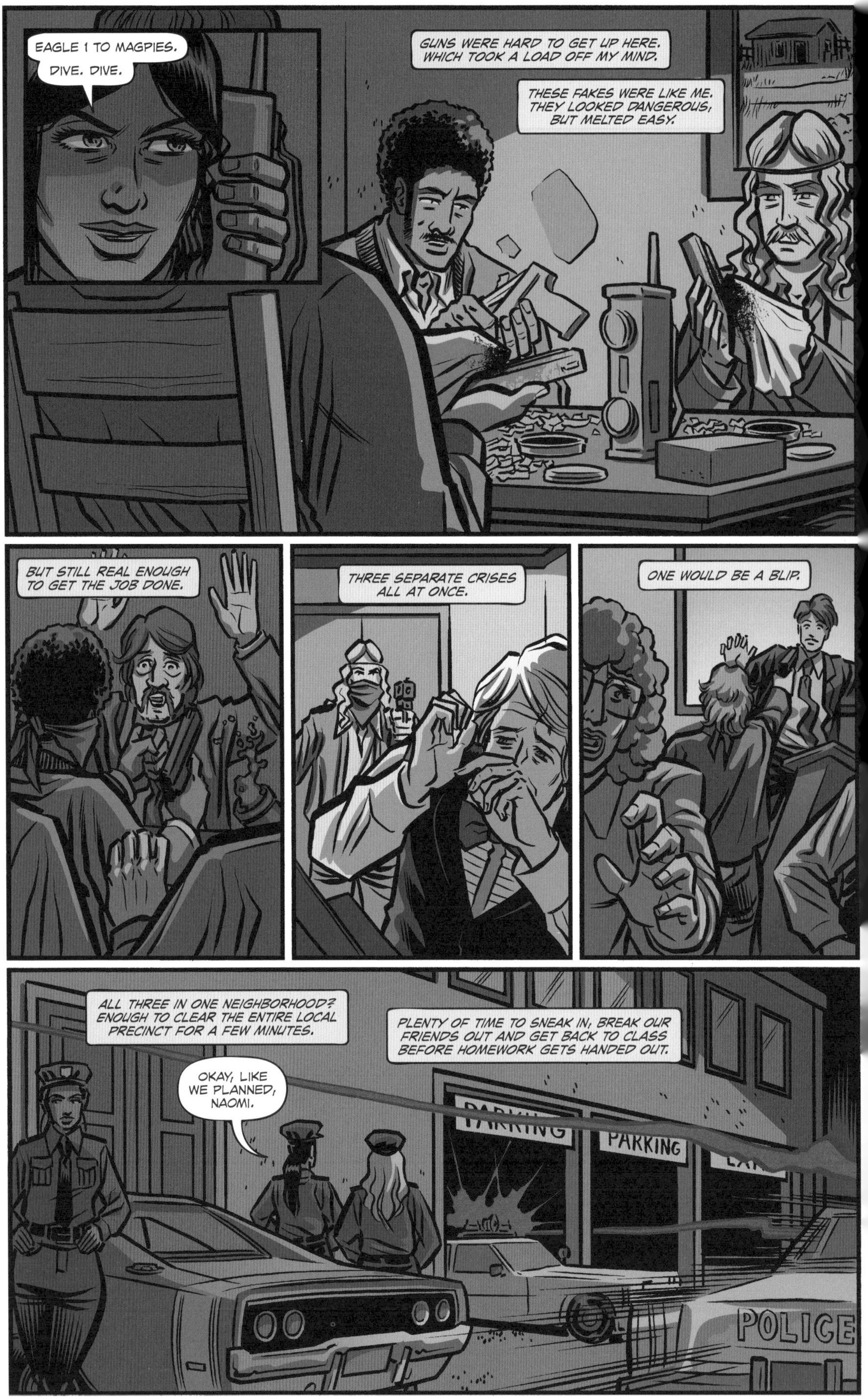
EAGLE 1 TO MAGPIES.
DIVE. DIVE.
GUNS WERE HARD TO GET UP HERE. WHICH TOOK A LOAD OFF MY MIND.
THESE FAKES WERE LIKE ME. THEY LOOKED DANGEROUS, BUT MELTED EASY.
BUT STILL REAL ENOUGH TO GET THE JOB DONE.
THREE SEPARATE CRISES ALL AT ONCE.
ONE WOULD BE A BLIP.
ALL THREE IN ONE NEIGHBORHOOD? ENOUGH TO CLEAR THE ENTIRE LOCAL PRECINCT FOR A FEW MINUTES.
PLENTY OF TIME TO SNEAK IN, BREAK OUR FRIENDS OUT AND GET BACK TO CLASS BEFORE HOMEWORK GETS HANDED OUT.
OKAY, LIKE WE PLANNED, NAOMI.
PARKING
PARKING
POLICE

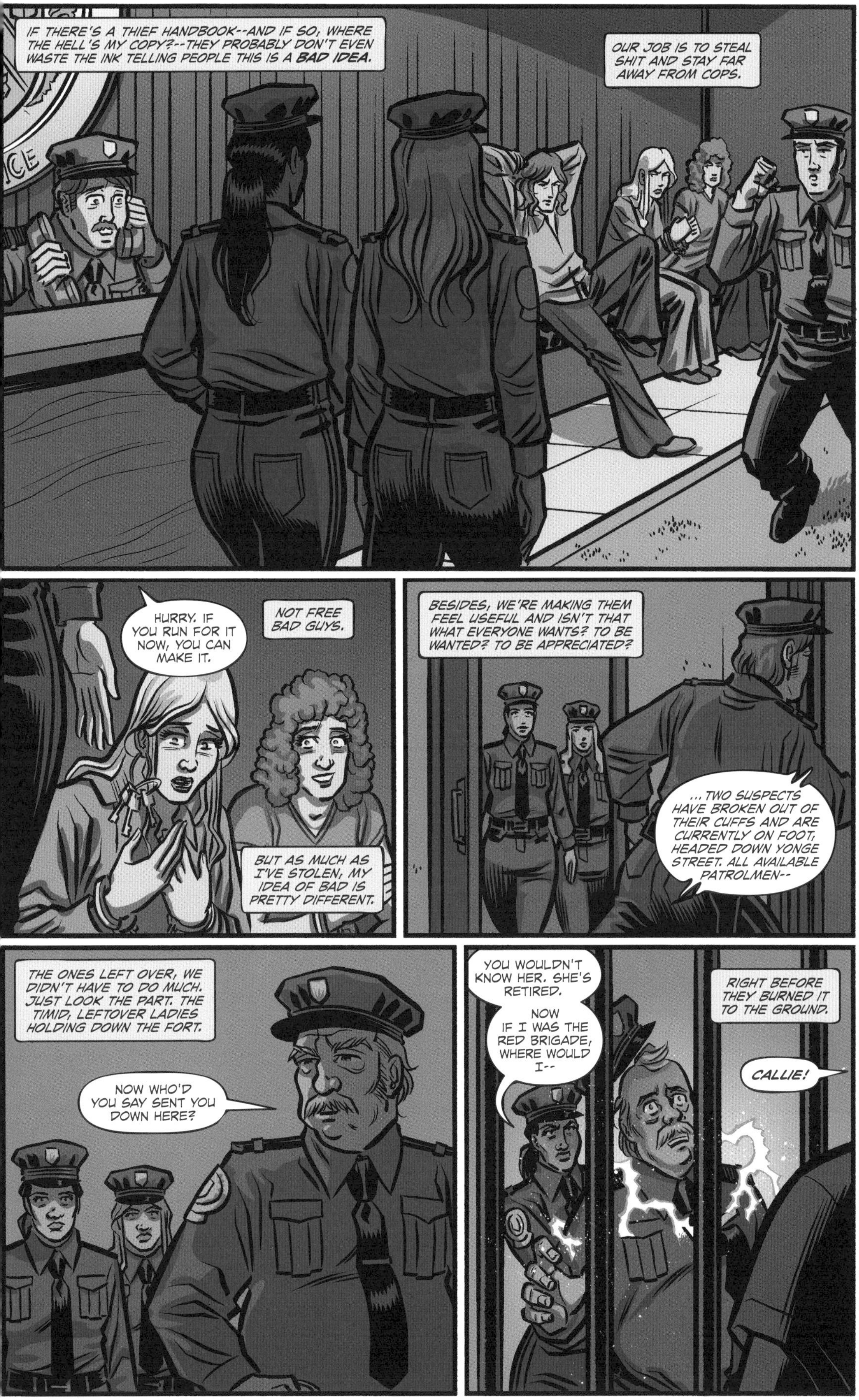

IF THERE'S A THIEF HANDBOOK--AND IF SO, WHERE THE HELL'S MY COPY?--THEY PROBABLY DON'T EVEN WASTE THE INK TELLING PEOPLE THIS IS A **BAD IDEA.**
OUR JOB IS TO STEAL SHIT AND STAY FAR AWAY FROM COPS.
HURRY. IF YOU RUN FOR IT NOW, YOU CAN MAKE IT.
NOT FREE BAD GUYS.
BUT AS MUCH AS I'VE STOLEN, MY IDEA OF BAD IS PRETTY DIFFERENT.
BESIDES, WE'RE MAKING THEM FEEL USEFUL AND ISN'T THAT WHAT EVERYONE WANTS? TO BE WANTED? TO BE APPRECIATED?
...TWO SUSPECTS HAVE BROKEN OUT OF THEIR CUFFS AND ARE CURRENTLY ON FOOT, HEADED DOWN YONGE STREET. ALL AVAILABLE PATROLMEN--
THE ONES LEFT OVER, WE DIDN'T HAVE TO DO MUCH. JUST LOOK THE PART. THE TIMID, LEFTOVER LADIES HOLDING DOWN THE FORT.
NOW WHO'D YOU SAY SENT YOU DOWN HERE?
YOU WOULDN'T KNOW HER. SHE'S RETIRED.
NOW IF I WAS THE RED BRIGADE, WHERE WOULD I--
RIGHT BEFORE THEY BURNED IT TO THE GROUND.
CALLIE!

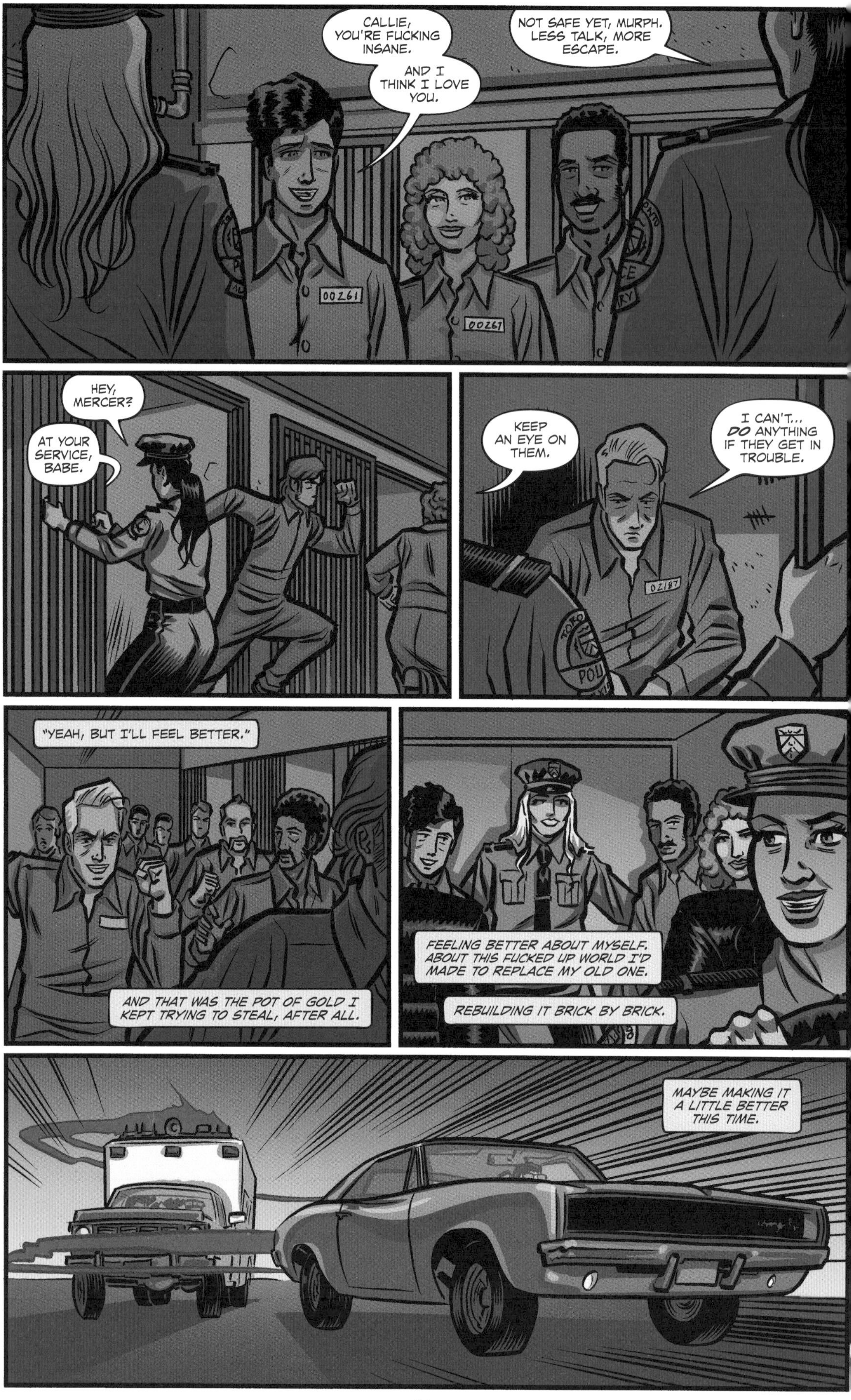

CALLIE, YOU'RE FUCKING INSANE.
AND I THINK I LOVE YOU.
NOT SAFE YET, MURPH. LESS TALK, MORE ESCAPE.
HEY, MERCER?
AT YOUR SERVICE, BABE.
KEEP AN EYE ON THEM.
I CAN'T... DO ANYTHING IF THEY GET IN TROUBLE.
"YEAH, BUT I'LL FEEL BETTER."
AND THAT WAS THE POT OF GOLD I KEPT TRYING TO STEAL, AFTER ALL.
FEELING BETTER ABOUT MYSELF. ABOUT THIS FUCKED UP WORLD I'D MADE TO REPLACE MY OLD ONE.
REBUILDING IT BRICK BY BRICK.
MAYBE MAKING IT A LITTLE BETTER THIS TIME.

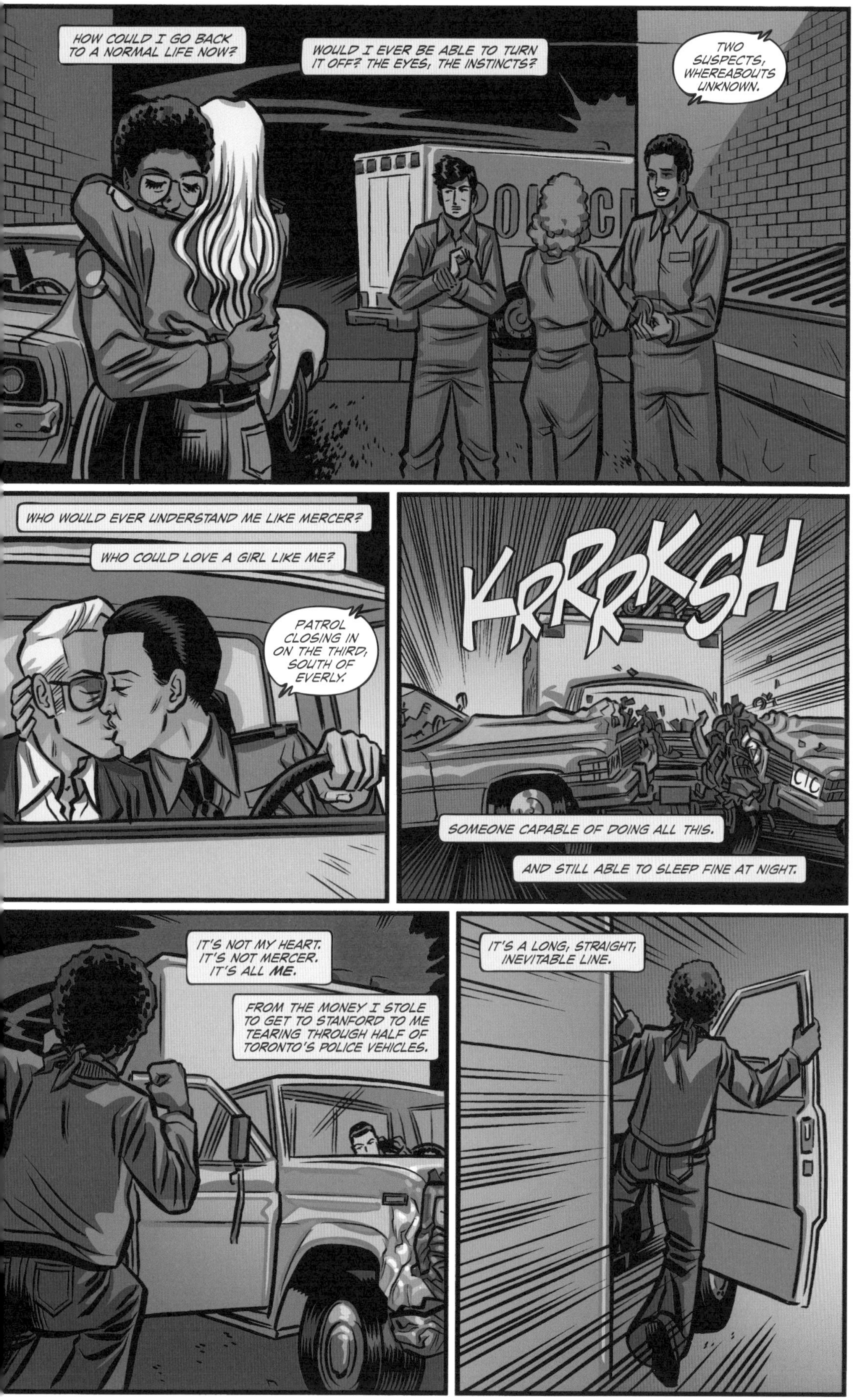
HOW COULD I GO BACK TO A NORMAL LIFE NOW?
WOULD I EVER BE ABLE TO TURN IT OFF? THE EYES, THE INSTINCTS?
TWO SUSPECTS, WHEREABOUTS UNKNOWN.
POLICE
WHO WOULD EVER UNDERSTAND ME LIKE MERCER?
WHO COULD LOVE A GIRL LIKE ME?
PATROL CLOSING IN ON THE THIRD, SOUTH OF EVERLY.
KRRRKSH
SOMEONE CAPABLE OF DOING ALL THIS.
AND STILL ABLE TO SLEEP FINE AT NIGHT.
IT'S NOT MY HEART. IT'S NOT MERCER. IT'S ALL **ME.**
FROM THE MONEY I STOLE TO GET TO STANFORD TO ME TEARING THROUGH HALF OF TORONTO'S POLICE VEHICLES.
IT'S A LONG, STRAIGHT, INEVITABLE LINE.

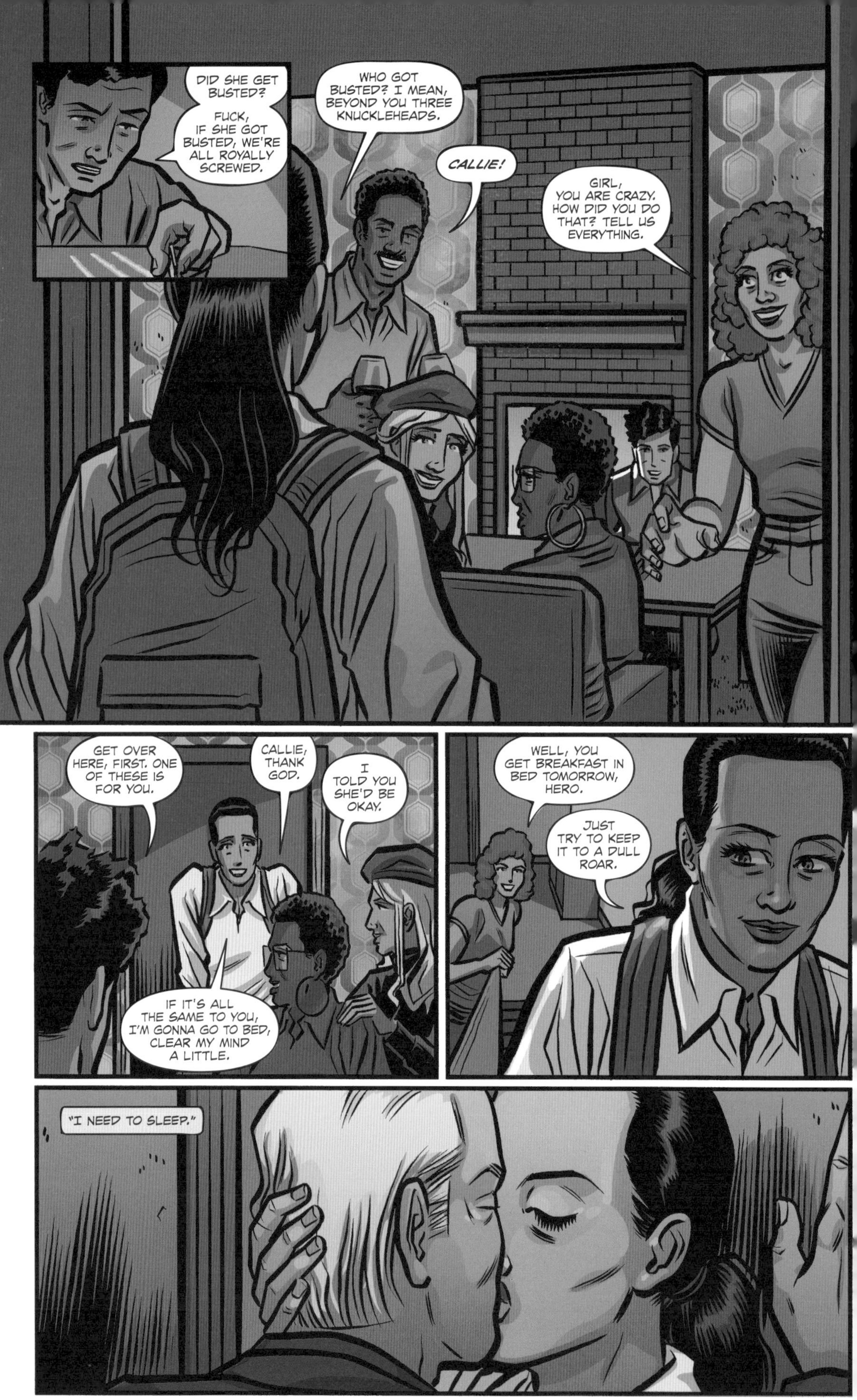
DID SHE GET BUSTED?
FUCK, IF SHE GOT BUSTED, WE'RE ALL ROYALLY SCREWED.
WHO GOT BUSTED? I MEAN, BEYOND YOU THREE KNUCKLEHEADS.
CALLIE!
GIRL, YOU ARE CRAZY. HOW DID YOU DO THAT? TELL US EVERYTHING.
GET OVER HERE, FIRST. ONE OF THESE IS FOR YOU.
CALLIE, THANK GOD.
I TOLD YOU SHE'D BE OKAY.
IF IT'S ALL THE SAME TO YOU, I'M GONNA GO TO BED, CLEAR MY MIND A LITTLE.
WELL, YOU GET BREAKFAST IN BED TOMORROW, HERO.
JUST TRY TO KEEP IT TO A DULL ROAR.
"I NEED TO SLEEP."

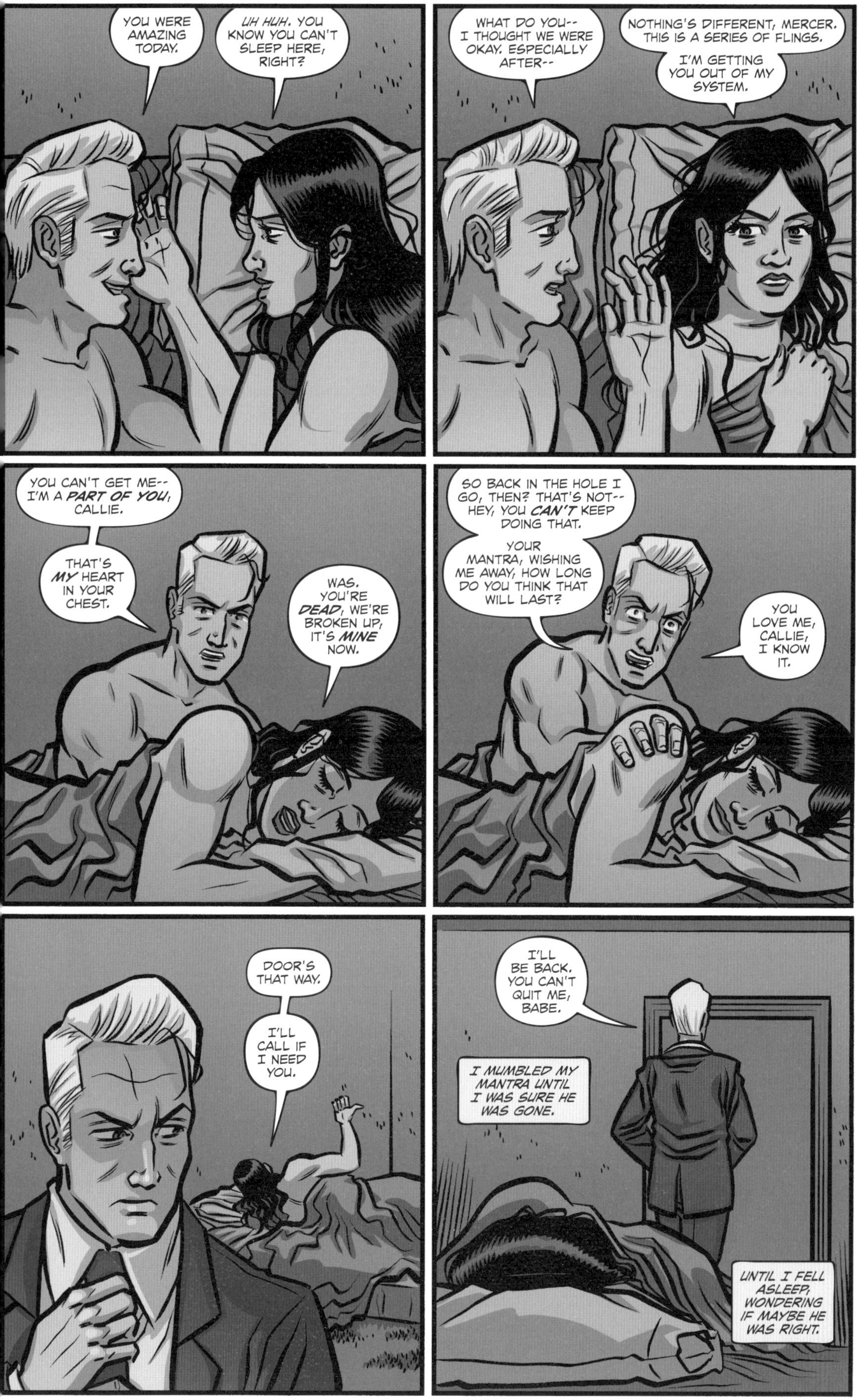
YOU WERE AMAZING TODAY.
UH HUH. YOU KNOW YOU CAN'T SLEEP HERE, RIGHT?
WHAT DO YOU-- I THOUGHT WE WERE OKAY. ESPECIALLY AFTER--
NOTHING'S DIFFERENT, MERCER. THIS IS A SERIES OF FLINGS.
I'M GETTING YOU OUT OF MY SYSTEM.
YOU CAN'T GET ME-- I'M A ***PART OF YOU***, CALLIE.
THAT'S ***MY*** HEART IN YOUR CHEST.
WAS. YOU'RE ***DEAD***, WE'RE BROKEN UP, IT'S ***MINE*** NOW.
SO BACK IN THE HOLE I GO, THEN? THAT'S NOT-- HEY, YOU ***CAN'T*** KEEP DOING THAT.
YOUR MANTRA, WISHING ME AWAY, HOW LONG DO YOU THINK THAT WILL LAST?
YOU LOVE ME, CALLIE, I KNOW IT.
DOOR'S THAT WAY.
I'LL CALL IF I NEED YOU.
I'LL BE BACK. YOU CAN'T QUIT ME, BABE.
I MUMBLED MY MANTRA UNTIL I WAS SURE HE WAS GONE.
UNTIL I FELL ASLEEP, WONDERING IF MAYBE HE WAS RIGHT.

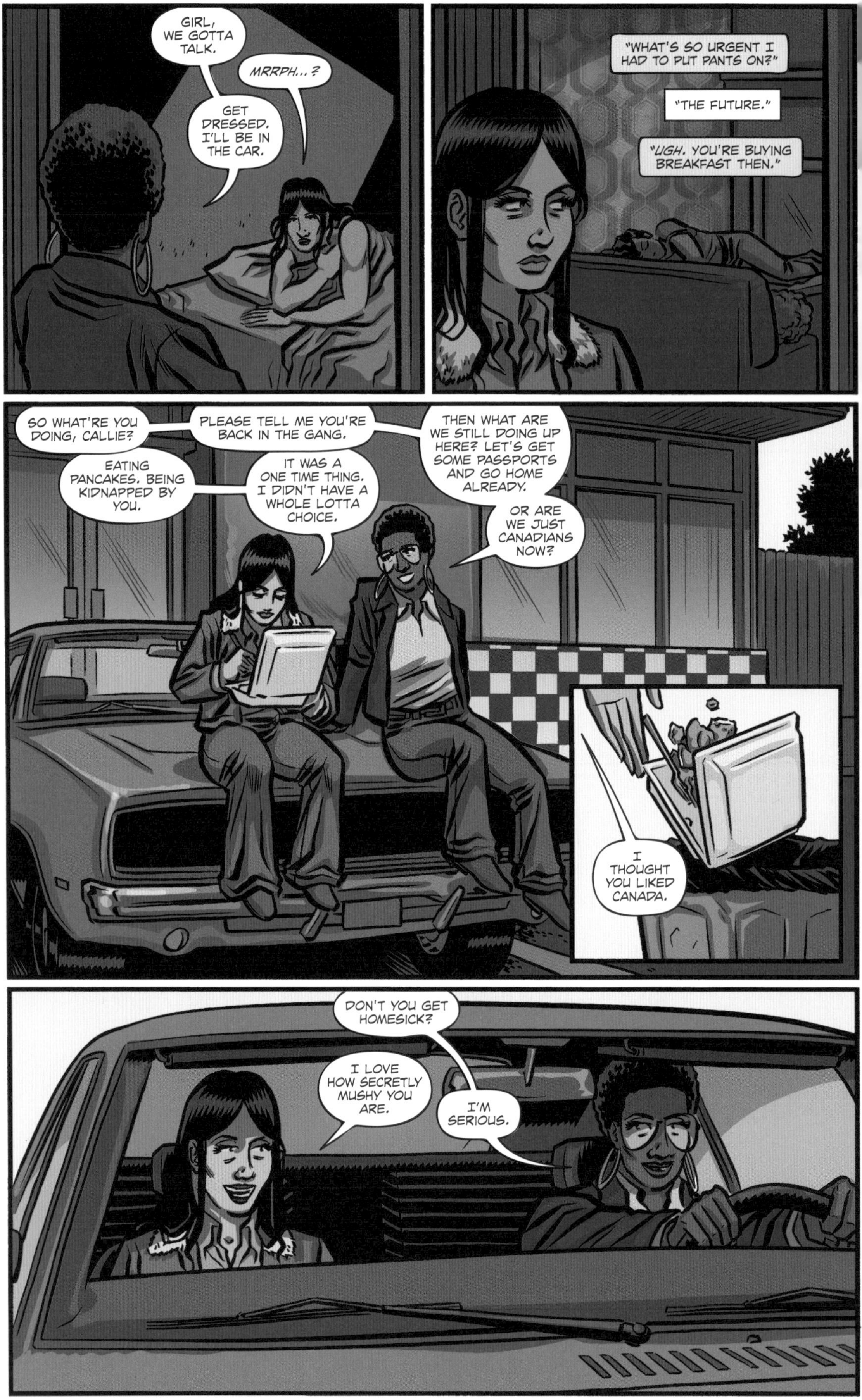
GIRL, WE GOTTA TALK.
MRRPH...?
GET DRESSED. I'LL BE IN THE CAR.
"WHAT'S SO URGENT I HAD TO PUT PANTS ON?"
"THE FUTURE."
"UGH. YOU'RE BUYING BREAKFAST THEN."
SO WHAT'RE YOU DOING, CALLIE?
EATING PANCAKES. BEING KIDNAPPED BY YOU.
PLEASE TELL ME YOU'RE BACK IN THE GANG.
IT WAS A ONE TIME THING. I DIDN'T HAVE A WHOLE LOTTA CHOICE.
THEN WHAT ARE WE STILL DOING UP HERE? LET'S GET SOME PASSPORTS AND GO HOME ALREADY.
OR ARE WE JUST CANADIANS NOW?
I THOUGHT YOU LIKED CANADA.
DON'T YOU GET HOMESICK?
I LOVE HOW SECRETLY MUSHY YOU ARE.
I'M SERIOUS.

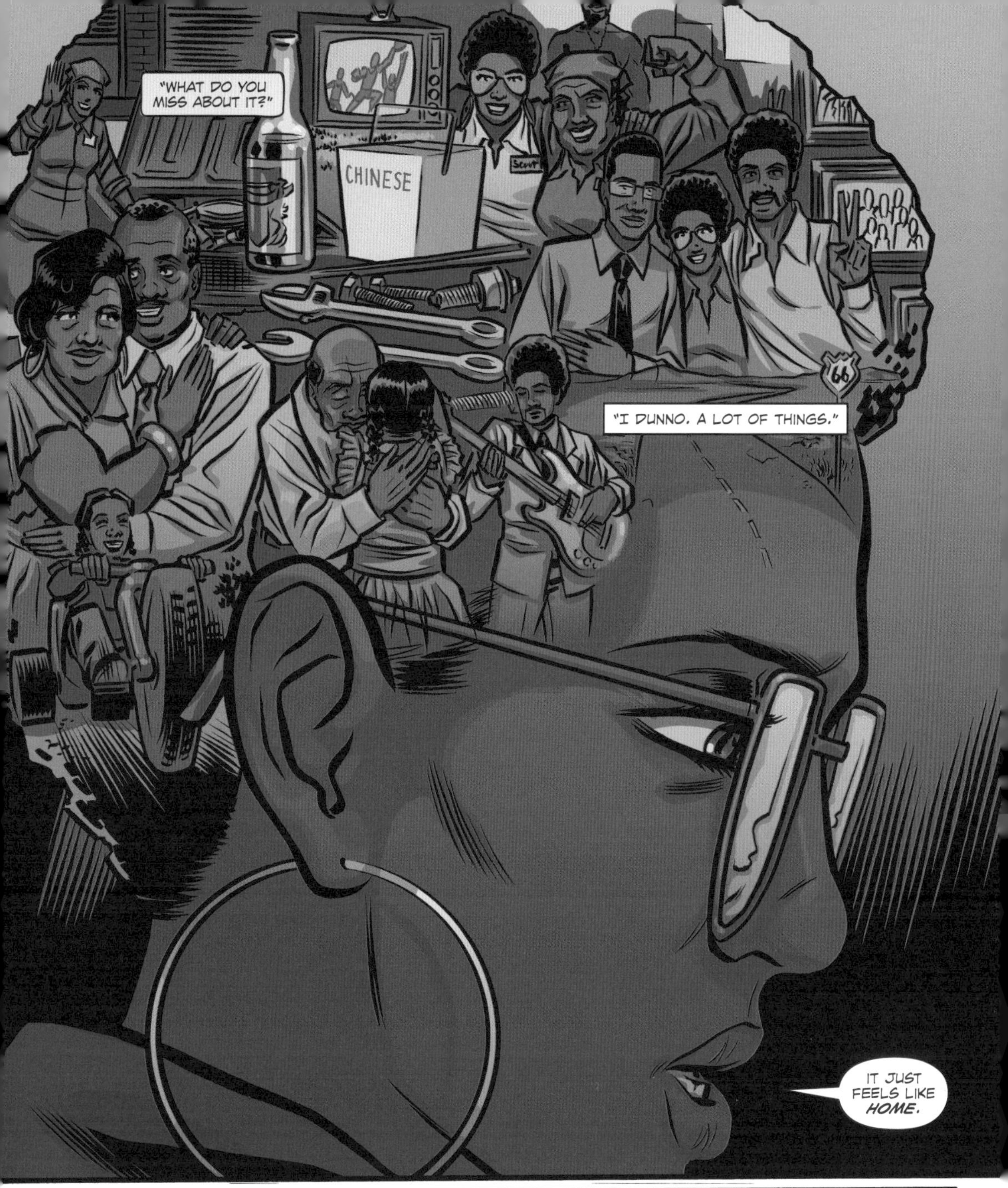
"WHAT DO YOU MISS ABOUT IT?"
CHINESE
"I DUNNO. A LOT OF THINGS."
IT JUST FEELS LIKE *HOME.*

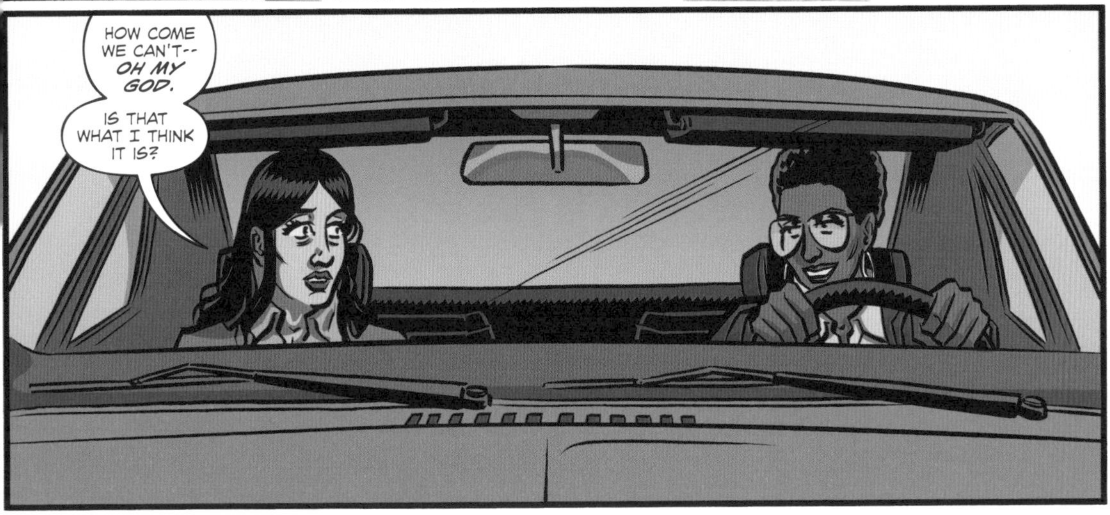
HOW COME WE CAN'T-- *OH MY GOD.*
IS THAT WHAT I THINK IT IS?

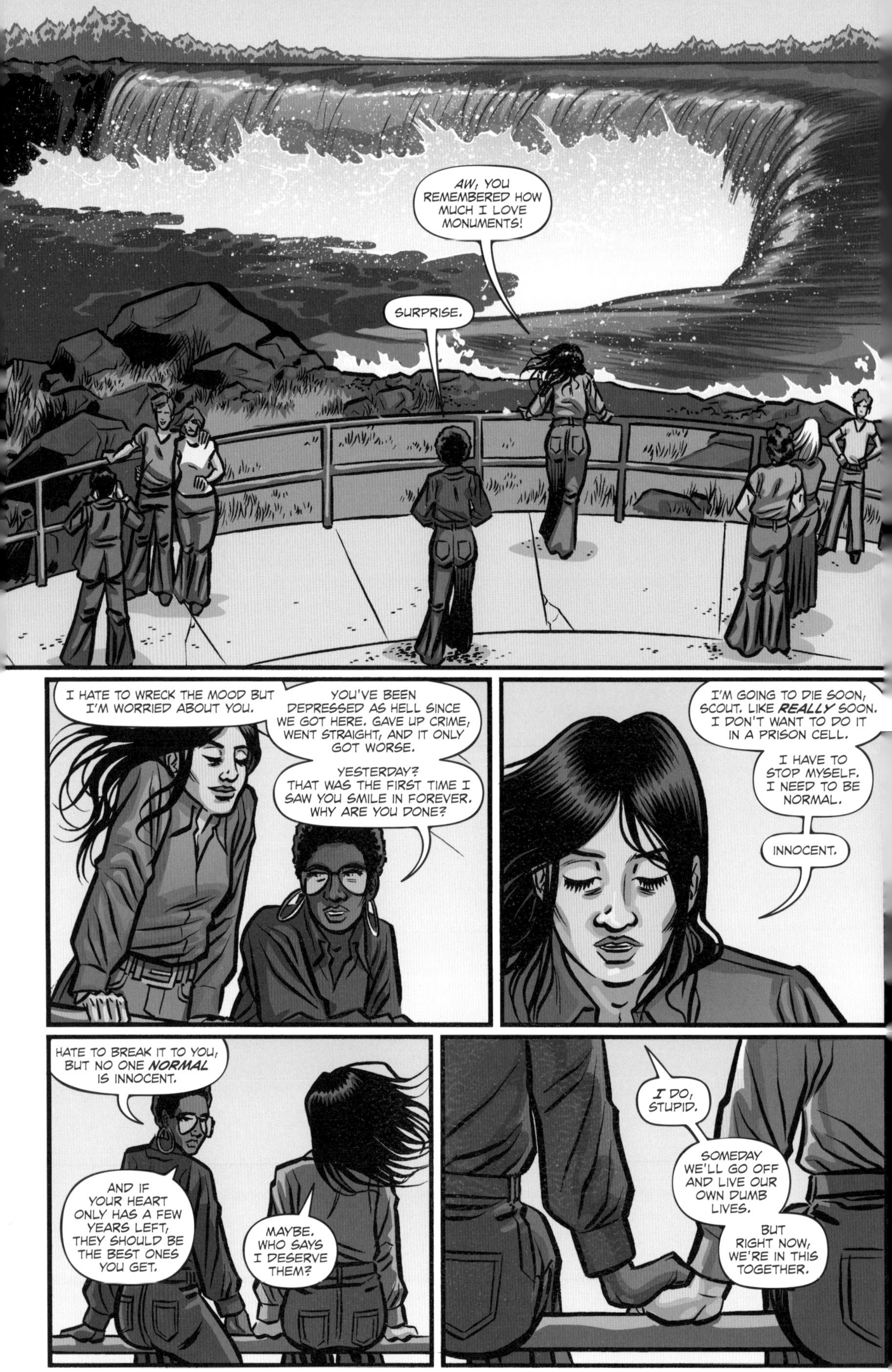
AW, YOU REMEMBERED HOW MUCH I LOVE MONUMENTS!
SURPRISE.
I HATE TO WRECK THE MOOD BUT I'M WORRIED ABOUT YOU.
YOU'VE BEEN DEPRESSED AS HELL SINCE WE GOT HERE. GAVE UP CRIME, WENT STRAIGHT, AND IT ONLY GOT WORSE.
YESTERDAY? THAT WAS THE FIRST TIME I SAW YOU SMILE IN FOREVER. WHY ARE YOU DONE?
I'M GOING TO DIE SOON, SCOUT. LIKE REALLY SOON. I DON'T WANT TO DO IT IN A PRISON CELL.
I HAVE TO STOP MYSELF. I NEED TO BE NORMAL.
INNOCENT.
HATE TO BREAK IT TO YOU, BUT NO ONE NORMAL IS INNOCENT.
AND IF YOUR HEART ONLY HAS A FEW YEARS LEFT, THEY SHOULD BE THE BEST ONES YOU GET.
MAYBE. WHO SAYS I DESERVE THEM?
I DO, STUPID.
SOMEDAY WE'LL GO OFF AND LIVE OUR OWN DUMB LIVES.
BUT RIGHT NOW, WE'RE IN THIS TOGETHER.

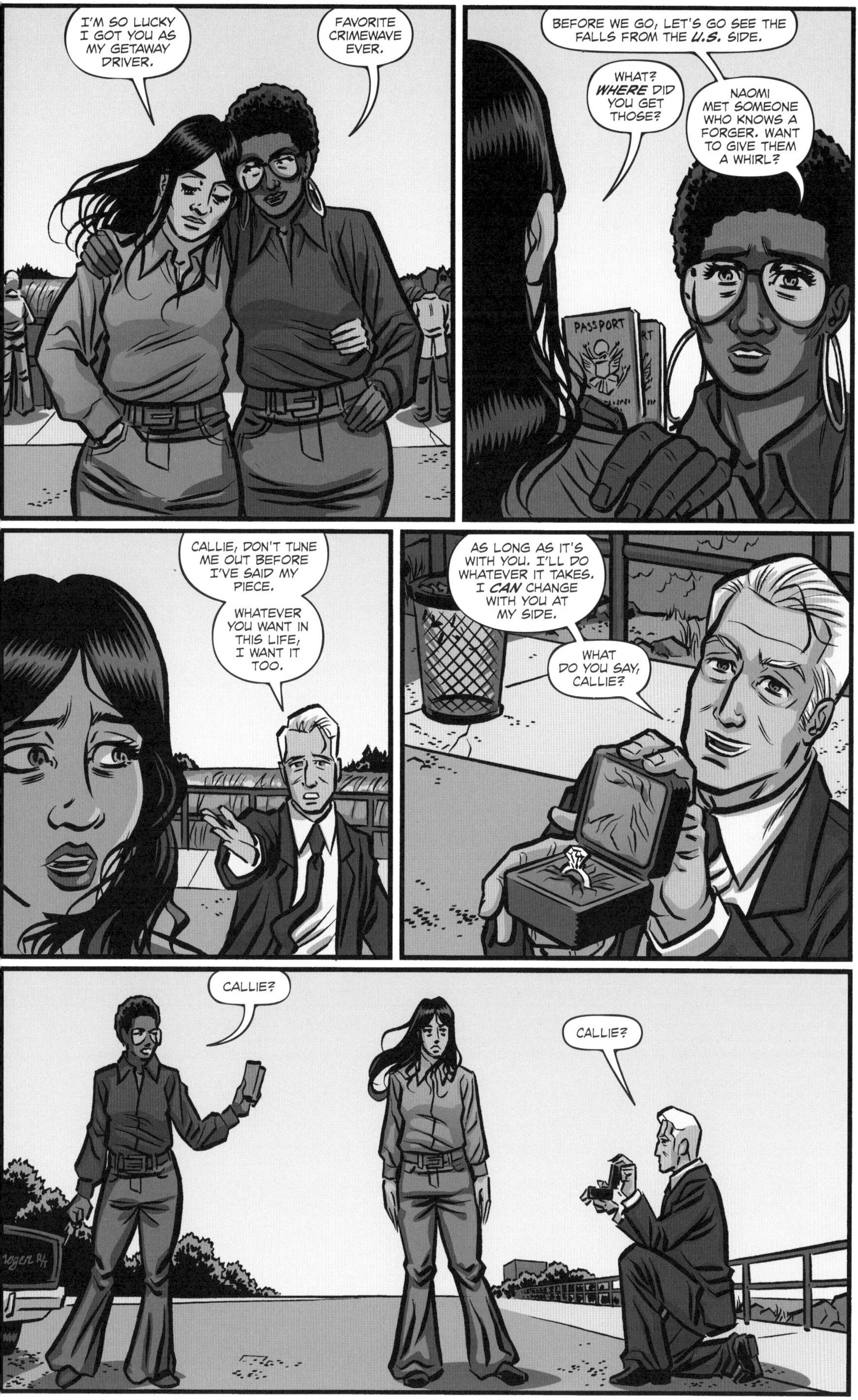
I'M SO LUCKY I GOT YOU AS MY GETAWAY DRIVER.
FAVORITE CRIMEWAVE EVER.
BEFORE WE GO, LET'S GO SEE THE FALLS FROM THE *U.S.* SIDE.
WHAT? ***WHERE*** DID YOU GET THOSE?
NAOMI MET SOMEONE WHO KNOWS A FORGER. WANT TO GIVE THEM A WHIRL?
PASSPORT
CALLIE, DON'T TUNE ME OUT BEFORE I'VE SAID MY PIECE.
WHATEVER YOU WANT IN THIS LIFE, I WANT IT TOO.
AS LONG AS IT'S WITH YOU. I'LL DO WHATEVER IT TAKES. I *CAN* CHANGE WITH YOU AT MY SIDE.
WHAT DO YOU SAY, CALLIE?
CALLIE?
CALLIE?

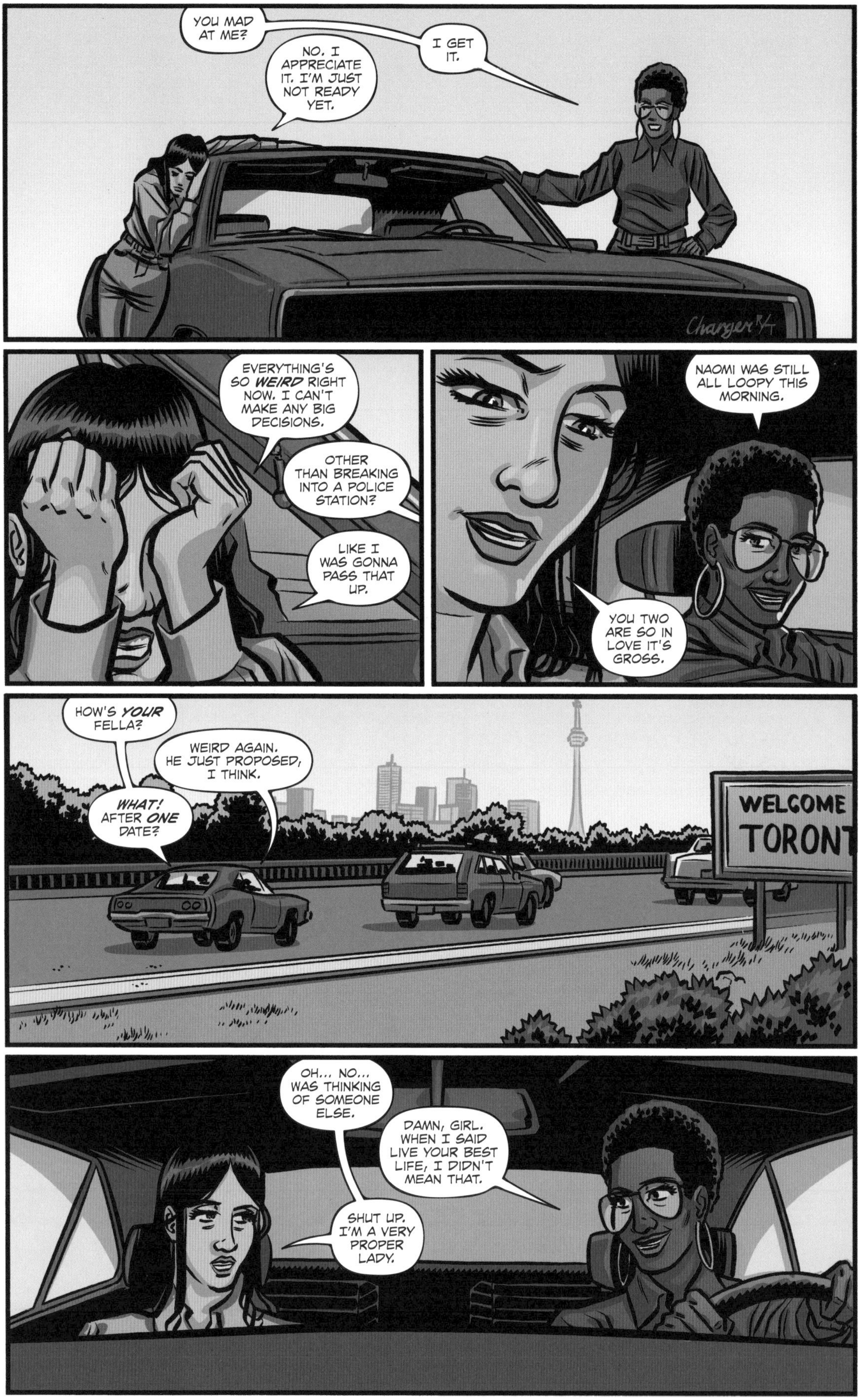
YOU MAD AT ME?
NO. I APPRECIATE IT. I'M JUST NOT READY YET.
I GET IT.
Charger R/T
EVERYTHING'S SO WEIRD RIGHT NOW. I CAN'T MAKE ANY BIG DECISIONS.
OTHER THAN BREAKING INTO A POLICE STATION?
LIKE I WAS GONNA PASS THAT UP.
NAOMI WAS STILL ALL LOOPY THIS MORNING.
YOU TWO ARE SO IN LOVE IT'S GROSS.
HOW'S YOUR FELLA?
WEIRD AGAIN. HE JUST PROPOSED, I THINK.
WHAT! AFTER ONE DATE?
WELCOME
TORONT
OH... NO... WAS THINKING OF SOMEONE ELSE.
DAMN, GIRL. WHEN I SAID LIVE YOUR BEST LIFE, I DIDN'T MEAN THAT.
SHUT UP. I'M A VERY PROPER LADY.

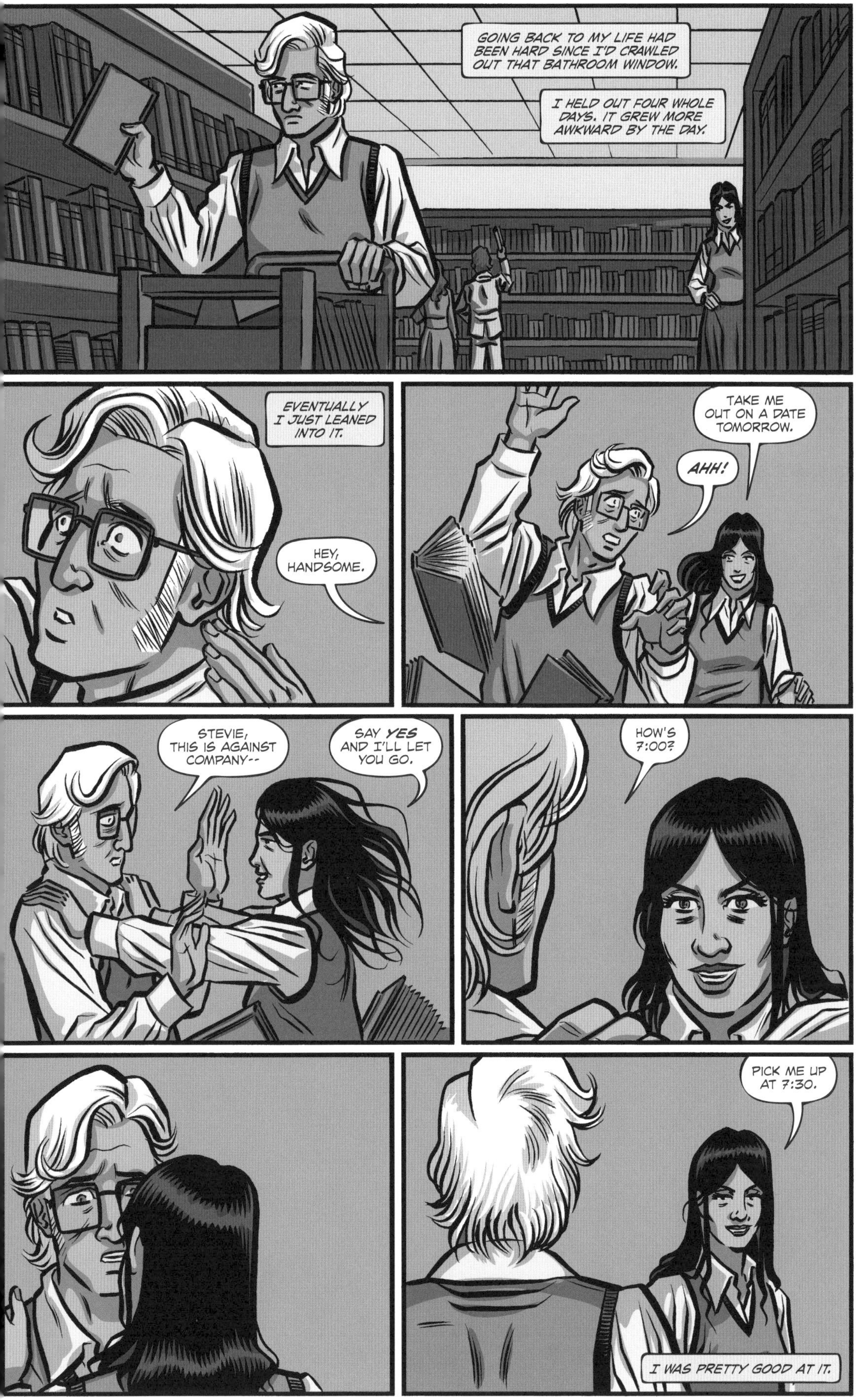
GOING BACK TO MY LIFE HAD BEEN HARD SINCE I'D CRAWLED OUT THAT BATHROOM WINDOW.
I HELD OUT FOUR WHOLE DAYS. IT GREW MORE AWKWARD BY THE DAY.
EVENTUALLY I JUST LEANED INTO IT.
HEY, HANDSOME.
TAKE ME OUT ON A DATE TOMORROW.
AHH!
STEVIE, THIS IS AGAINST COMPANY--
SAY YES AND I'LL LET YOU GO.
HOW'S 7:00?
PICK ME UP AT 7:30.
I WAS PRETTY GOOD AT IT.

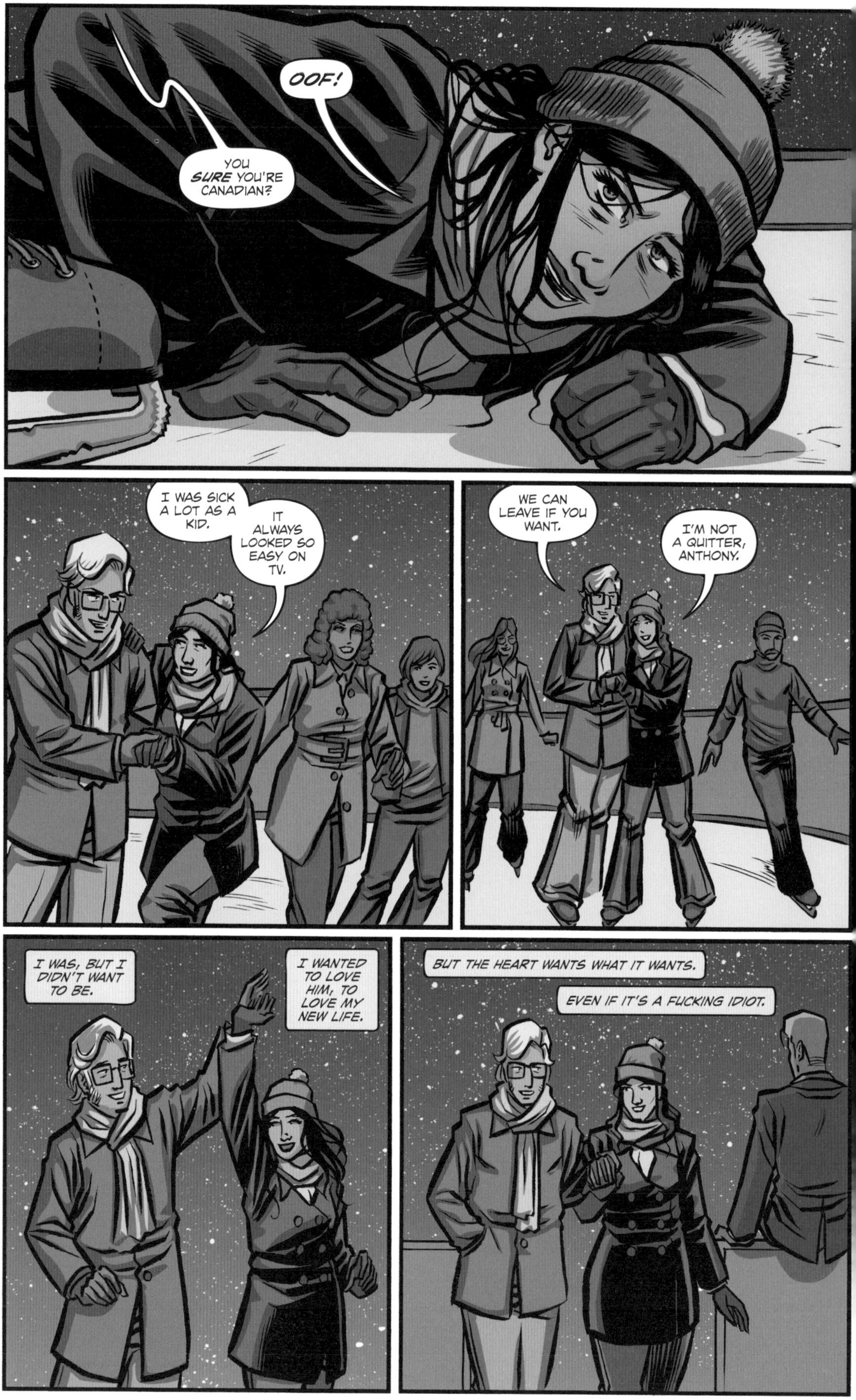
OOF!
YOU SURE YOU'RE CANADIAN?
I WAS SICK A LOT AS A KID.
IT ALWAYS LOOKED SO EASY ON TV.
WE CAN LEAVE IF YOU WANT.
I'M NOT A QUITTER, ANTHONY.
I WAS, BUT I DIDN'T WANT TO BE.
I WANTED TO LOVE HIM, TO LOVE MY NEW LIFE.
BUT THE HEART WANTS WHAT IT WANTS.
EVEN IF IT'S A FUCKING IDIOT.

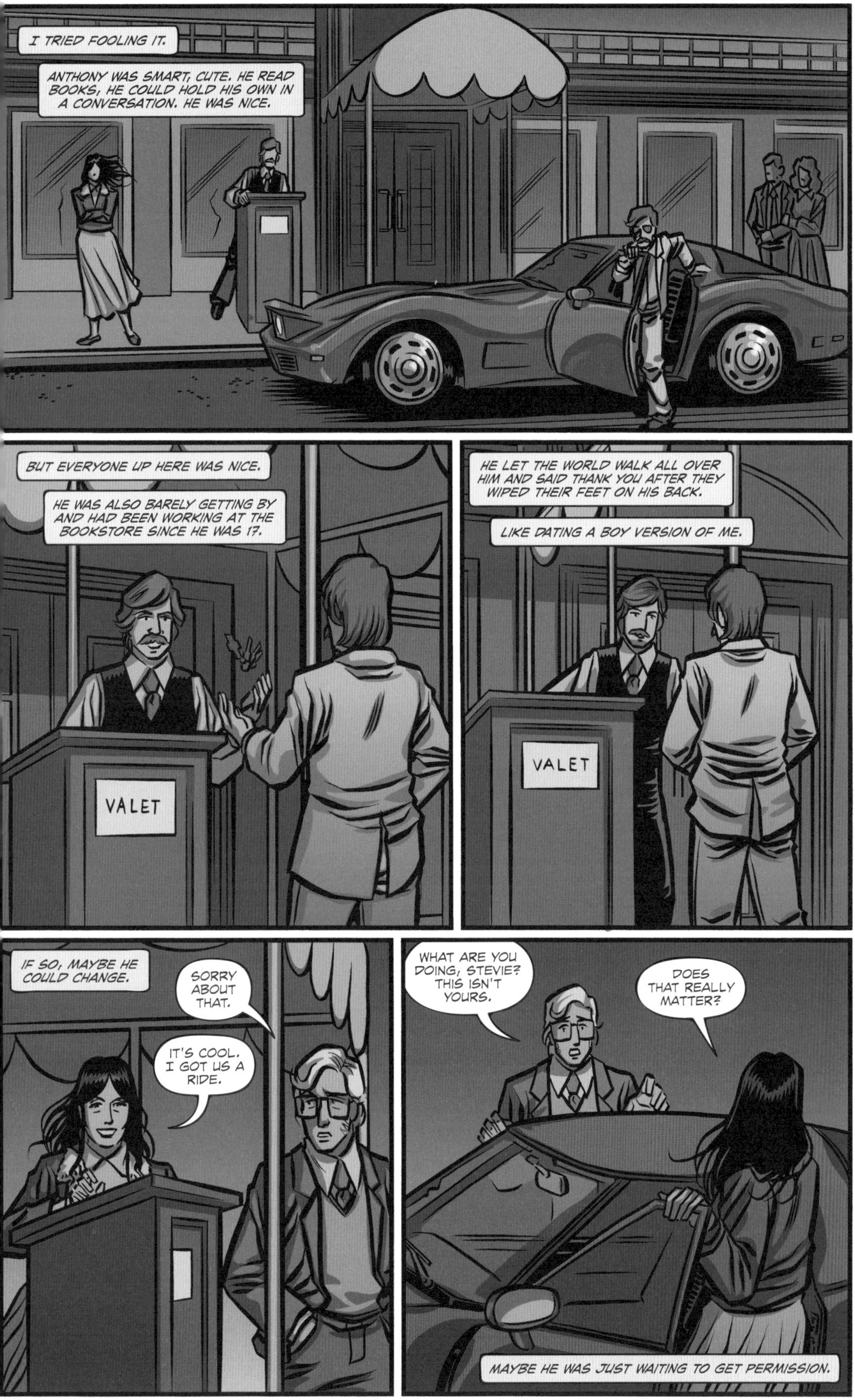
I TRIED FOOLING IT.
ANTHONY WAS SMART, CUTE. HE READ BOOKS, HE COULD HOLD HIS OWN IN A CONVERSATION. HE WAS NICE.
BUT EVERYONE UP HERE WAS NICE.
HE WAS ALSO BARELY GETTING BY AND HAD BEEN WORKING AT THE BOOKSTORE SINCE HE WAS 17.
VALET
HE LET THE WORLD WALK ALL OVER HIM AND SAID THANK YOU AFTER THEY WIPED THEIR FEET ON HIS BACK.
LIKE DATING A BOY VERSION OF ME.
VALET
IF SO, MAYBE HE COULD CHANGE.
SORRY ABOUT THAT.
IT'S COOL. I GOT US A RIDE.
WHAT ARE YOU DOING, STEVIE? THIS ISN'T YOURS.
DOES THAT REALLY MATTER?
MAYBE HE WAS JUST WAITING TO GET PERMISSION.

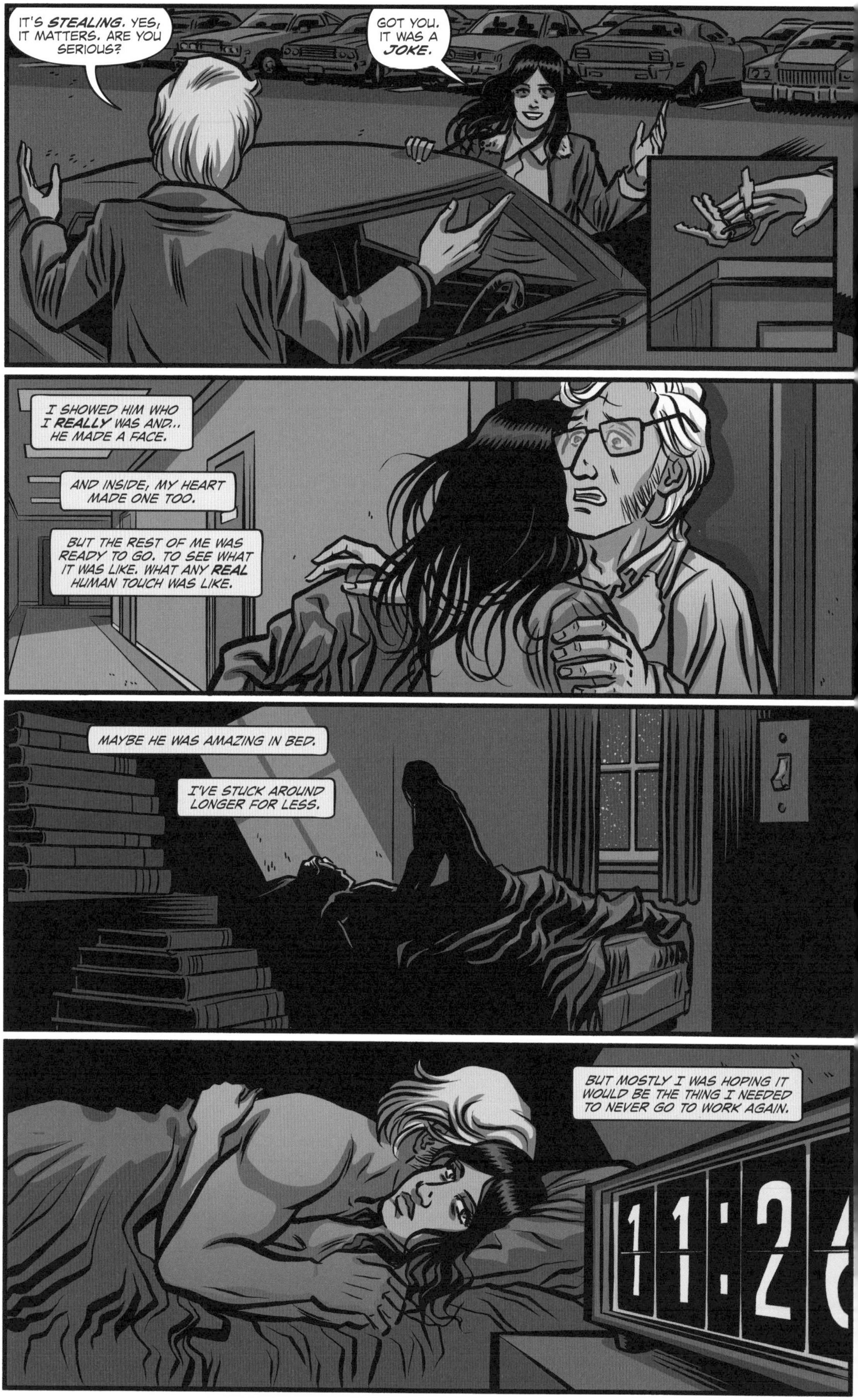
IT'S STEALING. YES, IT MATTERS. ARE YOU SERIOUS?
GOT YOU. IT WAS A JOKE.
I SHOWED HIM WHO I REALLY WAS AND... HE MADE A FACE.
AND INSIDE, MY HEART MADE ONE TOO.
BUT THE REST OF ME WAS READY TO GO. TO SEE WHAT IT WAS LIKE. WHAT ANY REAL HUMAN TOUCH WAS LIKE.
MAYBE HE WAS AMAZING IN BED.
I'VE STUCK AROUND LONGER FOR LESS.
BUT MOSTLY I WAS HOPING IT WOULD BE THE THING I NEEDED TO NEVER GO TO WORK AGAIN.

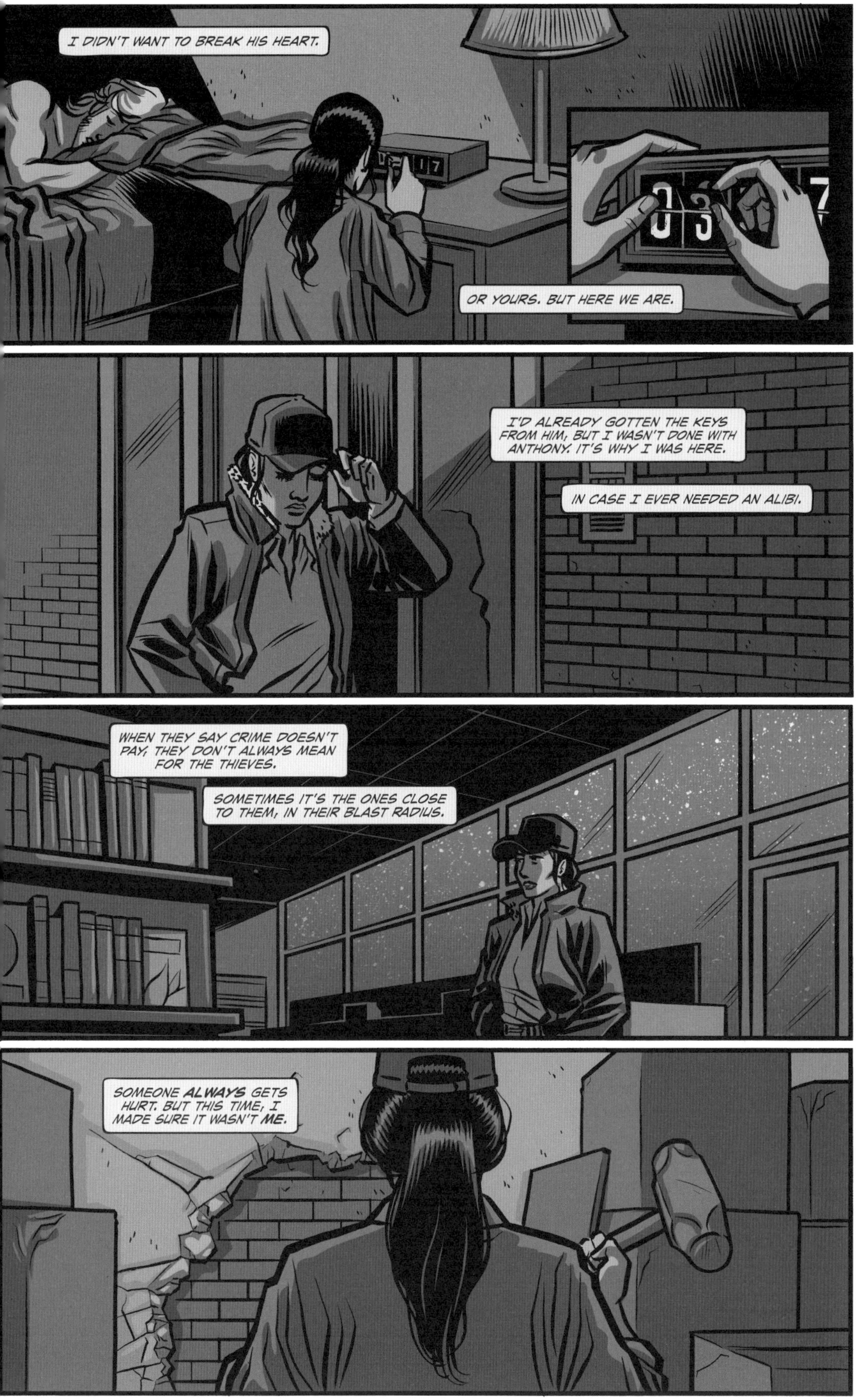
I DIDN'T WANT TO BREAK HIS HEART.
OR YOURS. BUT HERE WE ARE.
I'D ALREADY GOTTEN THE KEYS FROM HIM, BUT I WASN'T DONE WITH ANTHONY. IT'S WHY I WAS HERE.
IN CASE I EVER NEEDED AN ALIBI.
WHEN THEY SAY CRIME DOESN'T PAY, THEY DON'T ALWAYS MEAN FOR THE THIEVES.
SOMETIMES IT'S THE ONES CLOSE TO THEM, IN THEIR BLAST RADIUS.
SOMEONE ALWAYS GETS HURT. BUT THIS TIME, I MADE SURE IT WASN'T ME.

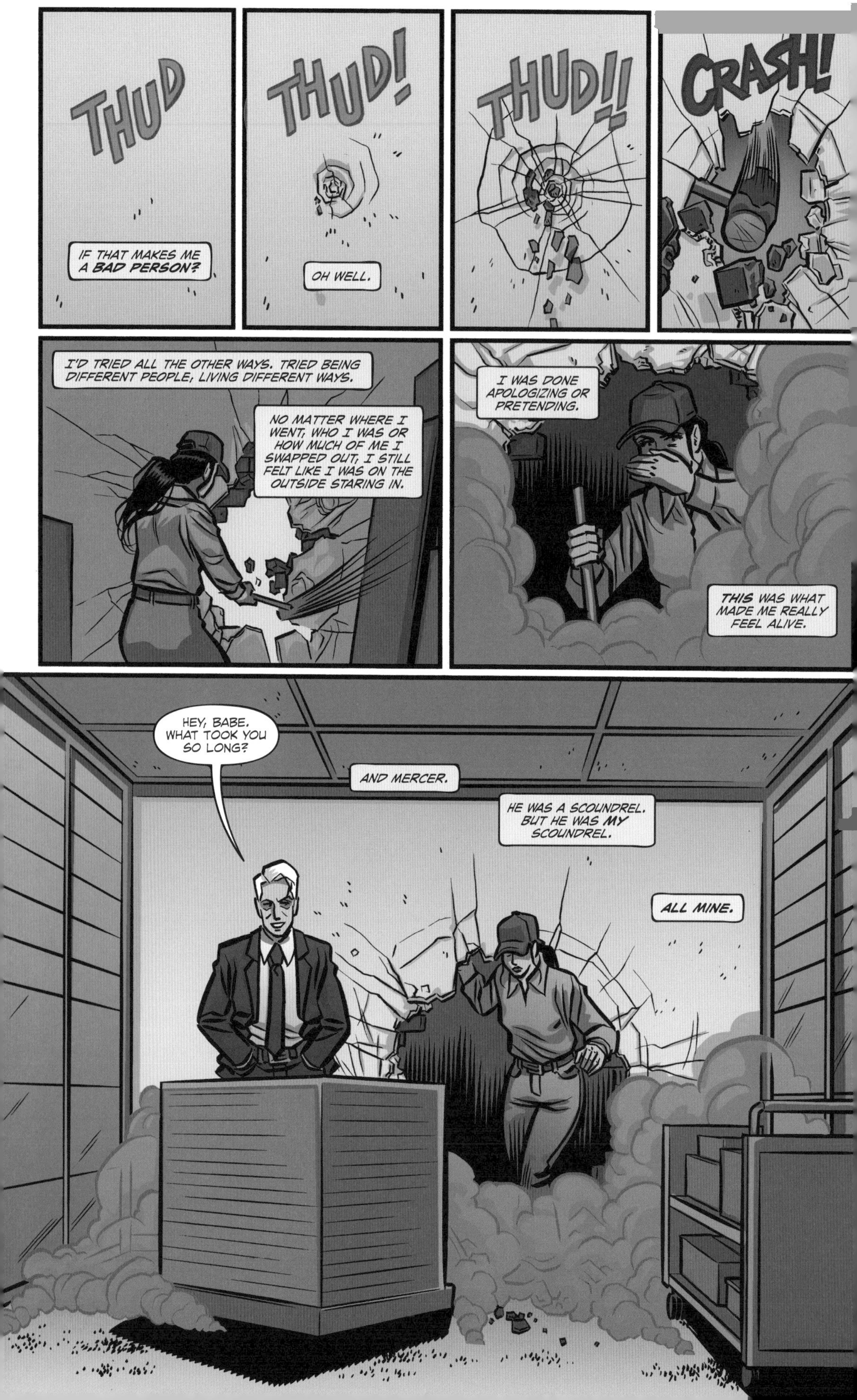
THUD
IF THAT MAKES ME A BAD PERSON?
THUD!
OH WELL.
THUD!!
CRASH!
I'D TRIED ALL THE OTHER WAYS. TRIED BEING DIFFERENT PEOPLE; LIVING DIFFERENT WAYS.
NO MATTER WHERE I WENT, WHO I WAS OR HOW MUCH OF ME I SWAPPED OUT, I STILL FELT LIKE I WAS ON THE OUTSIDE STARING IN.
I WAS DONE APOLOGIZING OR PRETENDING.
THIS WAS WHAT MADE ME REALLY FEEL ALIVE.
HEY, BABE. WHAT TOOK YOU SO LONG?
AND MERCER.
HE WAS A SCOUNDREL. BUT HE WAS MY SCOUNDREL.
ALL MINE.

CHAPTER 3

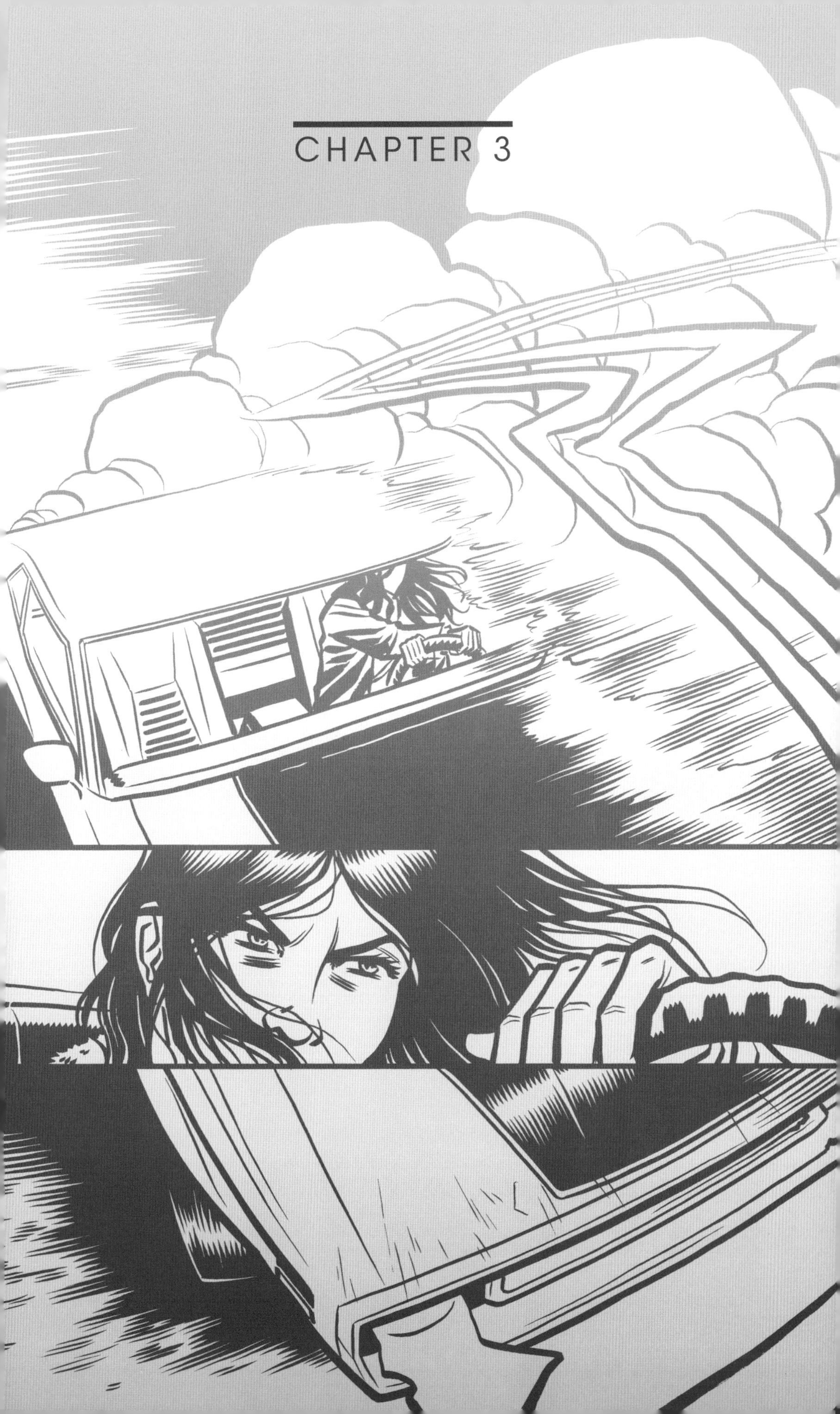

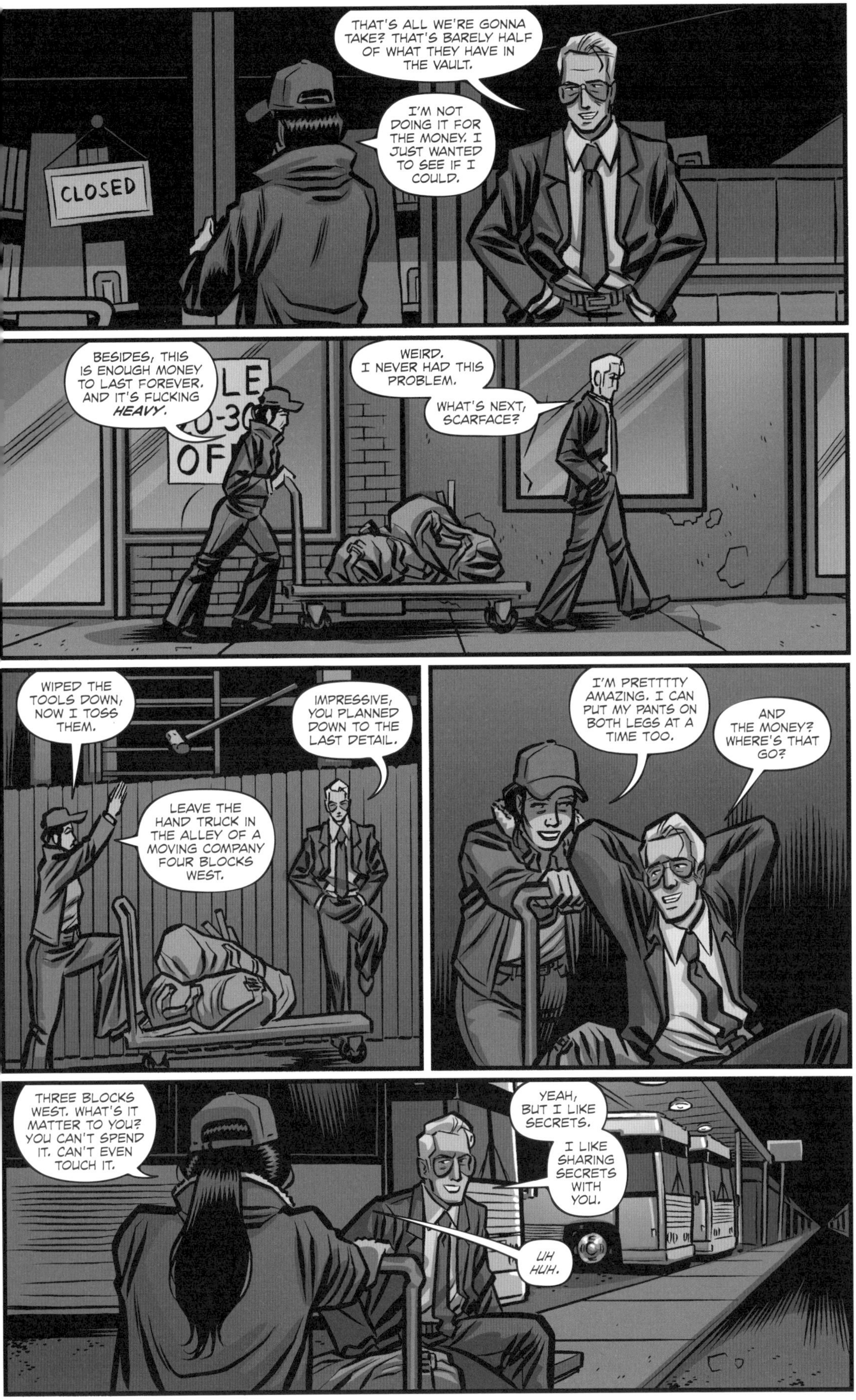
THAT'S ALL WE'RE GONNA TAKE? THAT'S BARELY HALF OF WHAT THEY HAVE IN THE VAULT.
I'M NOT DOING IT FOR THE MONEY. I JUST WANTED TO SEE IF I COULD.
CLOSED
BESIDES, THIS IS ENOUGH MONEY TO LAST FOREVER. AND IT'S FUCKING *HEAVY*.
WEIRD. I NEVER HAD THIS PROBLEM.
WHAT'S NEXT, SCARFACE?
WIPED THE TOOLS DOWN, NOW I TOSS THEM.
IMPRESSIVE, YOU PLANNED DOWN TO THE LAST DETAIL.
LEAVE THE HAND TRUCK IN THE ALLEY OF A MOVING COMPANY FOUR BLOCKS WEST.
I'M PRETTTTY AMAZING. I CAN PUT MY PANTS ON BOTH LEGS AT A TIME TOO.
AND THE MONEY? WHERE'S THAT GO?
THREE BLOCKS WEST. WHAT'S IT MATTER TO YOU? YOU CAN'T SPEND IT. CAN'T EVEN TOUCH IT.
YEAH, BUT I LIKE SECRETS.
I LIKE SHARING SECRETS WITH YOU.
UH HUH.

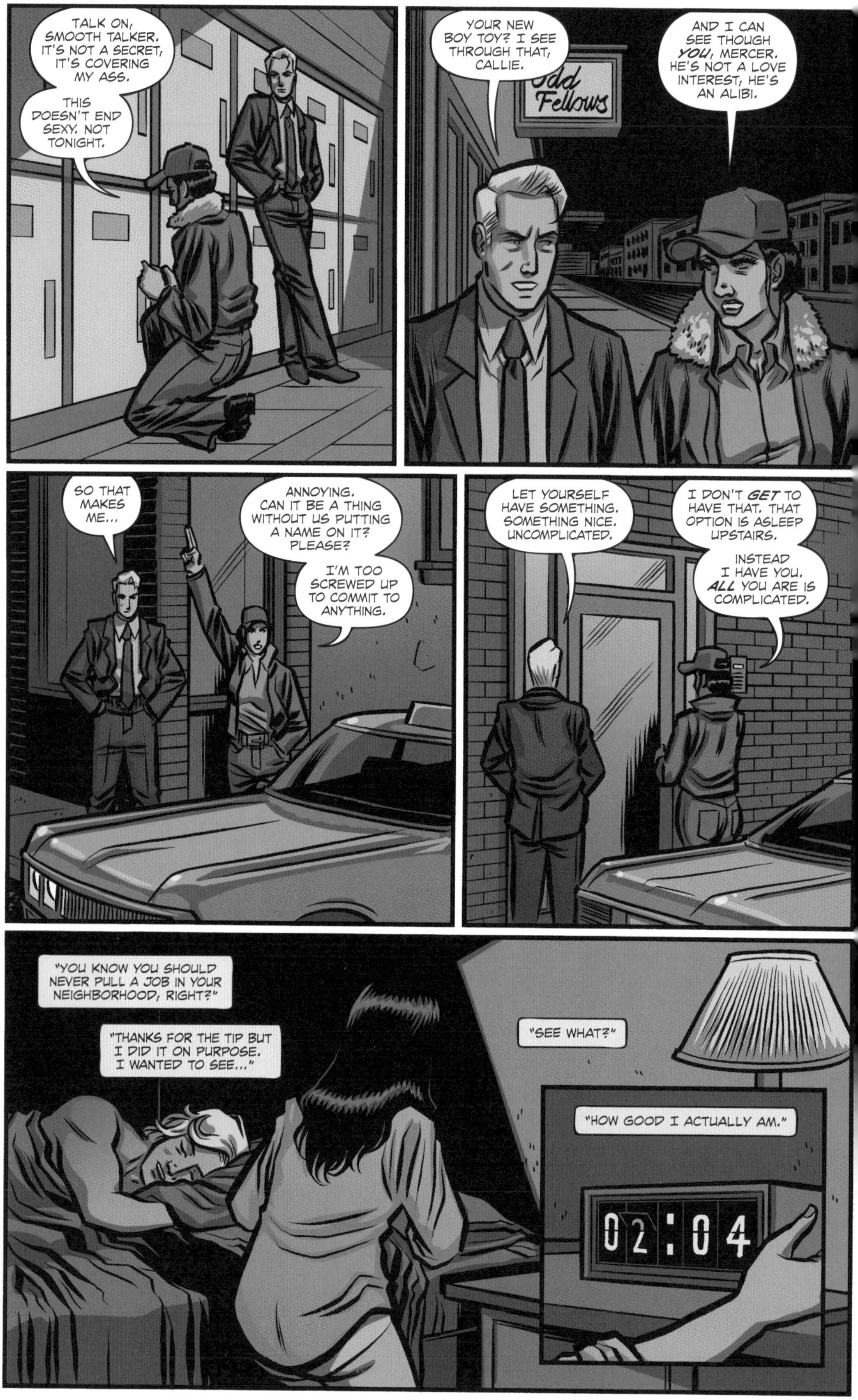
TALK ON, SMOOTH TALKER. IT'S NOT A SECRET, IT'S COVERING MY ASS.
THIS DOESN'T END SEXY. NOT TONIGHT.
YOUR NEW BOY TOY? I SEE THROUGH THAT, CALLIE.
Odd Fellows
AND I CAN SEE THOUGH YOU, MERCER. HE'S NOT A LOVE INTEREST, HE'S AN ALIBI.
SO THAT MAKES ME...
ANNOYING. CAN IT BE A THING WITHOUT US PUTTING A NAME ON IT? PLEASE?
I'M TOO SCREWED UP TO COMMIT TO ANYTHING.
LET YOURSELF HAVE SOMETHING. SOMETHING NICE. UNCOMPLICATED.
I DON'T GET TO HAVE THAT. THAT OPTION IS ASLEEP UPSTAIRS.
INSTEAD I HAVE YOU. ALL YOU ARE IS COMPLICATED.
"YOU KNOW YOU SHOULD NEVER PULL A JOB IN YOUR NEIGHBORHOOD, RIGHT?"
"THANKS FOR THE TIP BUT I DID IT ON PURPOSE. I WANTED TO SEE..."
"SEE WHAT?"
"HOW GOOD I ACTUALLY AM."
02:04

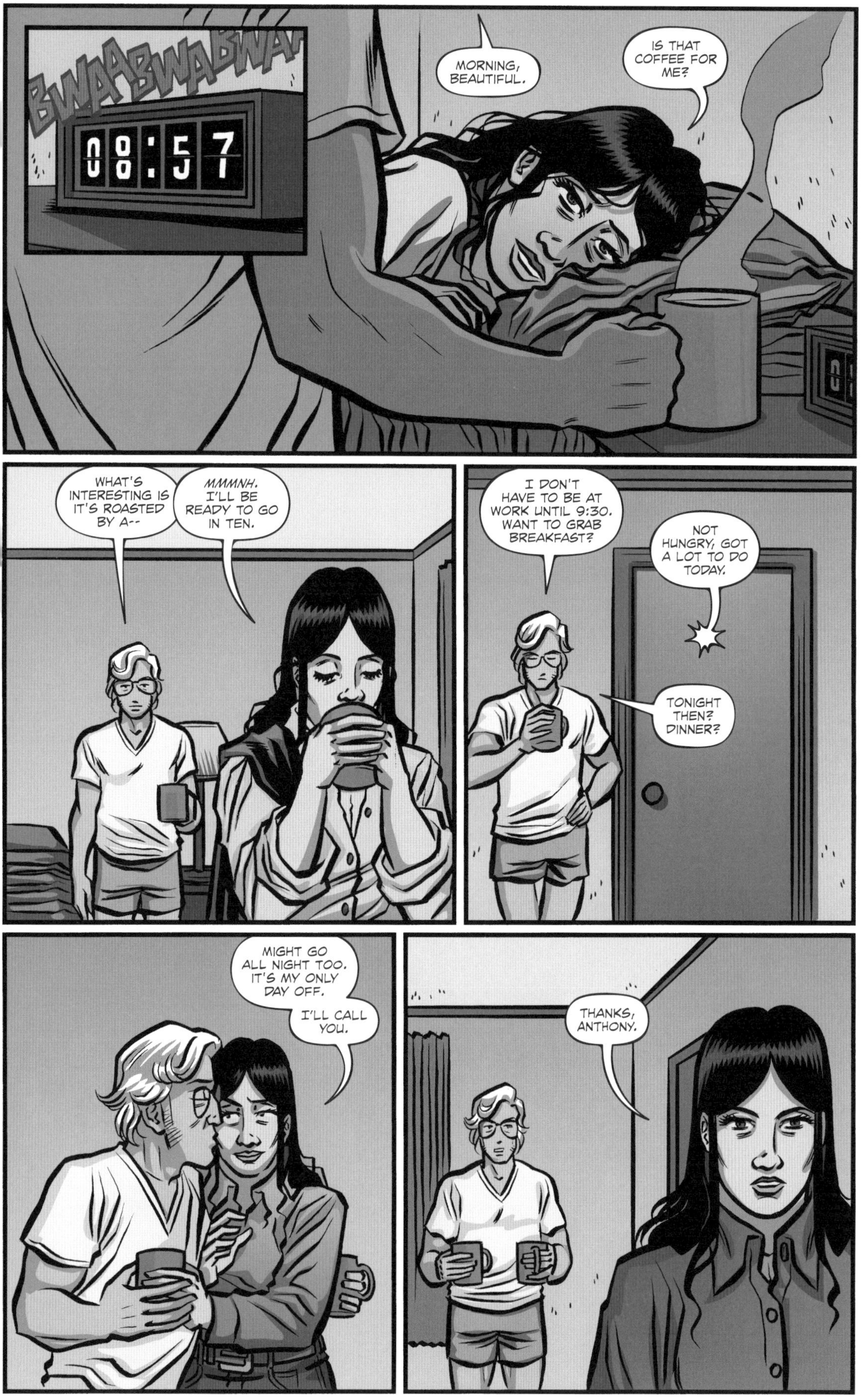
BWAABWABWA
08:57
MORNING, BEAUTIFUL.
IS THAT COFFEE FOR ME?
WHAT'S INTERESTING IS IT'S ROASTED BY A--
MMMNH. I'LL BE READY TO GO IN TEN.
I DON'T HAVE TO BE AT WORK UNTIL 9:30. WANT TO GRAB BREAKFAST?
NOT HUNGRY; GOT A LOT TO DO TODAY.
TONIGHT THEN? DINNER?
MIGHT GO ALL NIGHT TOO. IT'S MY ONLY DAY OFF.
I'LL CALL YOU.
THANKS, ANTHONY.

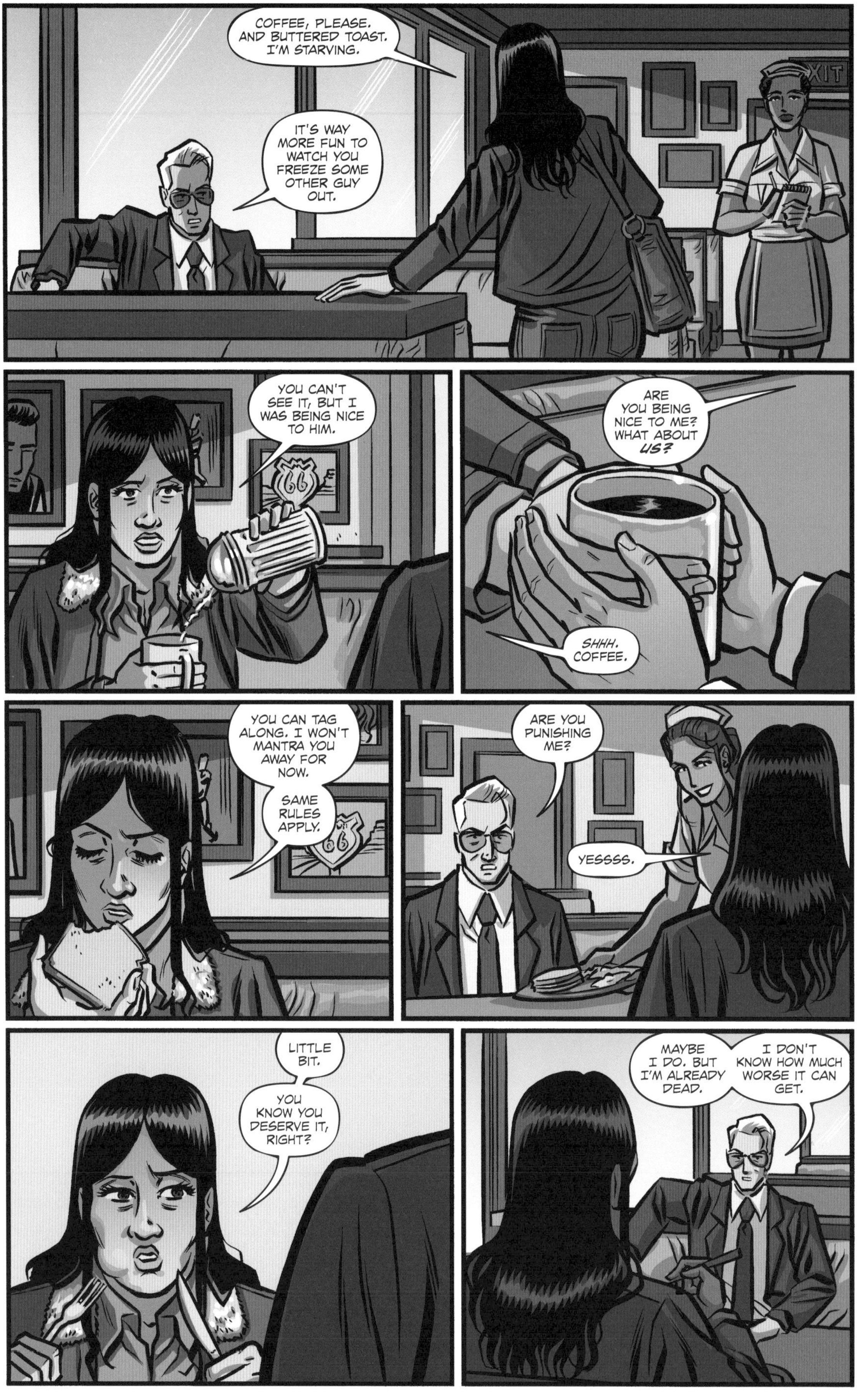
COFFEE, PLEASE. AND BUTTERED TOAST. I'M STARVING.
IT'S WAY MORE FUN TO WATCH YOU FREEZE SOME OTHER GUY OUT.
EXIT
YOU CAN'T SEE IT, BUT I WAS BEING NICE TO HIM.
ARE YOU BEING NICE TO ME? WHAT ABOUT US?
SHHH. COFFEE.
YOU CAN TAG ALONG. I WON'T MANTRA YOU AWAY FOR NOW.
SAME RULES APPLY.
ARE YOU PUNISHING ME?
YESSSS.
LITTLE BIT.
YOU KNOW YOU DESERVE IT, RIGHT?
MAYBE I DO. BUT I'M ALREADY DEAD.
I DON'T KNOW HOW MUCH WORSE IT CAN GET.

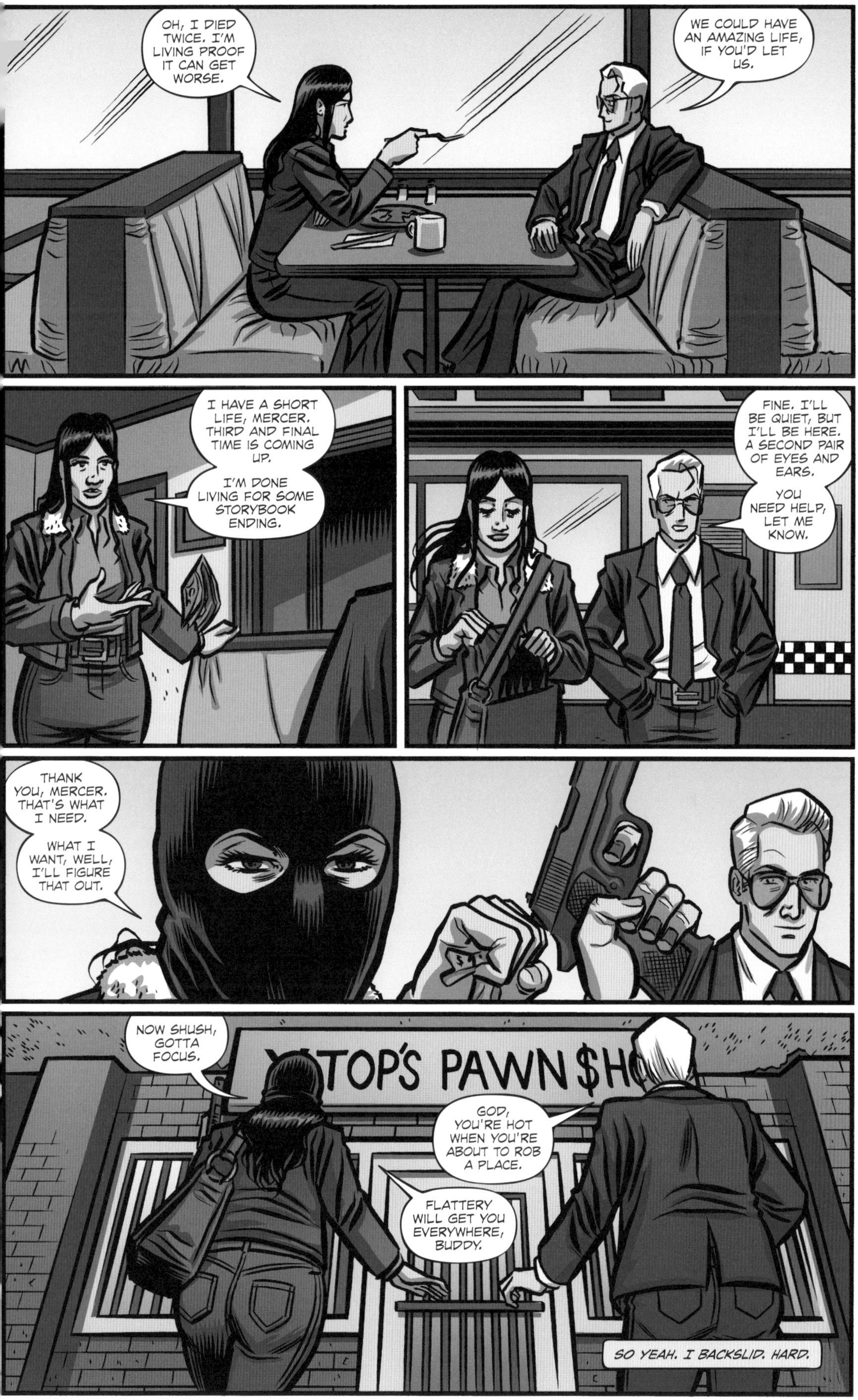
OH, I DIED TWICE. I'M LIVING PROOF IT CAN GET WORSE.
WE COULD HAVE AN AMAZING LIFE, IF YOU'D LET US.
I HAVE A SHORT LIFE, MERCER. THIRD AND FINAL TIME IS COMING UP.
I'M DONE LIVING FOR SOME STORYBOOK ENDING.
FINE. I'LL BE QUIET, BUT I'LL BE HERE. A SECOND PAIR OF EYES AND EARS.
YOU NEED HELP, LET ME KNOW.
THANK YOU, MERCER. THAT'S WHAT I NEED.
WHAT I WANT, WELL, I'LL FIGURE THAT OUT.
NOW SHUSH, GOTTA FOCUS.
TOP'S PAWN
GOD, YOU'RE HOT WHEN YOU'RE ABOUT TO ROB A PLACE.
FLATTERY WILL GET YOU EVERYWHERE, BUDDY.
SO YEAH. I BACKSLID. HARD.

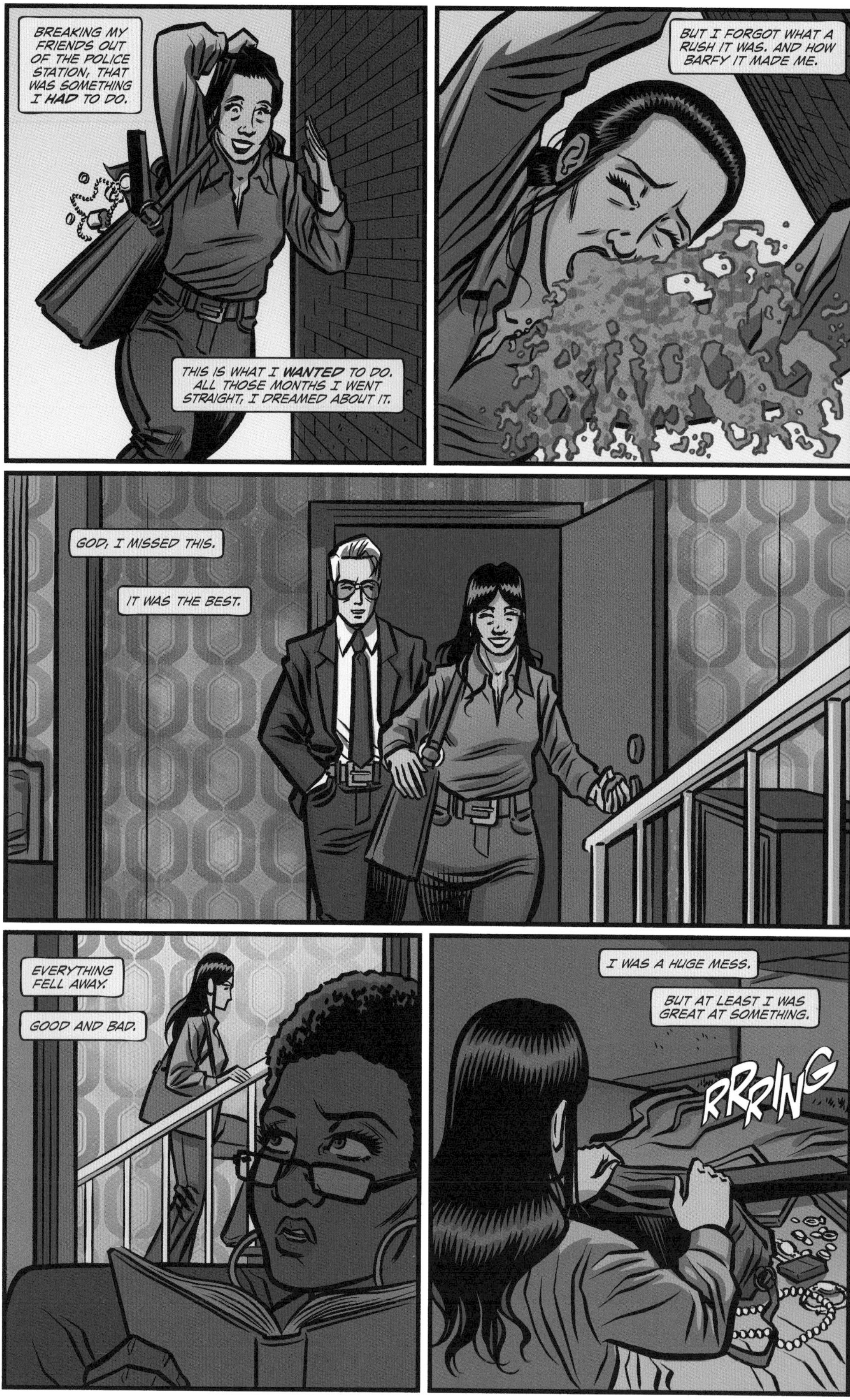
BREAKING MY FRIENDS OUT OF THE POLICE STATION, THAT WAS SOMETHING I HAD TO DO.
THIS IS WHAT I WANTED TO DO. ALL THOSE MONTHS I WENT STRAIGHT, I DREAMED ABOUT IT.
BUT I FORGOT WHAT A RUSH IT WAS. AND HOW BARFY IT MADE ME.
GOD, I MISSED THIS.
IT WAS THE BEST.
EVERYTHING FELL AWAY.
GOOD AND BAD.
I WAS A HUGE MESS.
BUT AT LEAST I WAS GREAT AT SOMETHING.
RRRING

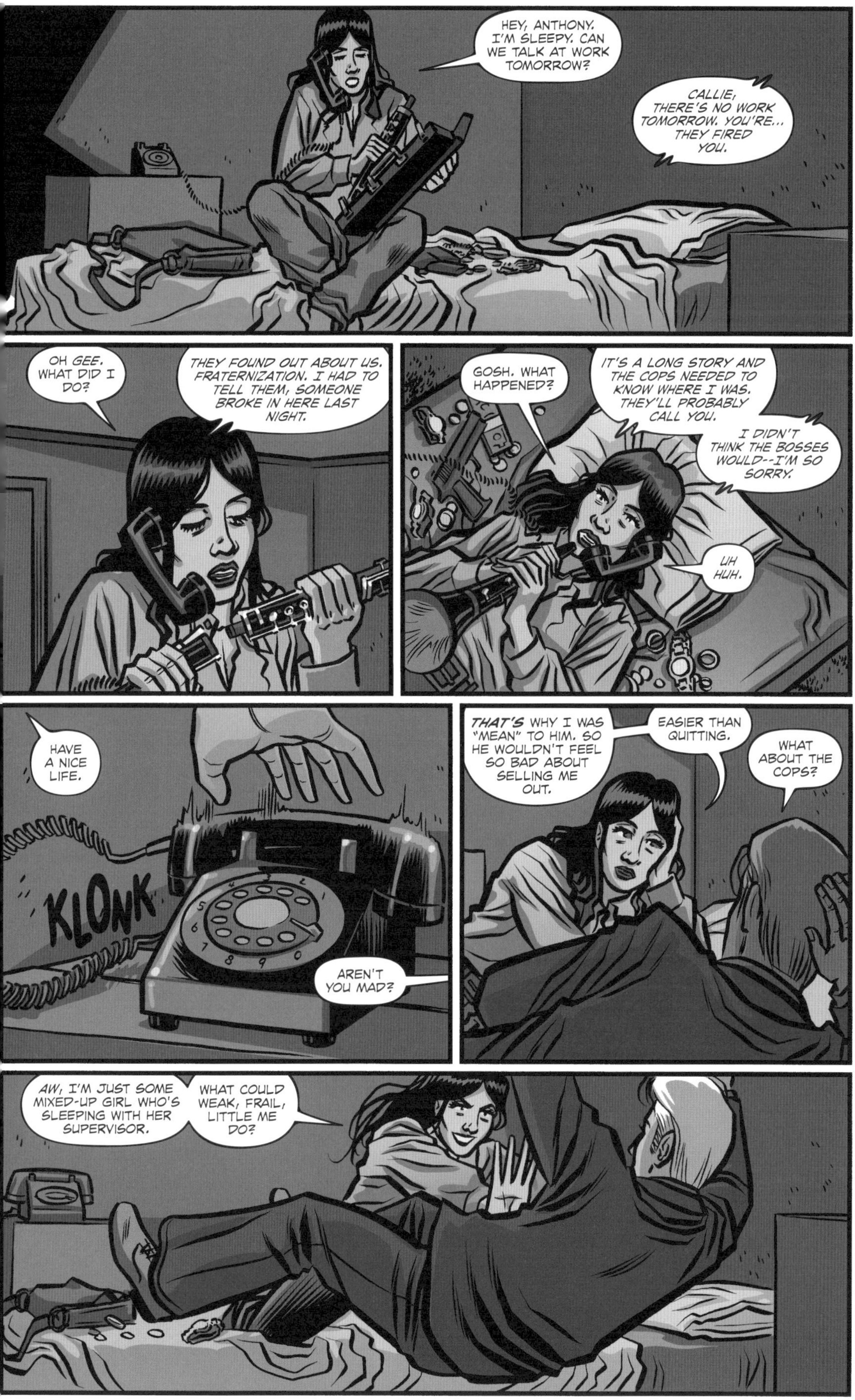
HEY, ANTHONY. I'M SLEEPY. CAN WE TALK AT WORK TOMORROW?
CALLIE, THERE'S NO WORK TOMORROW. YOU'RE... THEY FIRED YOU.
OH GEE. WHAT DID I DO?
THEY FOUND OUT ABOUT US. FRATERNIZATION. I HAD TO TELL THEM, SOMEONE BROKE IN HERE LAST NIGHT.
GOSH. WHAT HAPPENED?
IT'S A LONG STORY AND THE COPS NEEDED TO KNOW WHERE I WAS. THEY'LL PROBABLY CALL YOU.
I DIDN'T THINK THE BOSSES WOULD--I'M SO SORRY.
UH HUH.
HAVE A NICE LIFE.
KLONK
AREN'T YOU MAD?
THAT'S WHY I WAS "MEAN" TO HIM. SO HE WOULDN'T FEEL SO BAD ABOUT SELLING ME OUT.
EASIER THAN QUITTING.
WHAT ABOUT THE COPS?
AW, I'M JUST SOME MIXED-UP GIRL WHO'S SLEEPING WITH HER SUPERVISOR.
WHAT COULD WEAK, FRAIL, LITTLE ME DO?

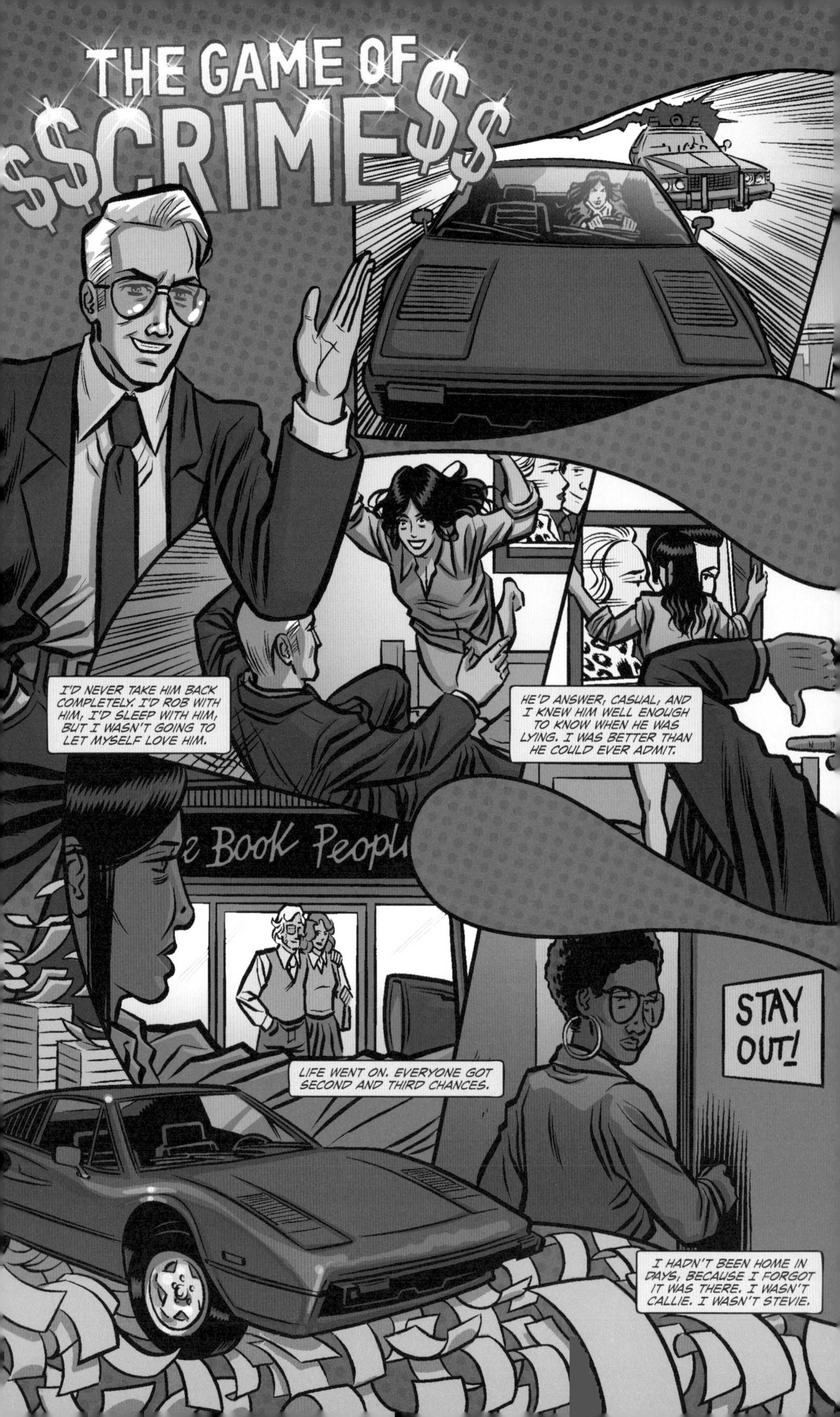
THE GAME OF $$CRIME$$
I'D NEVER TAKE HIM BACK COMPLETELY. I'D ROB WITH HIM, I'D SLEEP WITH HIM, BUT I WASN'T GOING TO LET MYSELF LOVE HIM.
HE'D ANSWER, CASUAL, AND I KNEW HIM WELL ENOUGH TO KNOW WHEN HE WAS LYING. I WAS BETTER THAN HE COULD EVER ADMIT.
e Book Peopl
LIFE WENT ON. EVERYONE GOT SECOND AND THIRD CHANCES.
STAY OUT!
I HADN'T BEEN HOME IN DAYS, BECAUSE I FORGOT IT WAS THERE. I WASN'T CALLIE. I WASN'T STEVIE.

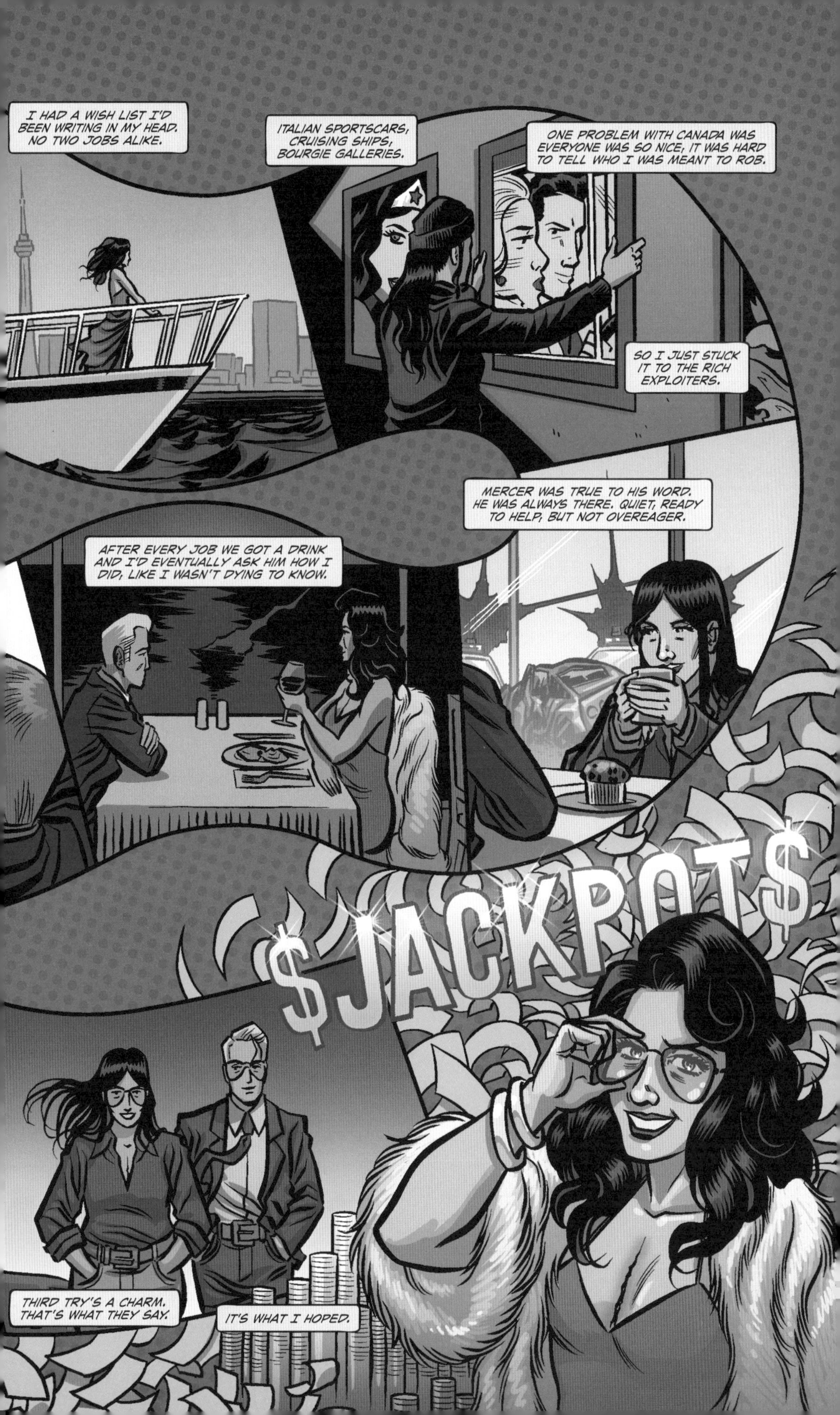
I HAD A WISH LIST I'D BEEN WRITING IN MY HEAD. NO TWO JOBS ALIKE.
ITALIAN SPORTSCARS, CRUISING SHIPS, BOURGIE GALLERIES.
ONE PROBLEM WITH CANADA WAS EVERYONE WAS SO NICE, IT WAS HARD TO TELL WHO I WAS MEANT TO ROB.
SO I JUST STUCK IT TO THE RICH EXPLOITERS.
MERCER WAS TRUE TO HIS WORD. HE WAS ALWAYS THERE. QUIET, READY TO HELP, BUT NOT OVEREAGER.
AFTER EVERY JOB WE GOT A DRINK AND I'D EVENTUALLY ASK HIM HOW I DID, LIKE I WASN'T DYING TO KNOW.
$JACKPOT$
THIRD TRY'S A CHARM. THAT'S WHAT THEY SAY.
IT'S WHAT I HOPED.

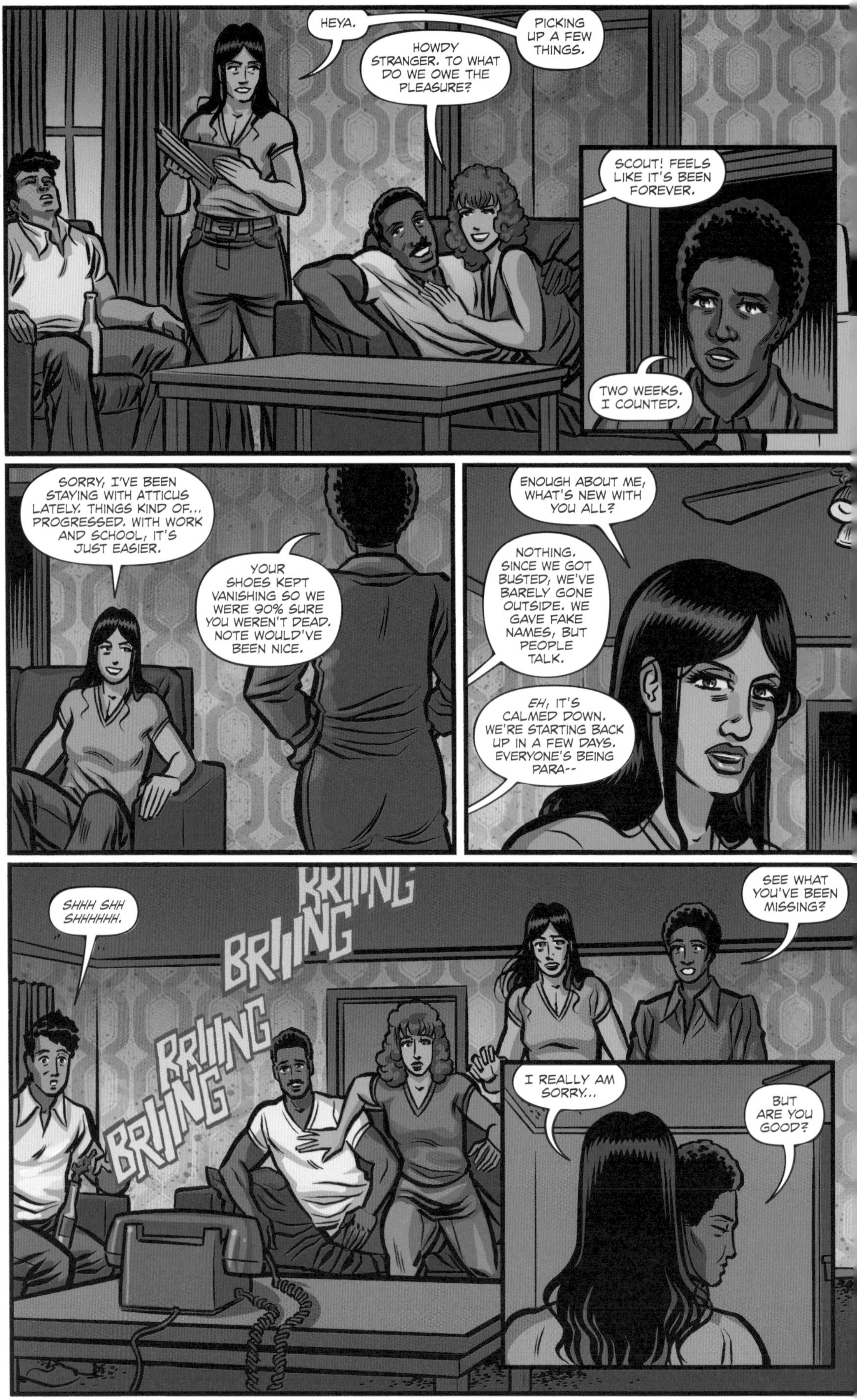
HEYA.
HOWDY STRANGER. TO WHAT DO WE OWE THE PLEASURE?
PICKING UP A FEW THINGS.
SCOUT! FEELS LIKE IT'S BEEN FOREVER.
TWO WEEKS. I COUNTED.
SORRY, I'VE BEEN STAYING WITH ATTICUS LATELY. THINGS KIND OF... PROGRESSED. WITH WORK AND SCHOOL, IT'S JUST EASIER.
YOUR SHOES KEPT VANISHING SO WE WERE 90% SURE YOU WEREN'T DEAD. NOTE WOULD'VE BEEN NICE.
ENOUGH ABOUT ME, WHAT'S NEW WITH YOU ALL?
NOTHING. SINCE WE GOT BUSTED, WE'VE BARELY GONE OUTSIDE. WE GAVE FAKE NAMES, BUT PEOPLE TALK.
EH, IT'S CALMED DOWN. WE'RE STARTING BACK UP IN A FEW DAYS. EVERYONE'S BEING PARA--
SHHH SHH SHHHHHH.
BRIIING
BRIIING
BRIIING
BRIIING
SEE WHAT YOU'VE BEEN MISSING?
I REALLY AM SORRY...
BUT ARE YOU GOOD?

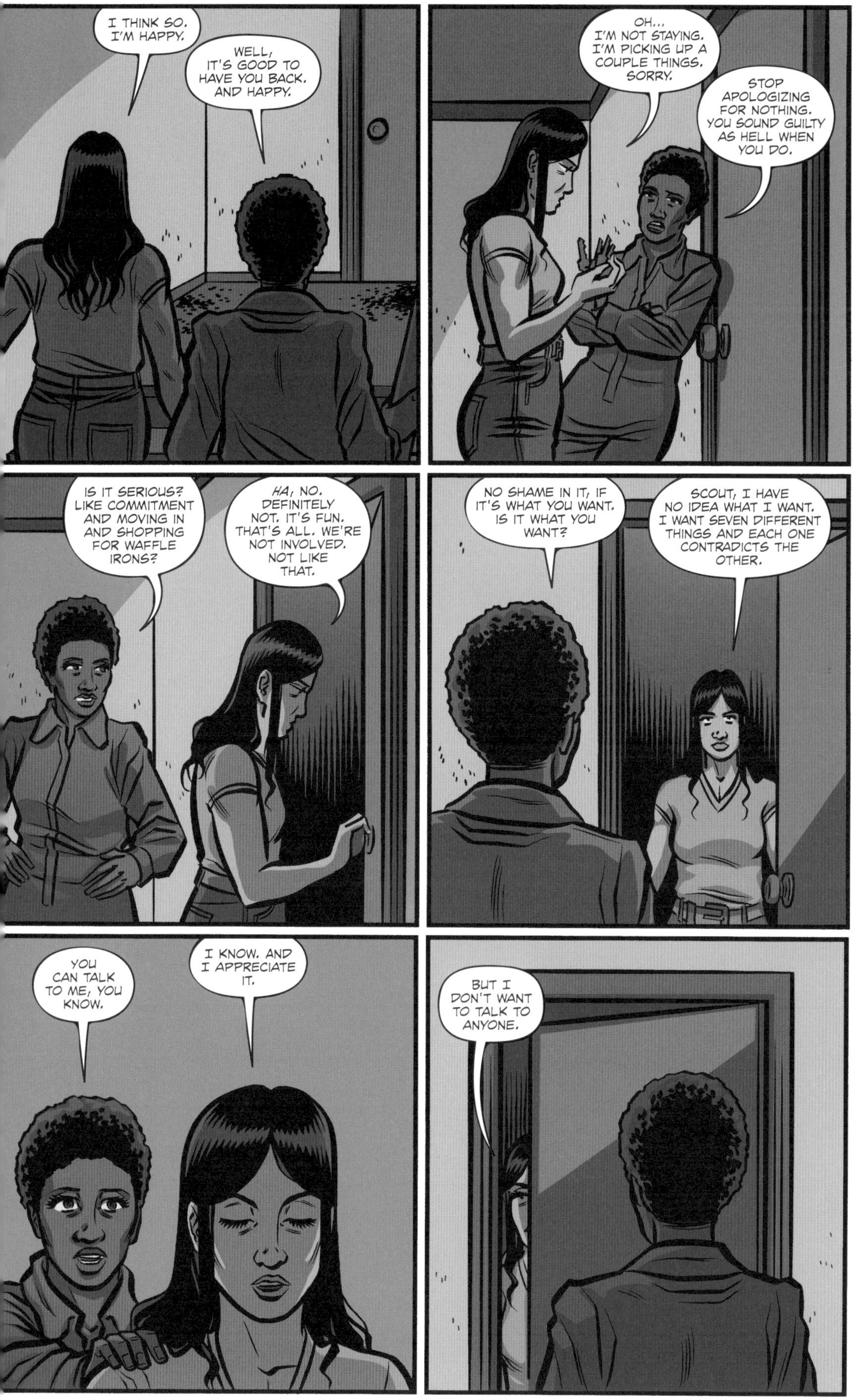
I THINK SO. I'M HAPPY.
WELL, IT'S GOOD TO HAVE YOU BACK. AND HAPPY.
OH... I'M NOT STAYING. I'M PICKING UP A COUPLE THINGS. SORRY.
STOP APOLOGIZING FOR NOTHING. YOU SOUND GUILTY AS HELL WHEN YOU DO.
IS IT SERIOUS? LIKE COMMITMENT AND MOVING IN AND SHOPPING FOR WAFFLE IRONS?
HA, NO. DEFINITELY NOT. IT'S FUN. THAT'S ALL. WE'RE NOT INVOLVED. NOT LIKE THAT.
NO SHAME IN IT, IF IT'S WHAT YOU WANT. IS IT WHAT YOU WANT?
SCOUT, I HAVE NO IDEA WHAT I WANT. I WANT SEVEN DIFFERENT THINGS AND EACH ONE CONTRADICTS THE OTHER.
YOU CAN TALK TO ME, YOU KNOW.
I KNOW. AND I APPRECIATE IT.
BUT I DON'T WANT TO TALK TO ANYONE.

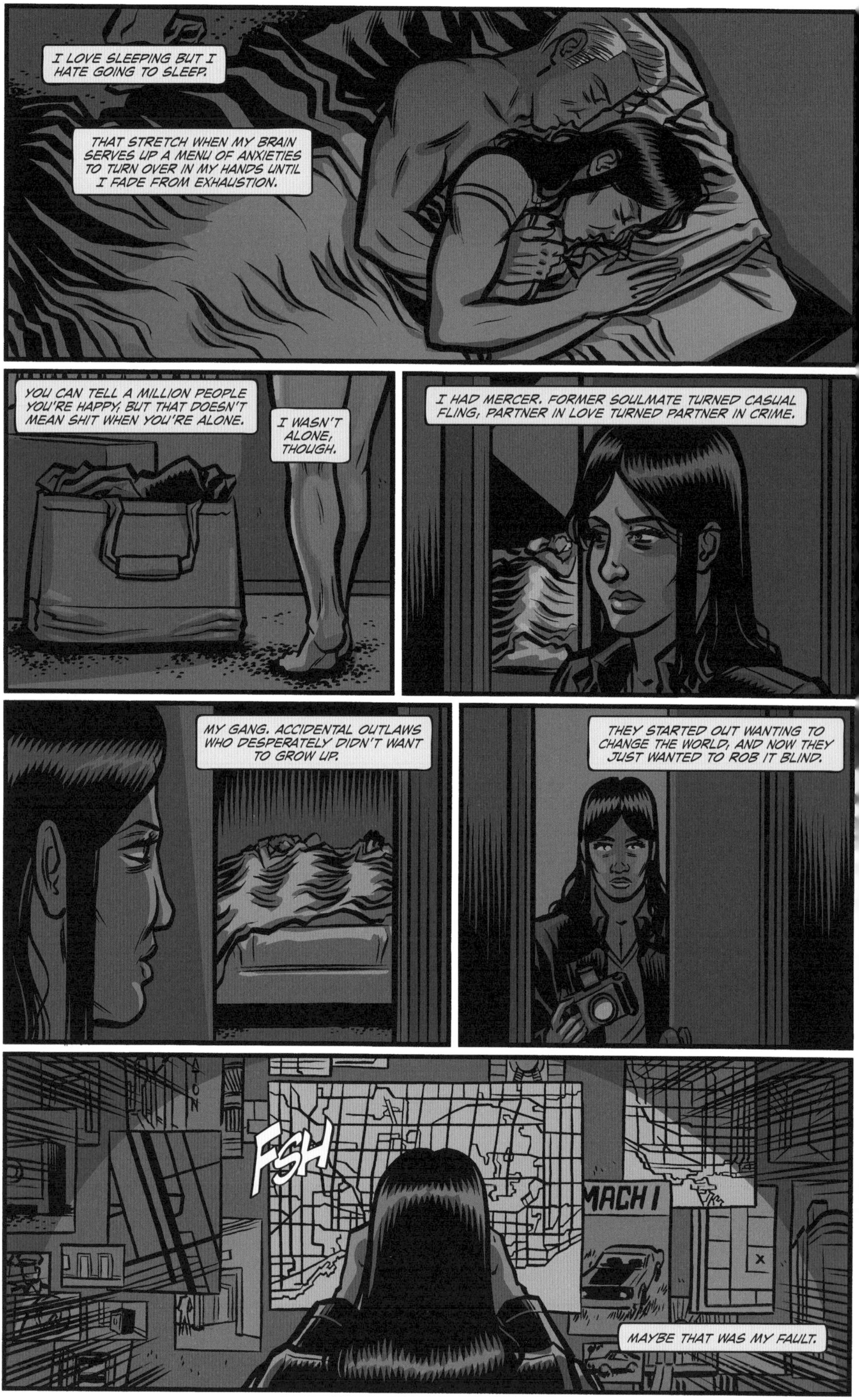
I LOVE SLEEPING BUT I HATE GOING TO SLEEP.
THAT STRETCH WHEN MY BRAIN SERVES UP A MENU OF ANXIETIES TO TURN OVER IN MY HANDS UNTIL I FADE FROM EXHAUSTION.
YOU CAN TELL A MILLION PEOPLE YOU'RE HAPPY, BUT THAT DOESN'T MEAN SHIT WHEN YOU'RE ALONE.
I WASN'T ALONE, THOUGH.
I HAD MERCER. FORMER SOULMATE TURNED CASUAL FLING, PARTNER IN LOVE TURNED PARTNER IN CRIME.
MY GANG. ACCIDENTAL OUTLAWS WHO DESPERATELY DIDN'T WANT TO GROW UP.
THEY STARTED OUT WANTING TO CHANGE THE WORLD, AND NOW THEY JUST WANTED TO ROB IT BLIND.
FSH
MACH I
MAYBE THAT WAS MY FAULT.

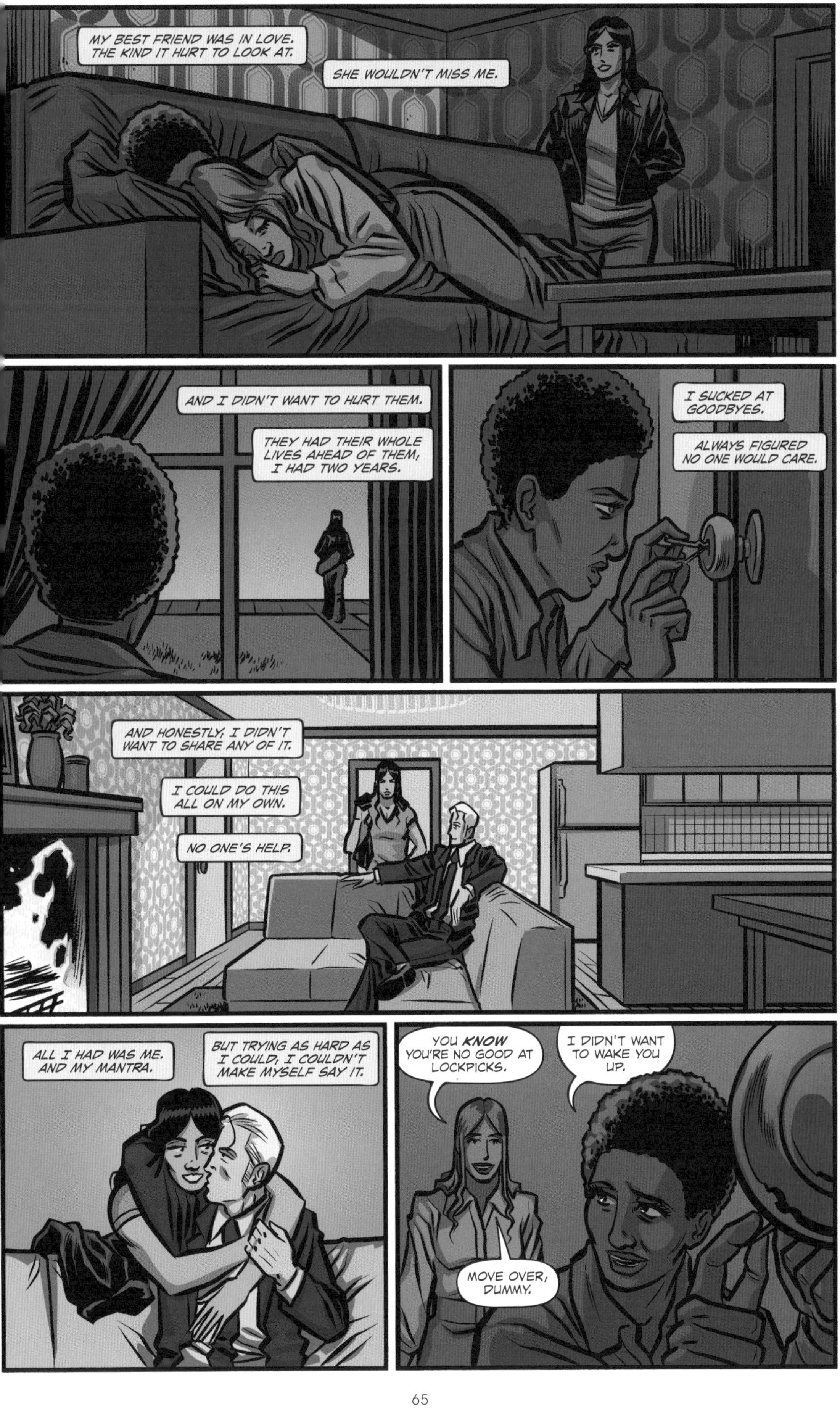
MY BEST FRIEND WAS IN LOVE. THE KIND IT HURT TO LOOK AT.
SHE WOULDN'T MISS ME.
AND I DIDN'T WANT TO HURT THEM.
THEY HAD THEIR WHOLE LIVES AHEAD OF THEM, I HAD TWO YEARS.
I SUCKED AT GOODBYES.
ALWAYS FIGURED NO ONE WOULD CARE.
AND HONESTLY, I DIDN'T WANT TO SHARE ANY OF IT.
I COULD DO THIS ALL ON MY OWN.
NO ONE'S HELP.
ALL I HAD WAS ME. AND MY MANTRA.
BUT TRYING AS HARD AS I COULD, I COULDN'T MAKE MYSELF SAY IT.
YOU KNOW YOU'RE NO GOOD AT LOCKPICKS.
I DIDN'T WANT TO WAKE YOU UP.
MOVE OVER, DUMMY.

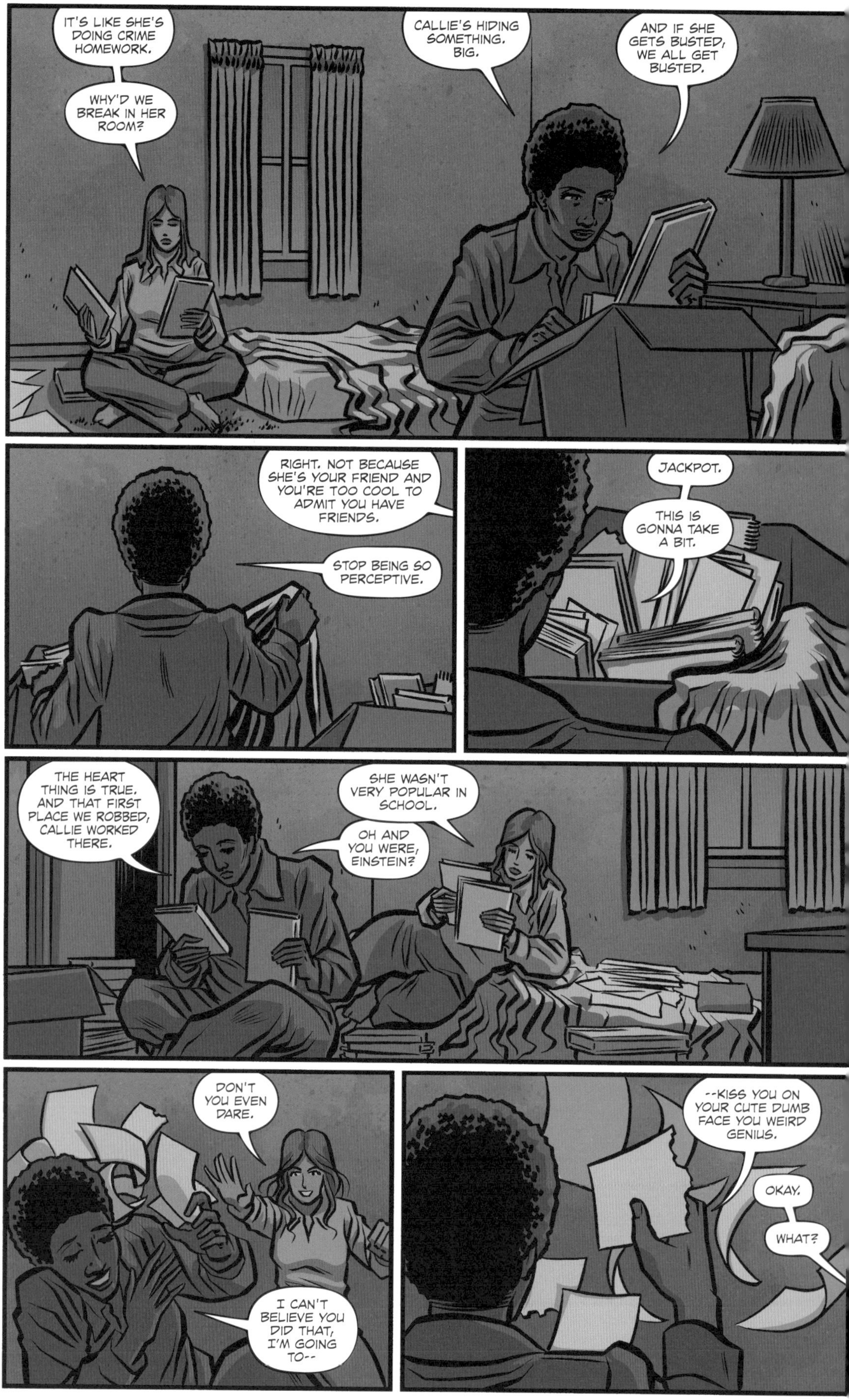
IT'S LIKE SHE'S DOING CRIME HOMEWORK.
WHY'D WE BREAK IN HER ROOM?
CALLIE'S HIDING SOMETHING. BIG.
AND IF SHE GETS BUSTED, WE ALL GET BUSTED.
RIGHT. NOT BECAUSE SHE'S YOUR FRIEND AND YOU'RE TOO COOL TO ADMIT YOU HAVE FRIENDS.
STOP BEING SO PERCEPTIVE.
JACKPOT.
THIS IS GONNA TAKE A BIT.
THE HEART THING IS TRUE. AND THAT FIRST PLACE WE ROBBED, CALLIE WORKED THERE.
SHE WASN'T VERY POPULAR IN SCHOOL.
OH AND YOU WERE, EINSTEIN?
DON'T YOU EVEN DARE.
I CAN'T BELIEVE YOU DID THAT, I'M GOING TO--
--KISS YOU ON YOUR CUTE DUMB FACE YOU WEIRD GENIUS.
OKAY.
WHAT?

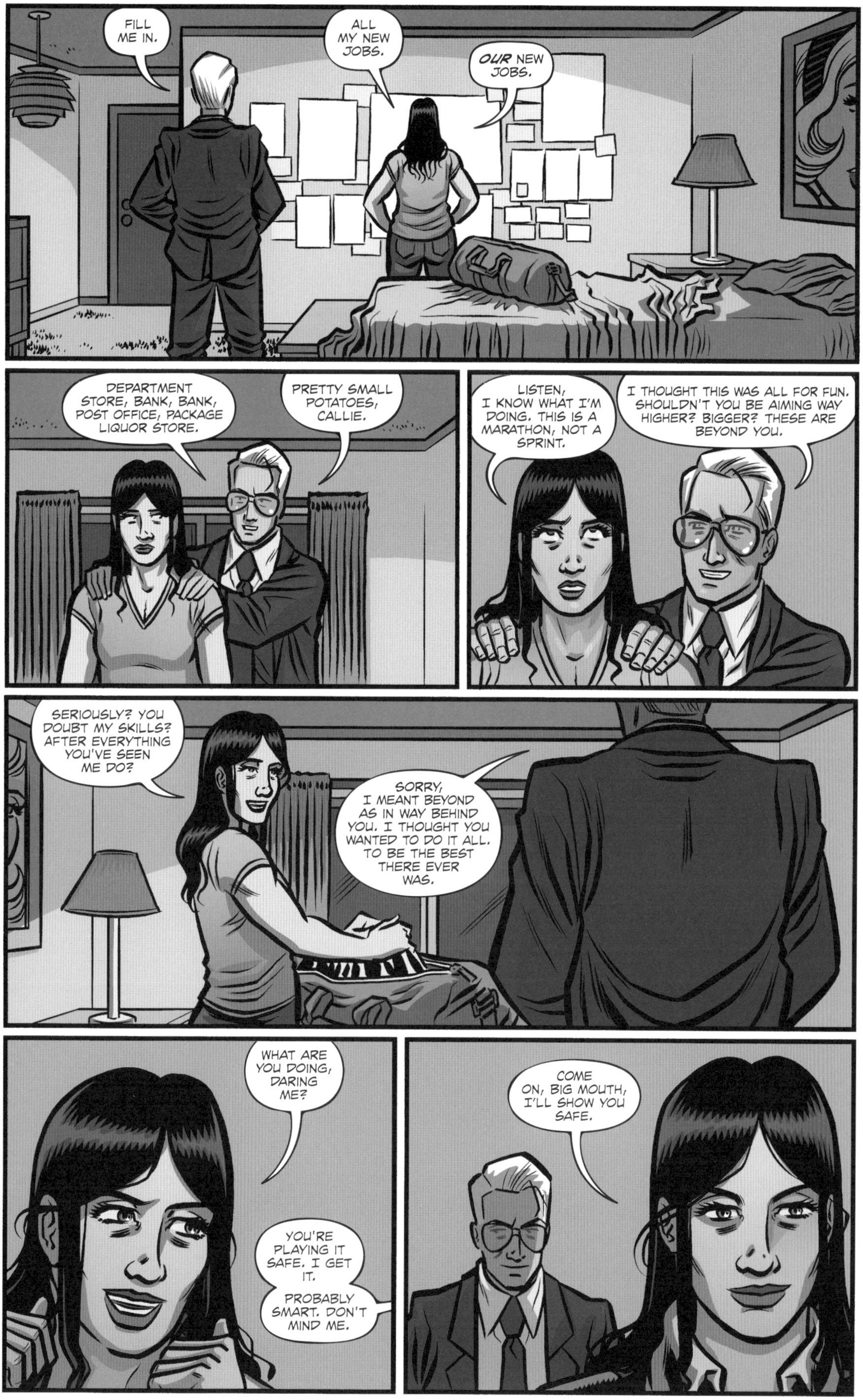
FILL ME IN.
ALL MY NEW JOBS.
OUR NEW JOBS.
DEPARTMENT STORE, BANK, BANK, POST OFFICE, PACKAGE LIQUOR STORE.
PRETTY SMALL POTATOES, CALLIE.
LISTEN, I KNOW WHAT I'M DOING. THIS IS A MARATHON, NOT A SPRINT.
I THOUGHT THIS WAS ALL FOR FUN. SHOULDN'T YOU BE AIMING WAY HIGHER? BIGGER? THESE ARE BEYOND YOU.
SERIOUSLY? YOU DOUBT MY SKILLS? AFTER EVERYTHING YOU'VE SEEN ME DO?
SORRY, I MEANT BEYOND AS IN WAY BEHIND YOU. I THOUGHT YOU WANTED TO DO IT ALL. TO BE THE BEST THERE EVER WAS.
WHAT ARE YOU DOING, DARING ME?
YOU'RE PLAYING IT SAFE. I GET IT.
PROBABLY SMART. DON'T MIND ME.
COME ON, BIG MOUTH, I'LL SHOW YOU SAFE.

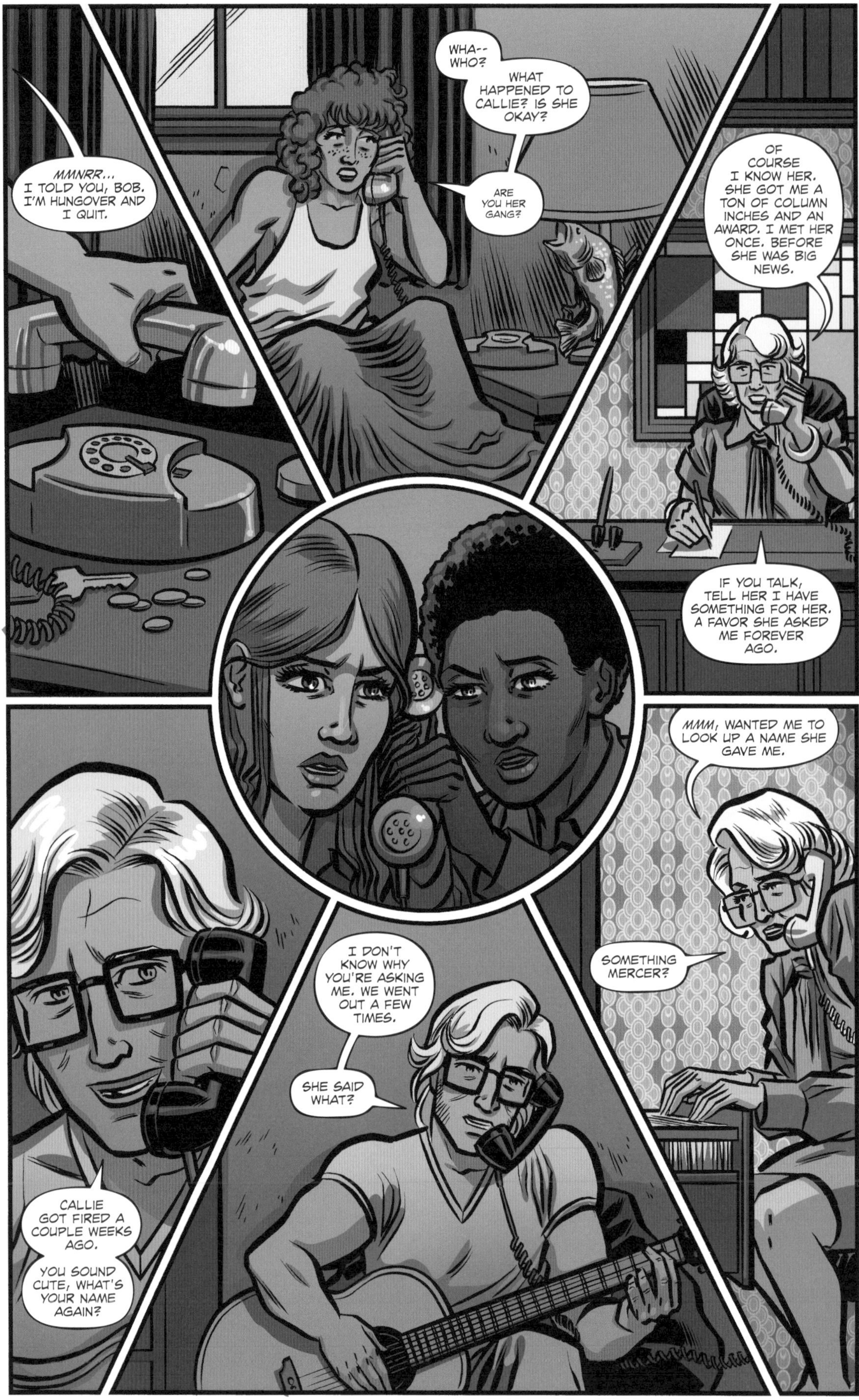
MMNRR... I TOLD YOU, BOB. I'M HUNGOVER AND I QUIT.
WHA-- WHO?
WHAT HAPPENED TO CALLIE? IS SHE OKAY?
ARE YOU HER GANG?
OF COURSE I KNOW HER. SHE GOT ME A TON OF COLUMN INCHES AND AN AWARD. I MET HER ONCE. BEFORE SHE WAS BIG NEWS.
IF YOU TALK, TELL HER I HAVE SOMETHING FOR HER. A FAVOR SHE ASKED ME FOREVER AGO.
MMM, WANTED ME TO LOOK UP A NAME SHE GAVE ME.
SOMETHING MERCER?
I DON'T KNOW WHY YOU'RE ASKING ME. WE WENT OUT A FEW TIMES.
SHE SAID WHAT?
CALLIE GOT FIRED A COUPLE WEEKS AGO.
YOU SOUND CUTE, WHAT'S YOUR NAME AGAIN?

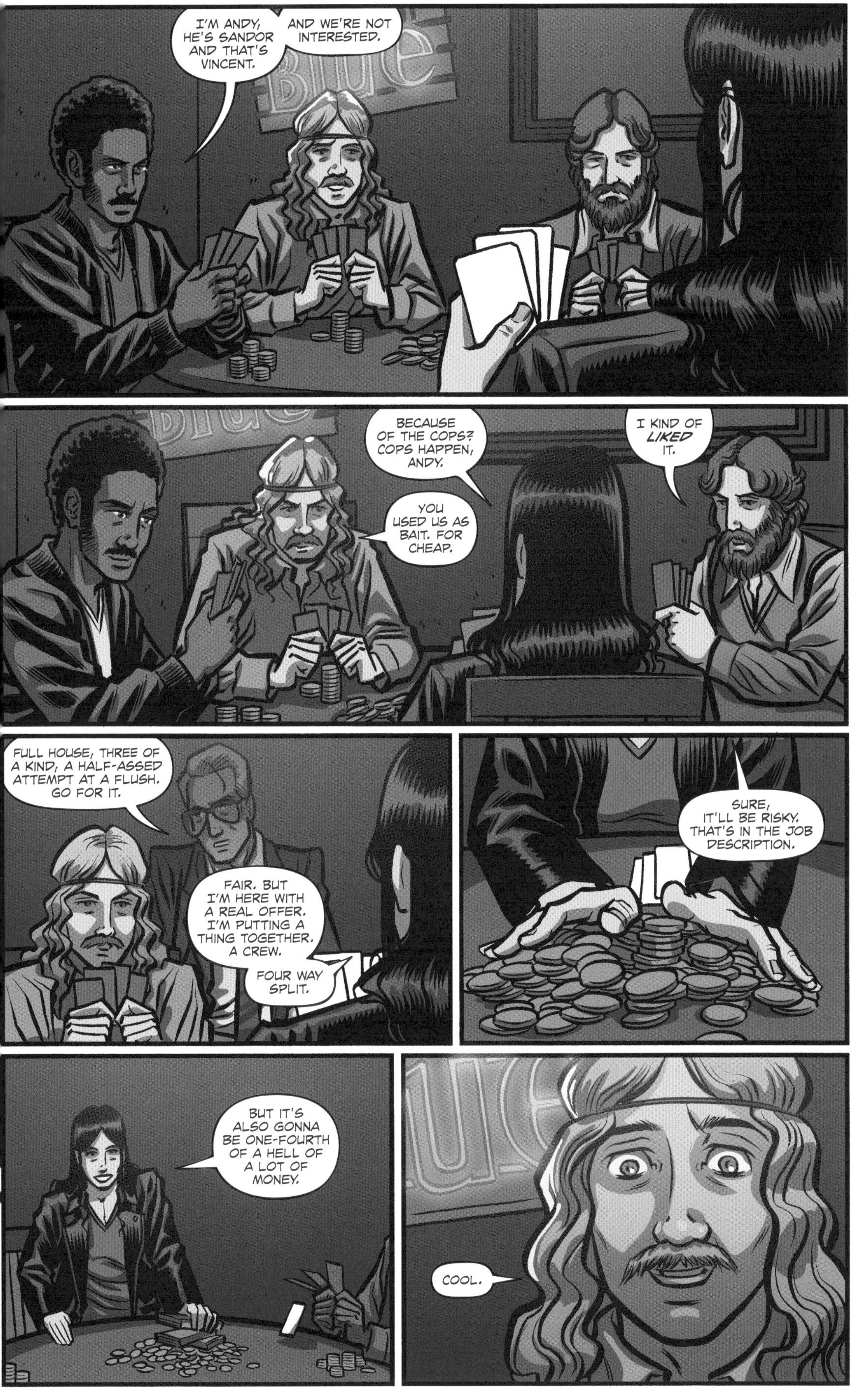
I'M ANDY, HE'S SANDOR AND THAT'S VINCENT.
AND WE'RE NOT INTERESTED.
BECAUSE OF THE COPS? COPS HAPPEN, ANDY.
YOU USED US AS BAIT. FOR CHEAP.
I KIND OF *LIKED* IT.
FULL HOUSE, THREE OF A KIND, A HALF-ASSED ATTEMPT AT A FLUSH. GO FOR IT.
FAIR. BUT I'M HERE WITH A REAL OFFER. I'M PUTTING A THING TOGETHER. A CREW.
FOUR WAY SPLIT.
SURE, IT'LL BE RISKY. THAT'S IN THE JOB DESCRIPTION.
BUT IT'S ALSO GONNA BE ONE-FOURTH OF A HELL OF A LOT OF MONEY.
COOL.

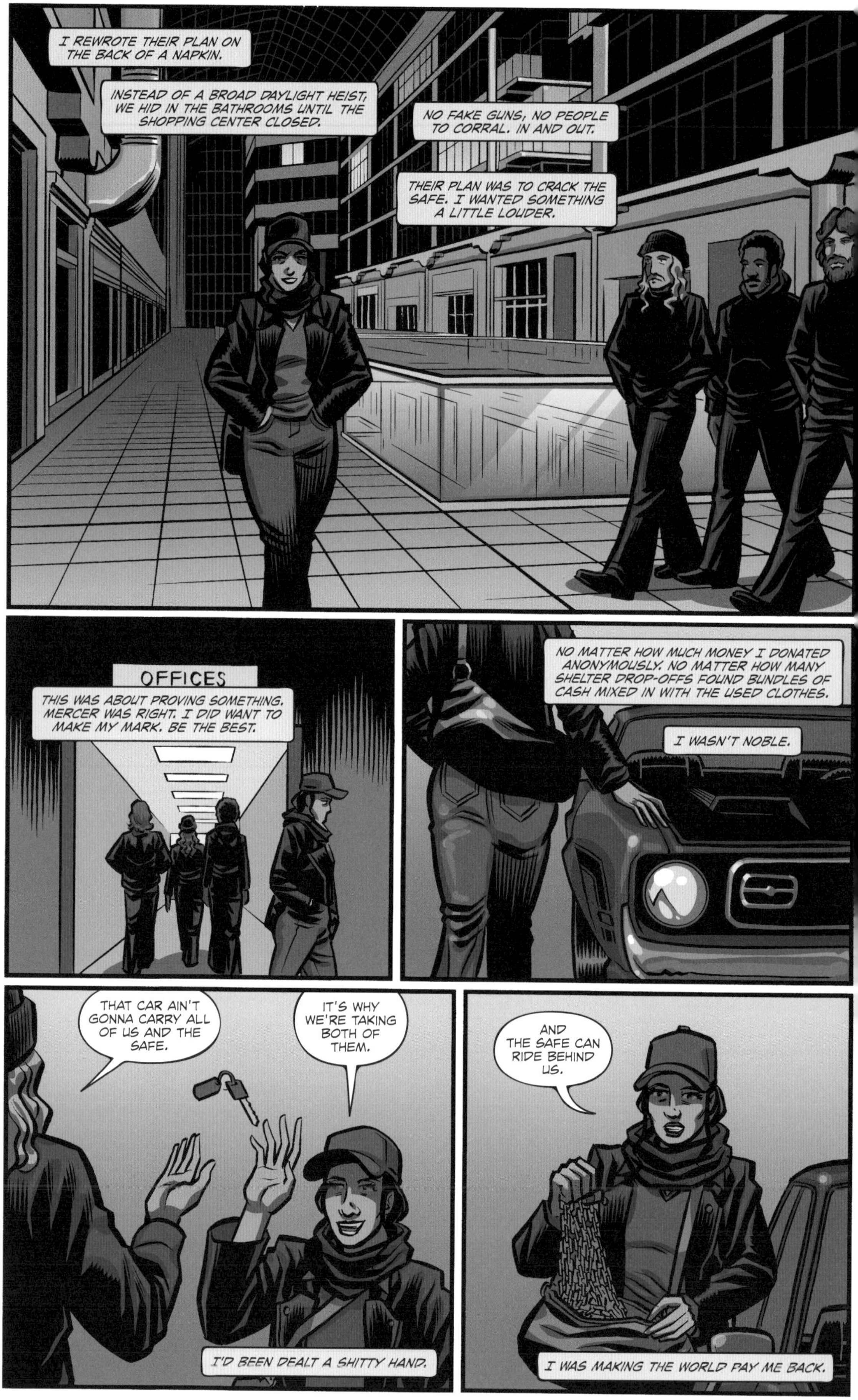
I REWROTE THEIR PLAN ON THE BACK OF A NAPKIN.
INSTEAD OF A BROAD DAYLIGHT HEIST, WE HID IN THE BATHROOMS UNTIL THE SHOPPING CENTER CLOSED.
NO FAKE GUNS, NO PEOPLE TO CORRAL. IN AND OUT.
THEIR PLAN WAS TO CRACK THE SAFE. I WANTED SOMETHING A LITTLE LOUDER.
OFFICES
THIS WAS ABOUT PROVING SOMETHING. MERCER WAS RIGHT. I DID WANT TO MAKE MY MARK. BE THE BEST.
NO MATTER HOW MUCH MONEY I DONATED ANONYMOUSLY. NO MATTER HOW MANY SHELTER DROP-OFFS FOUND BUNDLES OF CASH MIXED IN WITH THE USED CLOTHES.
I WASN'T NOBLE.
THAT CAR AIN'T GONNA CARRY ALL OF US AND THE SAFE.
IT'S WHY WE'RE TAKING BOTH OF THEM.
I'D BEEN DEALT A SHITTY HAND.
AND THE SAFE CAN RIDE BEHIND US.
I WAS MAKING THE WORLD PAY ME BACK.

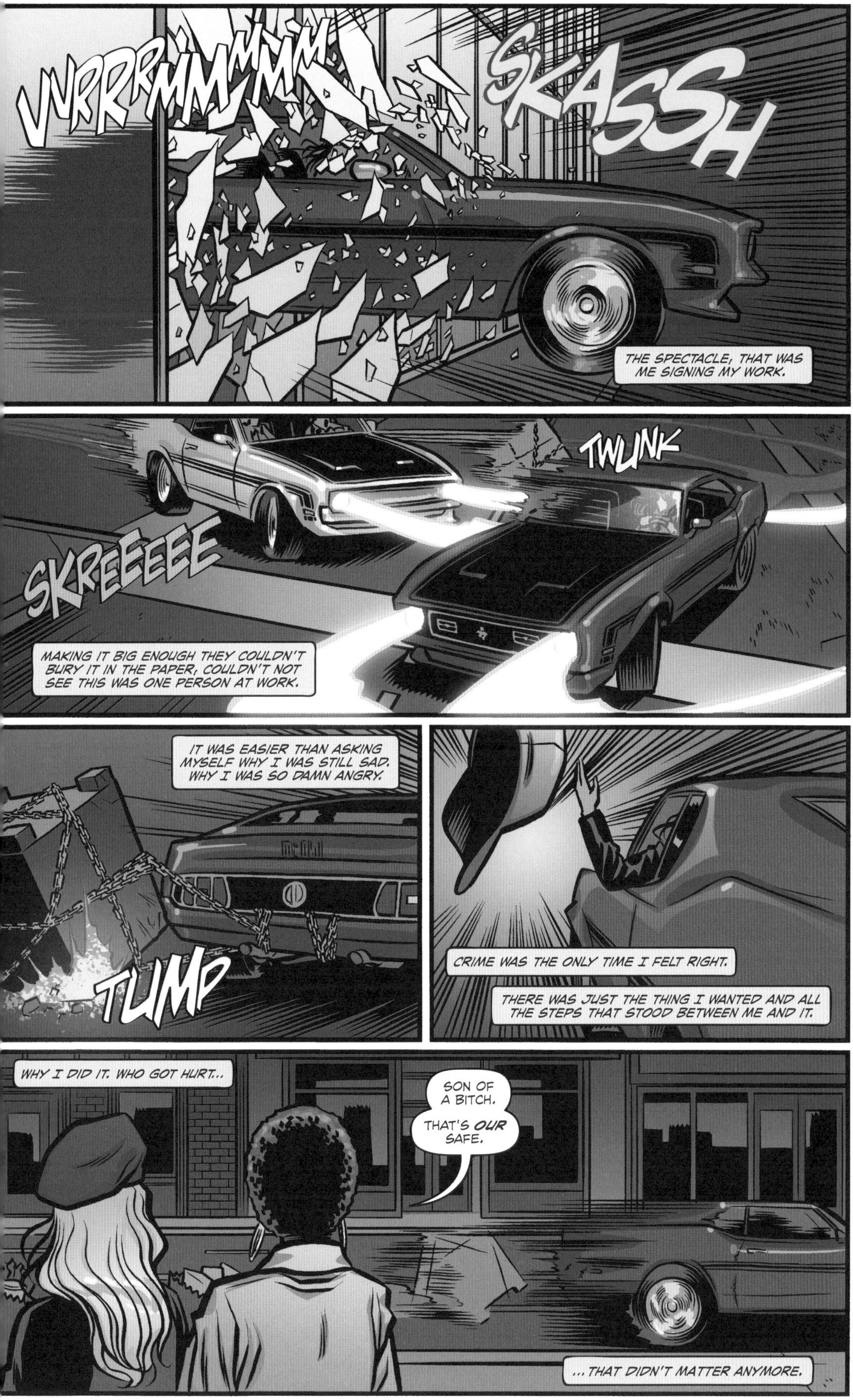
VVRRRMMMMM
SKASSH
THE SPECTACLE, THAT WAS ME SIGNING MY WORK.
TWUNK
SKREEEEE
MAKING IT BIG ENOUGH THEY COULDN'T BURY IT IN THE PAPER, COULDN'T NOT SEE THIS WAS ONE PERSON AT WORK.
IT WAS EASIER THAN ASKING MYSELF WHY I WAS STILL SAD. WHY I WAS SO DAMN ANGRY.
TUMP
CRIME WAS THE ONLY TIME I FELT RIGHT.
THERE WAS JUST THE THING I WANTED AND ALL THE STEPS THAT STOOD BETWEEN ME AND IT.
WHY I DID IT. WHO GOT HURT...
SON OF A BITCH.
THAT'S OUR SAFE.
...THAT DIDN'T MATTER ANYMORE.

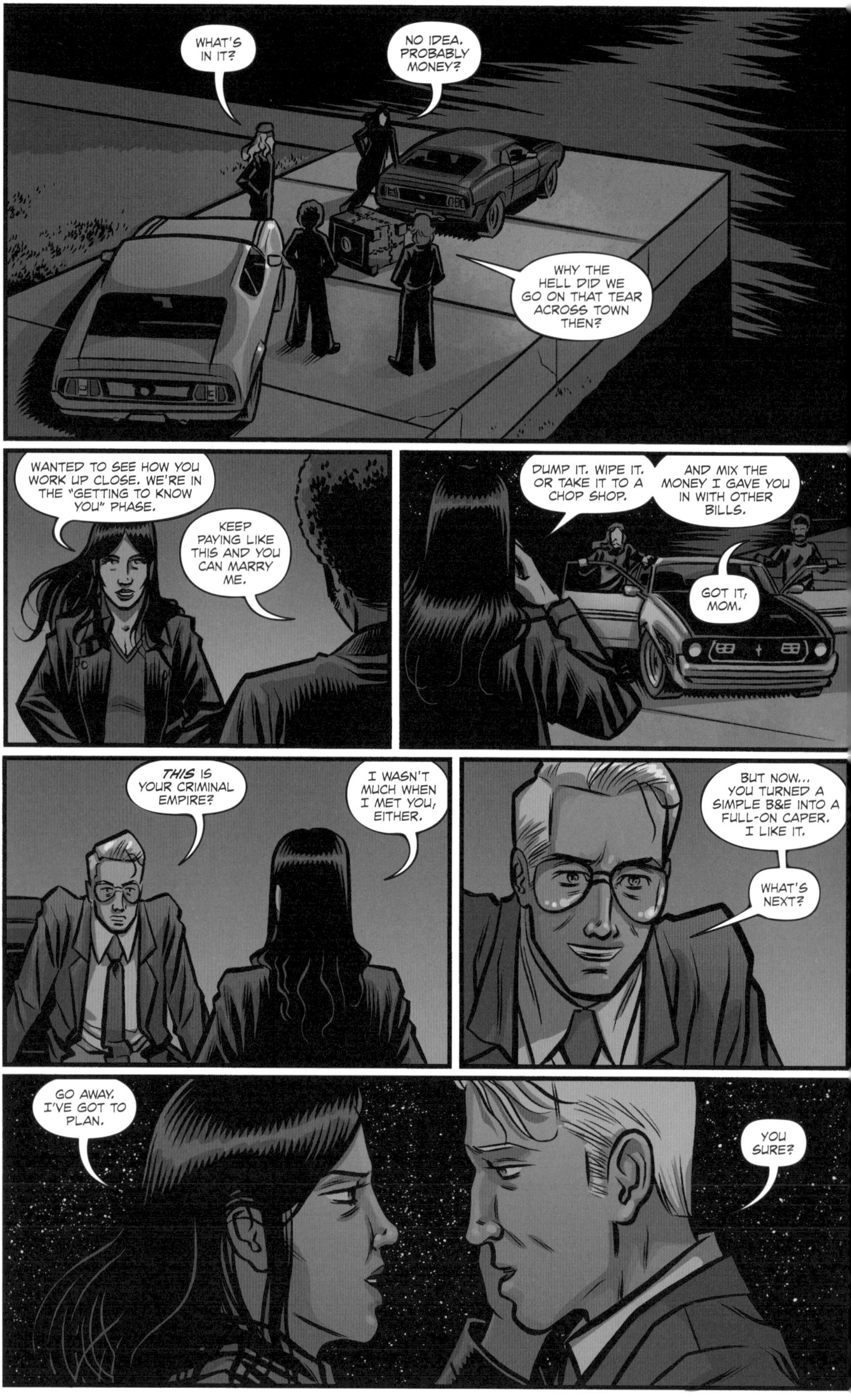
WHAT'S IN IT?
NO IDEA. PROBABLY MONEY?
WHY THE HELL DID WE GO ON THAT TEAR ACROSS TOWN THEN?
WANTED TO SEE HOW YOU WORK UP CLOSE. WE'RE IN THE "GETTING TO KNOW YOU" PHASE.
KEEP PAYING LIKE THIS AND YOU CAN MARRY ME.
DUMP IT. WIPE IT. OR TAKE IT TO A CHOP SHOP.
AND MIX THE MONEY I GAVE YOU IN WITH OTHER BILLS.
GOT IT, MOM.
THIS IS YOUR CRIMINAL EMPIRE?
I WASN'T MUCH WHEN I MET YOU, EITHER.
BUT NOW... YOU TURNED A SIMPLE B&E INTO A FULL-ON CAPER. I LIKE IT.
WHAT'S NEXT?
GO AWAY. I'VE GOT TO PLAN.
YOU SURE?

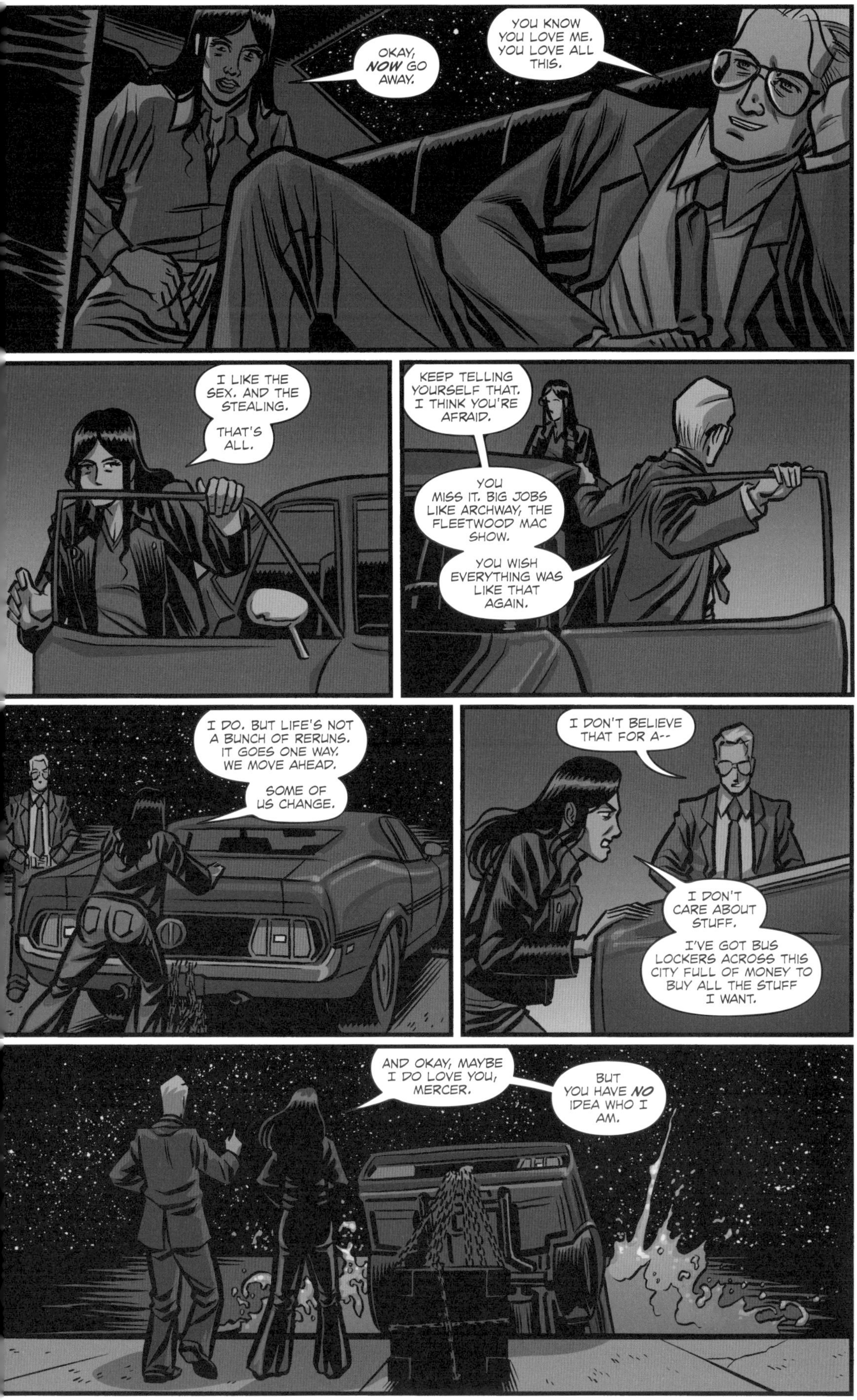
OKAY, NOW GO AWAY.
YOU KNOW YOU LOVE ME. YOU LOVE ALL THIS.
I LIKE THE SEX. AND THE STEALING.
THAT'S ALL.
KEEP TELLING YOURSELF THAT. I THINK YOU'RE AFRAID.
YOU MISS IT. BIG JOBS LIKE ARCHWAY, THE FLEETWOOD MAC SHOW.
YOU WISH EVERYTHING WAS LIKE THAT AGAIN.
I DO. BUT LIFE'S NOT A BUNCH OF RERUNS. IT GOES ONE WAY. WE MOVE AHEAD.
SOME OF US CHANGE.
I DON'T BELIEVE THAT FOR A--
I DON'T CARE ABOUT STUFF.
I'VE GOT BUS LOCKERS ACROSS THIS CITY FULL OF MONEY TO BUY ALL THE STUFF I WANT.
AND OKAY, MAYBE I DO LOVE YOU, MERCER.
BUT YOU HAVE NO IDEA WHO I AM.

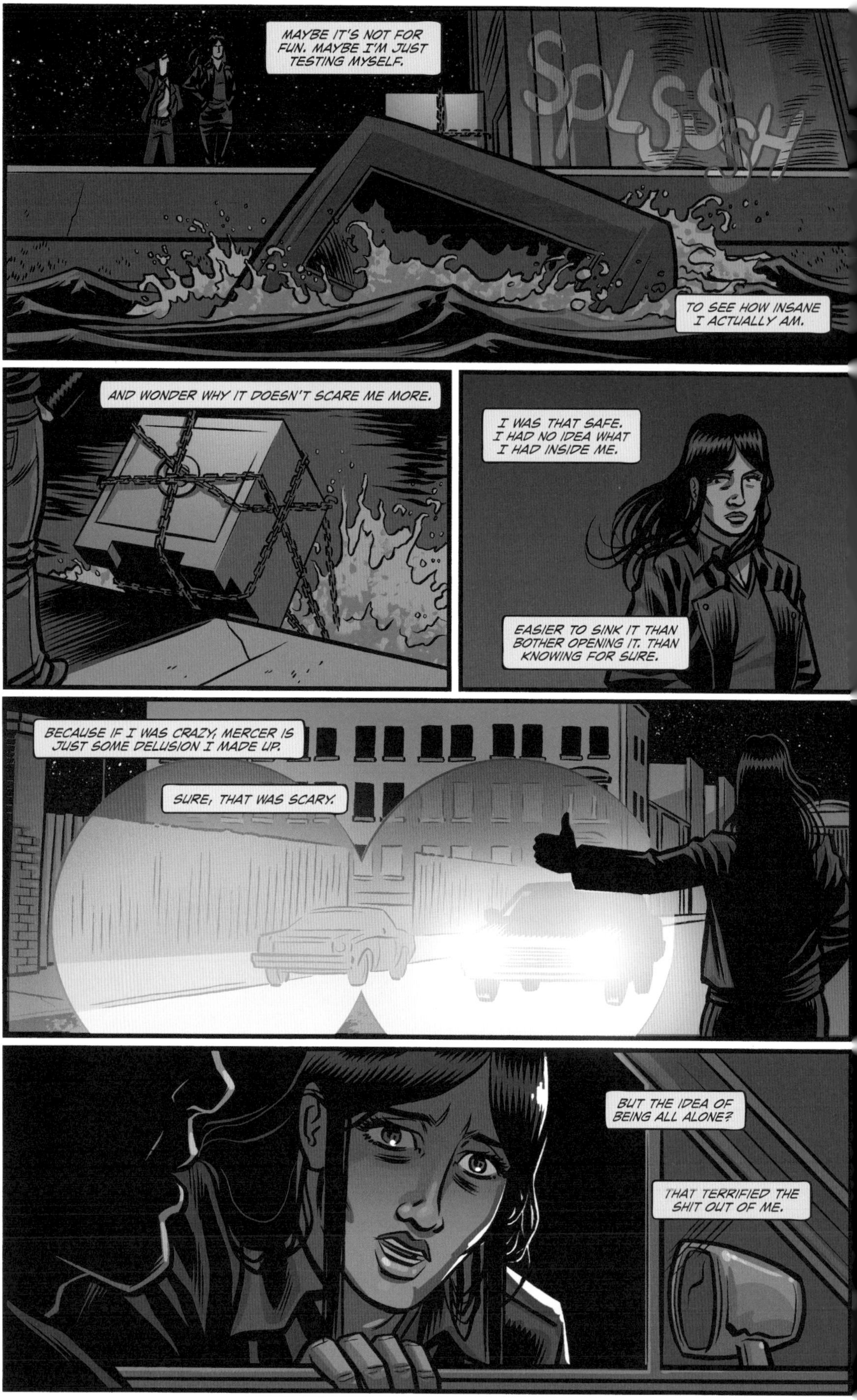
MAYBE IT'S NOT FOR FUN. MAYBE I'M JUST TESTING MYSELF.
SPLSSSH
TO SEE HOW INSANE I ACTUALLY AM.
AND WONDER WHY IT DOESN'T SCARE ME MORE.
I WAS THAT SAFE. I HAD NO IDEA WHAT I HAD INSIDE ME.
EASIER TO SINK IT THAN BOTHER OPENING IT. THAN KNOWING FOR SURE.
BECAUSE IF I WAS CRAZY, MERCER IS JUST SOME DELUSION I MADE UP.
SURE, THAT WAS SCARY.
BUT THE IDEA OF BEING ALL ALONE?
THAT TERRIFIED THE SHIT OUT OF ME.

CHAPTER 4

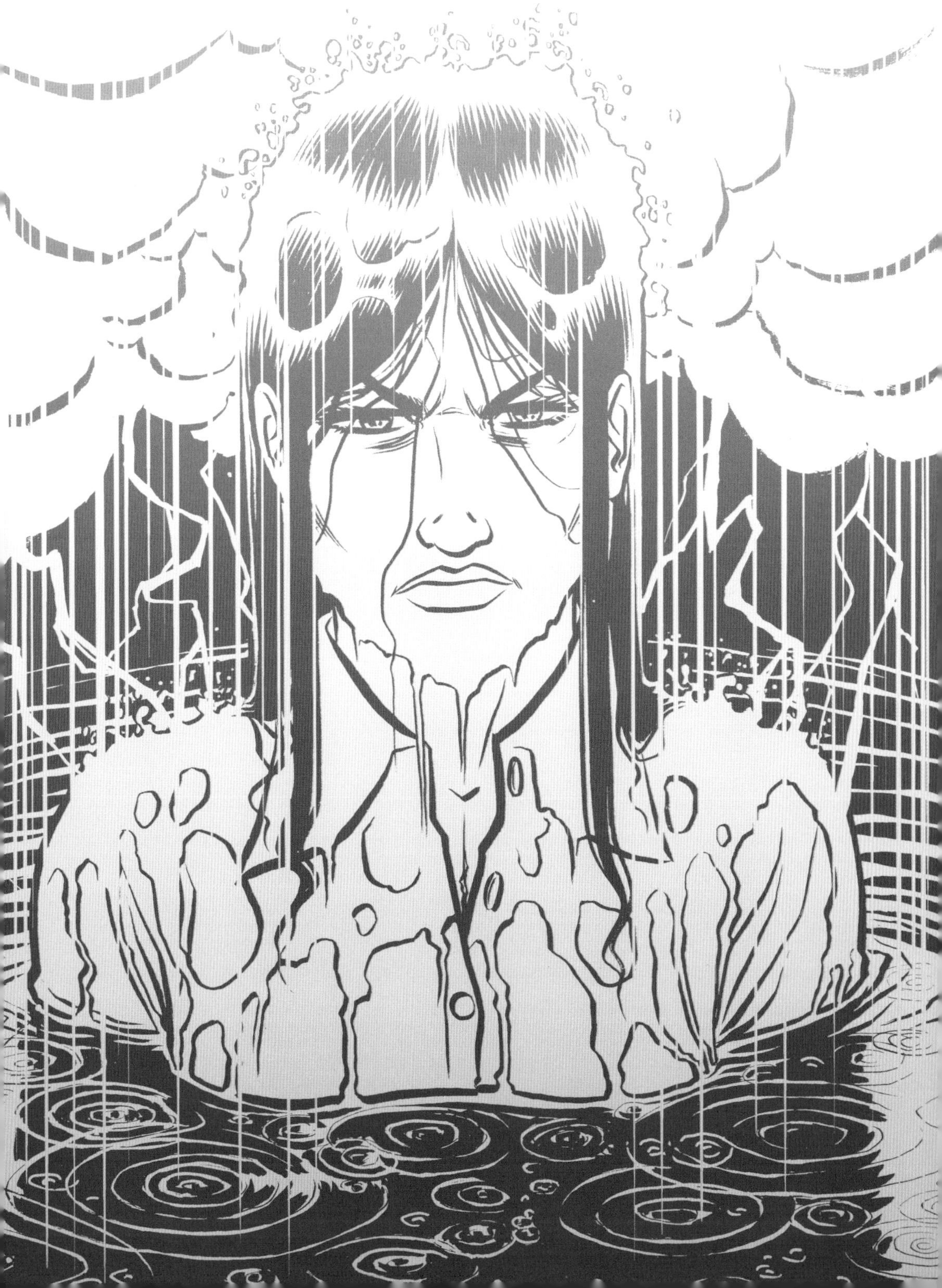

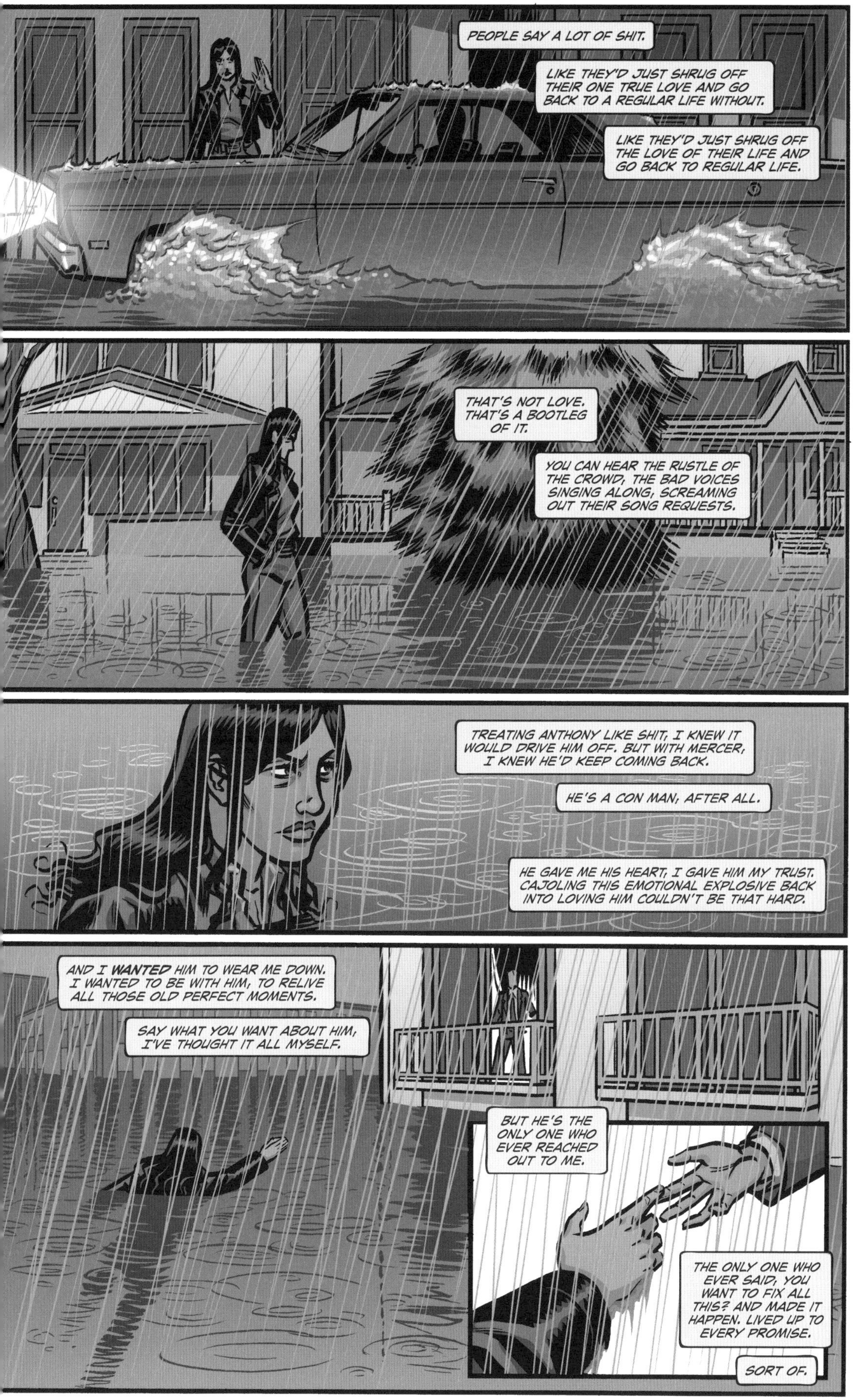
PEOPLE SAY A LOT OF SHIT.
LIKE THEY'D JUST SHRUG OFF THEIR ONE TRUE LOVE AND GO BACK TO A REGULAR LIFE WITHOUT.
LIKE THEY'D JUST SHRUG OFF THE LOVE OF THEIR LIFE AND GO BACK TO REGULAR LIFE.
THAT'S NOT LOVE. THAT'S A BOOTLEG OF IT.
YOU CAN HEAR THE RUSTLE OF THE CROWD, THE BAD VOICES SINGING ALONG, SCREAMING OUT THEIR SONG REQUESTS.
TREATING ANTHONY LIKE SHIT, I KNEW IT WOULD DRIVE HIM OFF. BUT WITH MERCER, I KNEW HE'D KEEP COMING BACK.
HE'S A CON MAN, AFTER ALL.
HE GAVE ME HIS HEART, I GAVE HIM MY TRUST. CAJOLING THIS EMOTIONAL EXPLOSIVE BACK INTO LOVING HIM COULDN'T BE THAT HARD.
AND I WANTED HIM TO WEAR ME DOWN. I WANTED TO BE WITH HIM, TO RELIVE ALL THOSE OLD PERFECT MOMENTS.
SAY WHAT YOU WANT ABOUT HIM, I'VE THOUGHT IT ALL MYSELF.
BUT HE'S THE ONLY ONE WHO EVER REACHED OUT TO ME.
THE ONLY ONE WHO EVER SAID, YOU WANT TO FIX ALL THIS? AND MADE IT HAPPEN. LIVED UP TO EVERY PROMISE.
SORT OF.

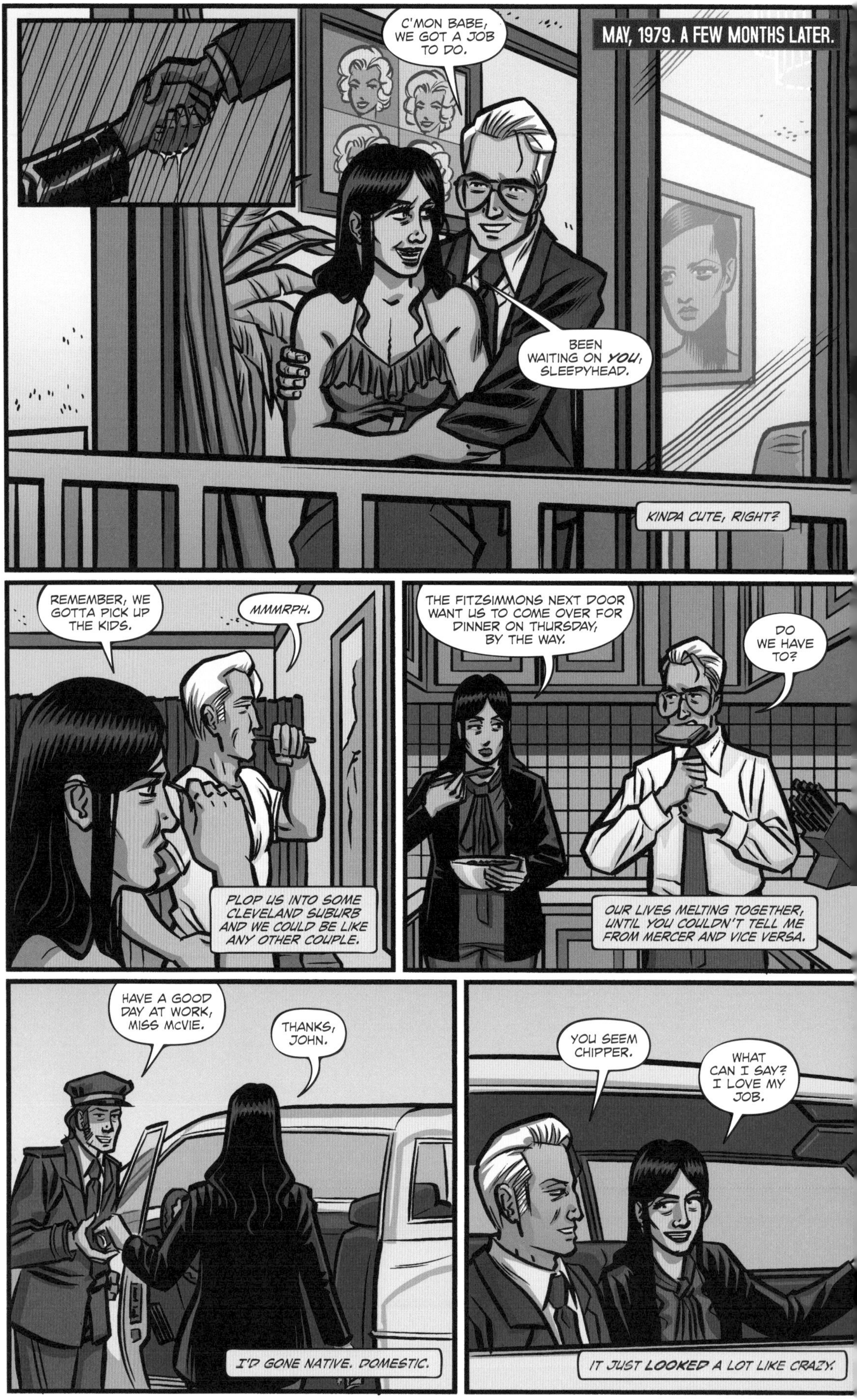
MAY, 1979. A FEW MONTHS LATER.
C'MON BABE, WE GOT A JOB TO DO.
BEEN WAITING ON YOU, SLEEPYHEAD.
KINDA CUTE, RIGHT?
REMEMBER, WE GOTTA PICK UP THE KIDS.
MMMRPH.
PLOP US INTO SOME CLEVELAND SUBURB AND WE COULD BE LIKE ANY OTHER COUPLE.
THE FITZSIMMONS NEXT DOOR WANT US TO COME OVER FOR DINNER ON THURSDAY, BY THE WAY.
DO WE HAVE TO?
OUR LIVES MELTING TOGETHER, UNTIL YOU COULDN'T TELL ME FROM MERCER AND VICE VERSA.
HAVE A GOOD DAY AT WORK, MISS McVIE.
THANKS, JOHN.
I'D GONE NATIVE. DOMESTIC.
YOU SEEM CHIPPER.
WHAT CAN I SAY? I LOVE MY JOB.
IT JUST LOOKED A LOT LIKE CRAZY.

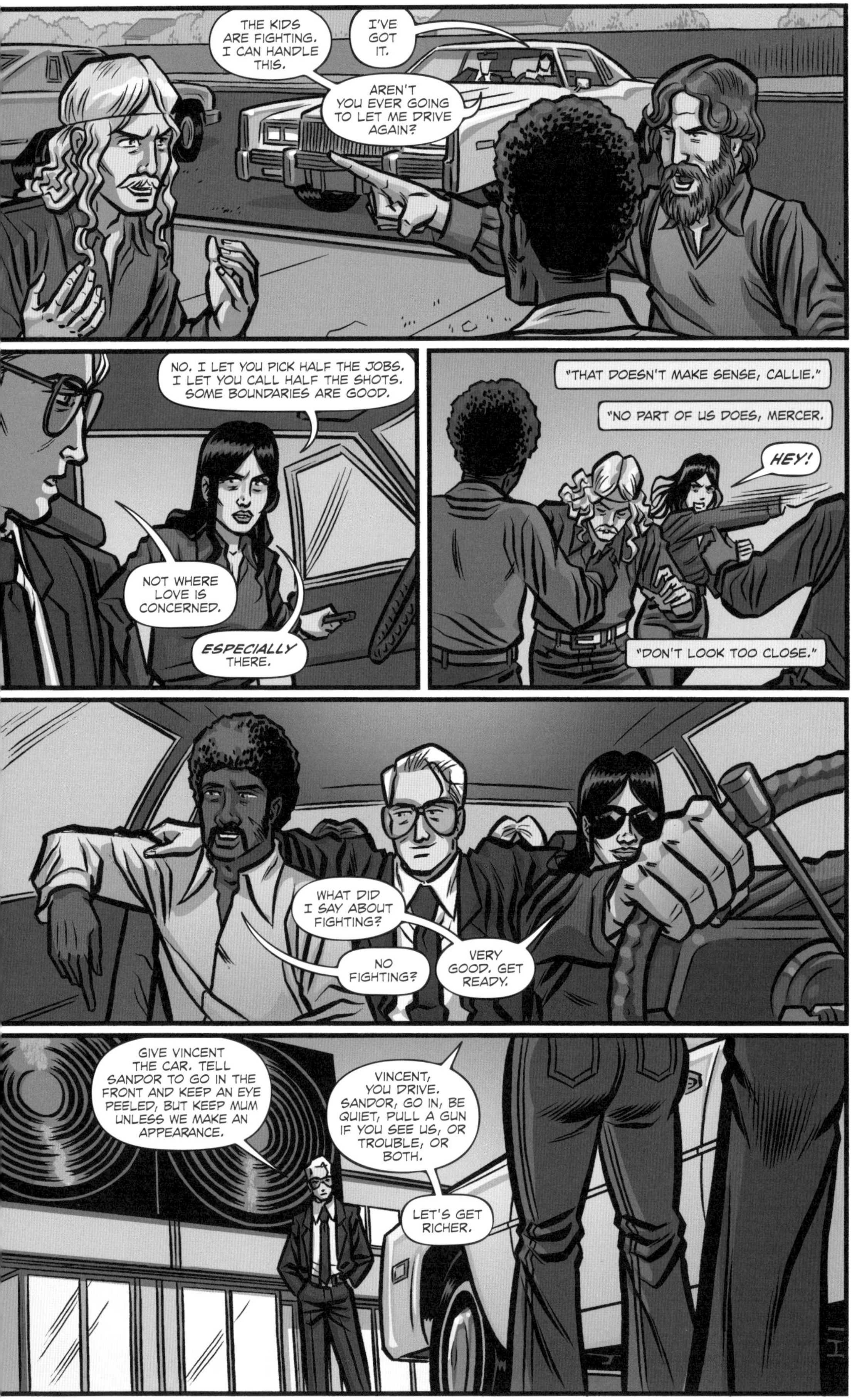
THE KIDS ARE FIGHTING. I CAN HANDLE THIS.
I'VE GOT IT.
AREN'T YOU EVER GOING TO LET ME DRIVE AGAIN?
NO. I LET YOU PICK HALF THE JOBS. I LET YOU CALL HALF THE SHOTS. SOME BOUNDARIES ARE GOOD.
NOT WHERE LOVE IS CONCERNED.
ESPECIALLY THERE.
"THAT DOESN'T MAKE SENSE, CALLIE."
"NO PART OF US DOES, MERCER.
HEY!
"DON'T LOOK TOO CLOSE."
WHAT DID I SAY ABOUT FIGHTING?
NO FIGHTING?
VERY GOOD. GET READY.
GIVE VINCENT THE CAR. TELL SANDOR TO GO IN THE FRONT AND KEEP AN EYE PEELED, BUT KEEP MUM UNLESS WE MAKE AN APPEARANCE.
VINCENT, YOU DRIVE. SANDOR, GO IN, BE QUIET, PULL A GUN IF YOU SEE US, OR TROUBLE, OR BOTH.
LET'S GET RICHER.

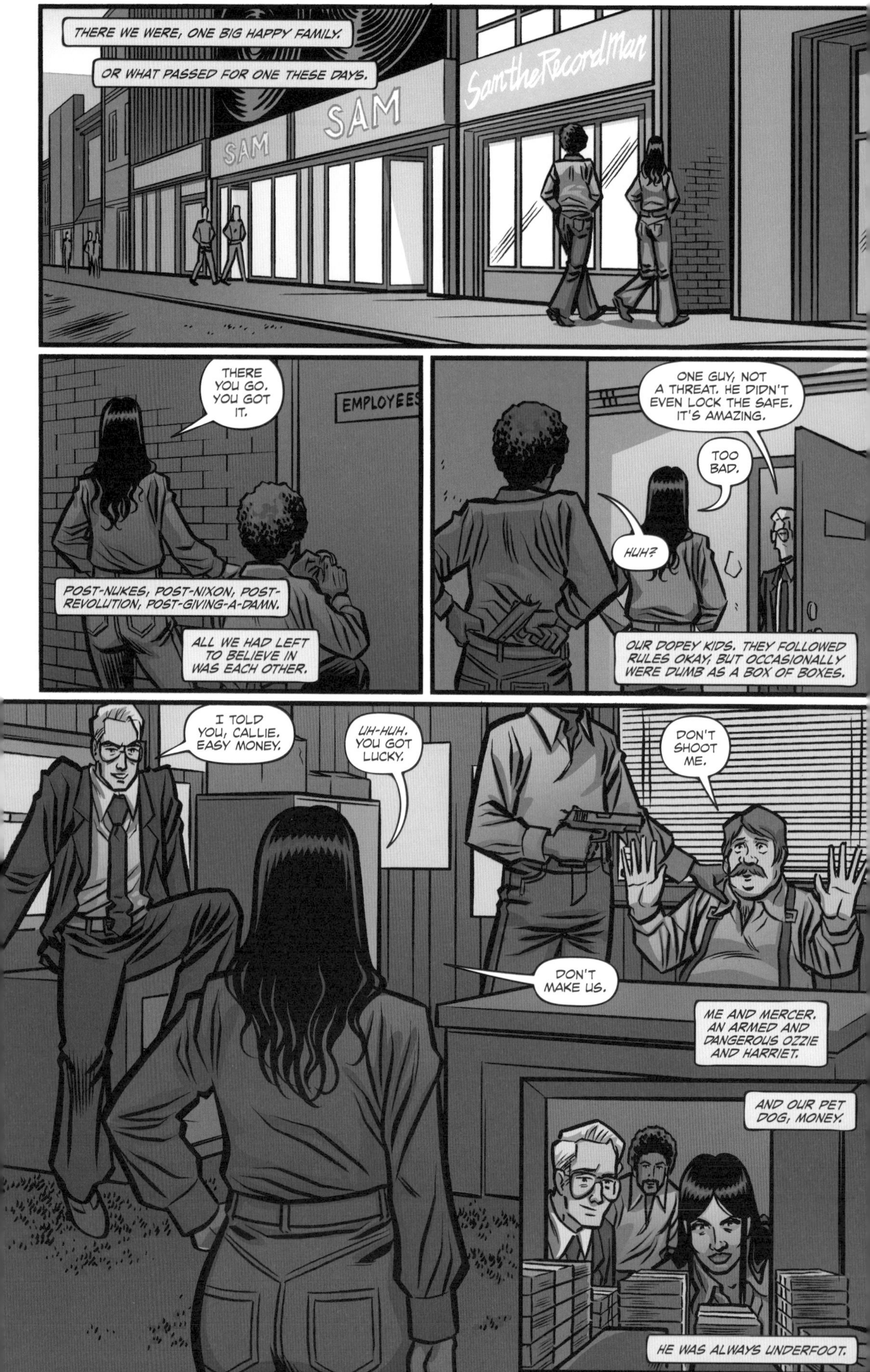
THERE WE WERE; ONE BIG HAPPY FAMILY.
OR WHAT PASSED FOR ONE THESE DAYS.
SAM
SAM
Sam the Record Man
THERE YOU GO. YOU GOT IT.
EMPLOYEES
POST-NUKES, POST-NIXON, POST-REVOLUTION, POST-GIVING-A-DAMN.
ALL WE HAD LEFT TO BELIEVE IN WAS EACH OTHER.
ONE GUY, NOT A THREAT. HE DIDN'T EVEN LOCK THE SAFE. IT'S AMAZING.
TOO BAD.
HUH?
OUR DOPEY KIDS. THEY FOLLOWED RULES OKAY, BUT OCCASIONALLY WERE DUMB AS A BOX OF BOXES.
I TOLD YOU, CALLIE. EASY MONEY.
UH-HUH. YOU GOT LUCKY.
DON'T SHOOT ME.
DON'T MAKE US.
ME AND MERCER. AN ARMED AND DANGEROUS OZZIE AND HARRIET.
AND OUR PET DOG, MONEY.
HE WAS ALWAYS UNDERFOOT.

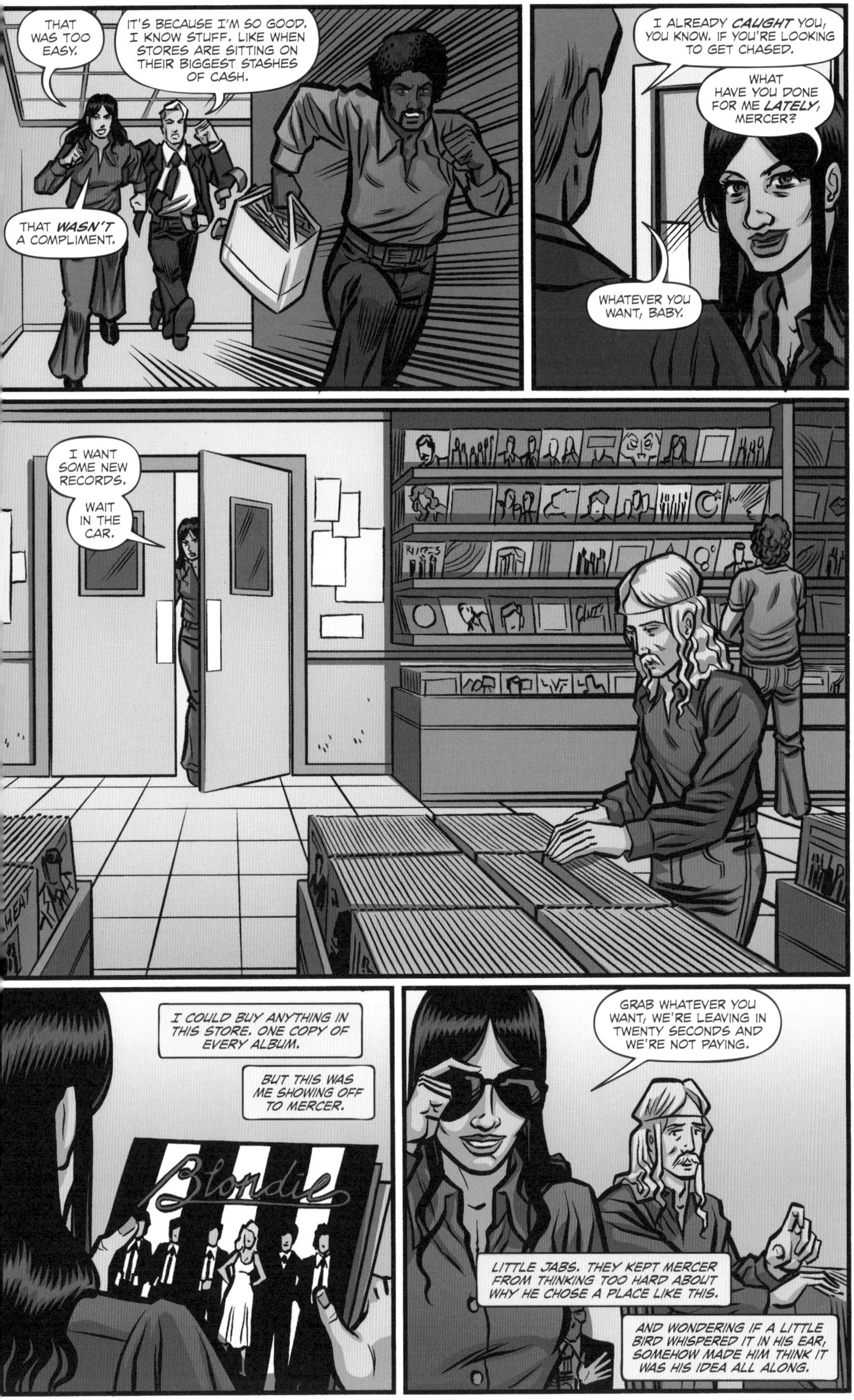
THAT WAS TOO EASY.
IT'S BECAUSE I'M SO GOOD. I KNOW STUFF. LIKE WHEN STORES ARE SITTING ON THEIR BIGGEST STASHES OF CASH.
THAT *WASN'T* A COMPLIMENT.
I ALREADY *CAUGHT* YOU, YOU KNOW. IF YOU'RE LOOKING TO GET CHASED.
WHAT HAVE YOU DONE FOR ME *LATELY*, MERCER?
WHATEVER YOU WANT, BABY.
I WANT SOME NEW RECORDS.
WAIT IN THE CAR.
I COULD BUY ANYTHING IN THIS STORE. ONE COPY OF EVERY ALBUM.
BUT THIS WAS ME SHOWING OFF TO MERCER.
Blondie
GRAB WHATEVER YOU WANT, WE'RE LEAVING IN TWENTY SECONDS AND WE'RE NOT PAYING.
LITTLE JABS. THEY KEPT MERCER FROM THINKING TOO HARD ABOUT WHY HE CHOSE A PLACE LIKE THIS.
AND WONDERING IF A LITTLE BIRD WHISPERED IT IN HIS EAR, SOMEHOW MADE HIM THINK IT WAS HIS IDEA ALL ALONG.

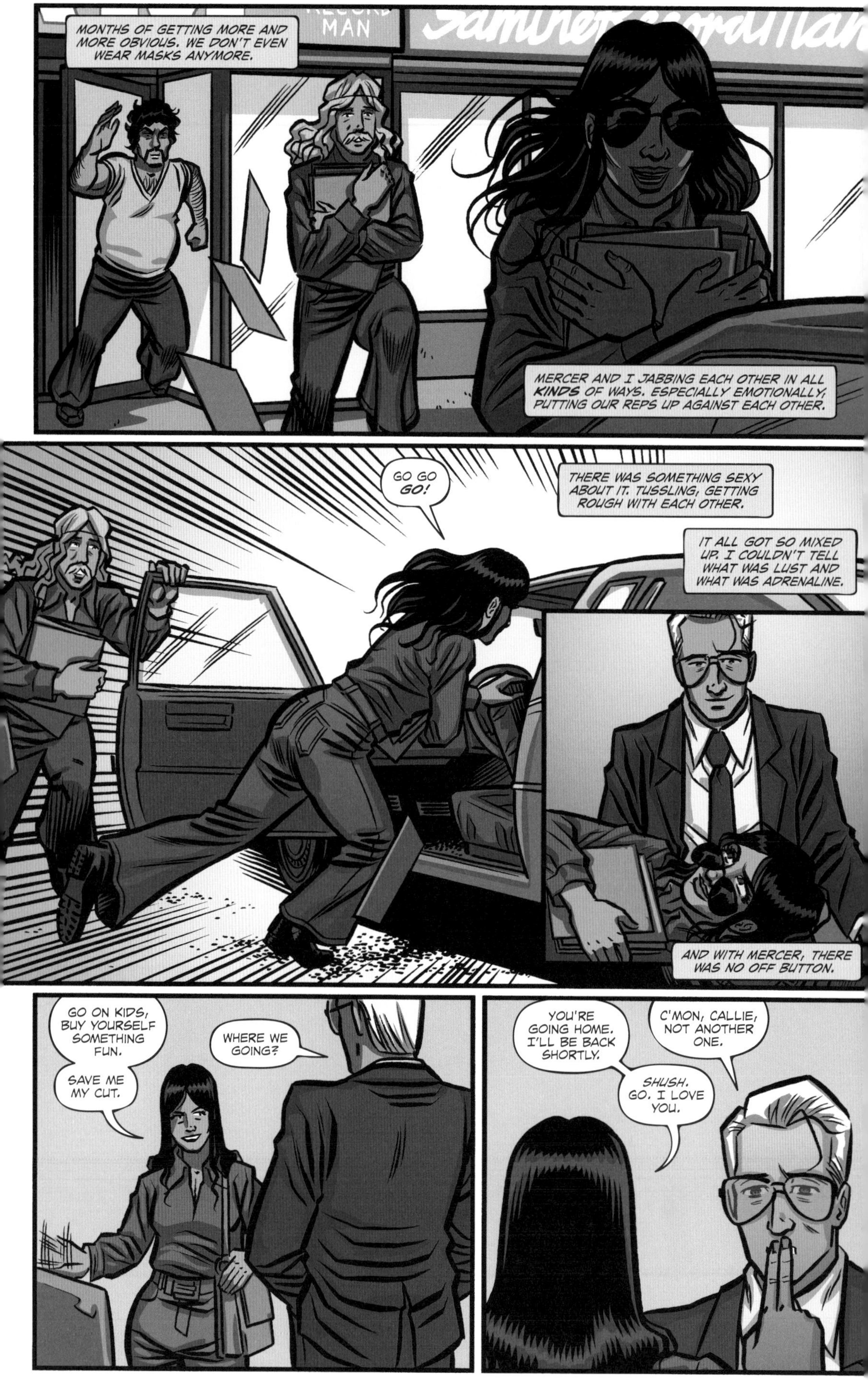
RECORD MAN
MONTHS OF GETTING MORE AND MORE OBVIOUS. WE DON'T EVEN WEAR MASKS ANYMORE.
MERCER AND I JABBING EACH OTHER IN ALL **KINDS** OF WAYS. ESPECIALLY EMOTIONALLY, PUTTING OUR REPS UP AGAINST EACH OTHER.
GO GO *GO!*
THERE WAS SOMETHING SEXY ABOUT IT. TUSSLING, GETTING ROUGH WITH EACH OTHER.
IT ALL GOT SO MIXED UP. I COULDN'T TELL WHAT WAS LUST AND WHAT WAS ADRENALINE.
AND WITH MERCER, THERE WAS NO OFF BUTTON.
GO ON KIDS, BUY YOURSELF SOMETHING FUN.
SAVE ME MY CUT.
WHERE WE GOING?
YOU'RE GOING HOME. I'LL BE BACK SHORTLY.
C'MON, CALLIE, NOT ANOTHER ONE.
SHUSH. GO. I LOVE YOU.

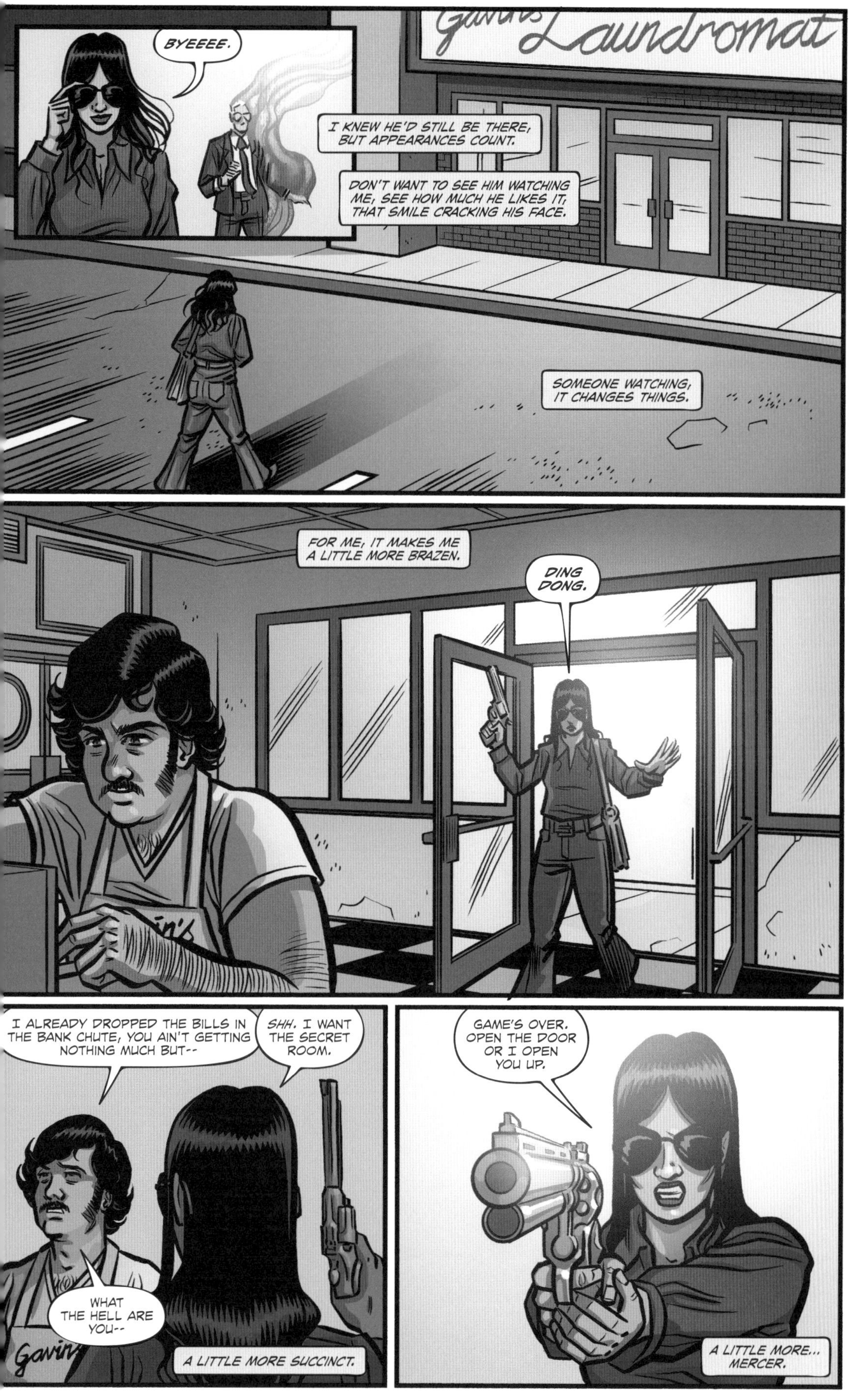
BYEEEE.
Gavin's Laundromat
I KNEW HE'D STILL BE THERE, BUT APPEARANCES COUNT.
DON'T WANT TO SEE HIM WATCHING ME; SEE HOW MUCH HE LIKES IT, THAT SMILE CRACKING HIS FACE.
SOMEONE WATCHING, IT CHANGES THINGS.
FOR ME, IT MAKES ME A LITTLE MORE BRAZEN.
DING DONG.
I ALREADY DROPPED THE BILLS IN THE BANK CHUTE, YOU AIN'T GETTING NOTHING MUCH BUT--
SHH. I WANT THE SECRET ROOM.
WHAT THE HELL ARE YOU--
A LITTLE MORE SUCCINCT.
GAME'S OVER. OPEN THE DOOR OR I OPEN YOU UP.
A LITTLE MORE... MERCER.

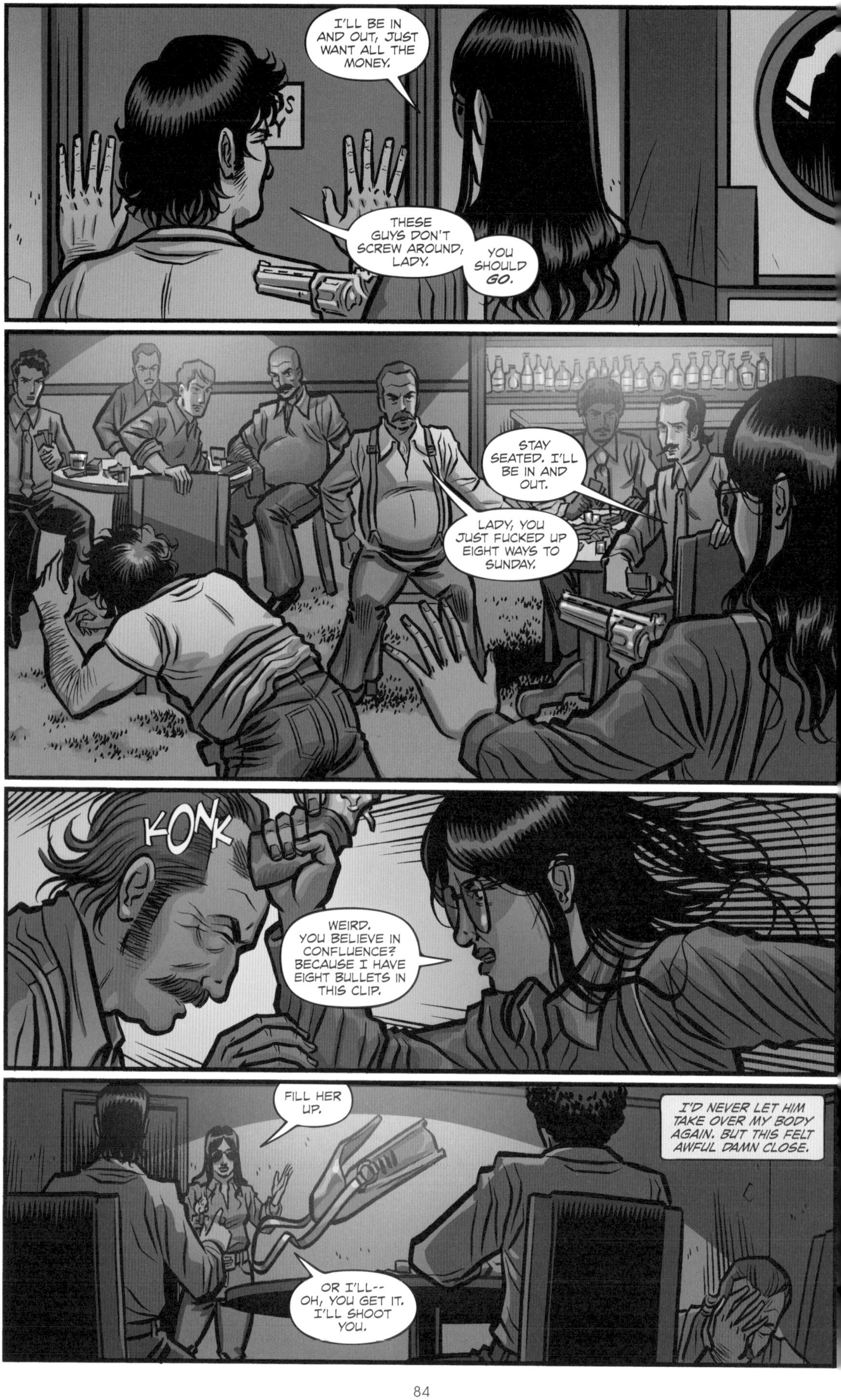

I'LL BE IN AND OUT, JUST WANT ALL THE MONEY.
THESE GUYS DON'T SCREW AROUND, LADY.
YOU SHOULD *GO.*
STAY SEATED. I'LL BE IN AND OUT.
LADY, YOU JUST FUCKED UP EIGHT WAYS TO SUNDAY.
KONK
WEIRD. YOU BELIEVE IN CONFLUENCE? BECAUSE I HAVE EIGHT BULLETS IN THIS CLIP.
FILL HER UP.
I'D NEVER LET HIM TAKE OVER MY BODY AGAIN. BUT THIS FELT AWFUL DAMN CLOSE.
OR I'LL-- OH, YOU GET IT. I'LL SHOOT YOU.

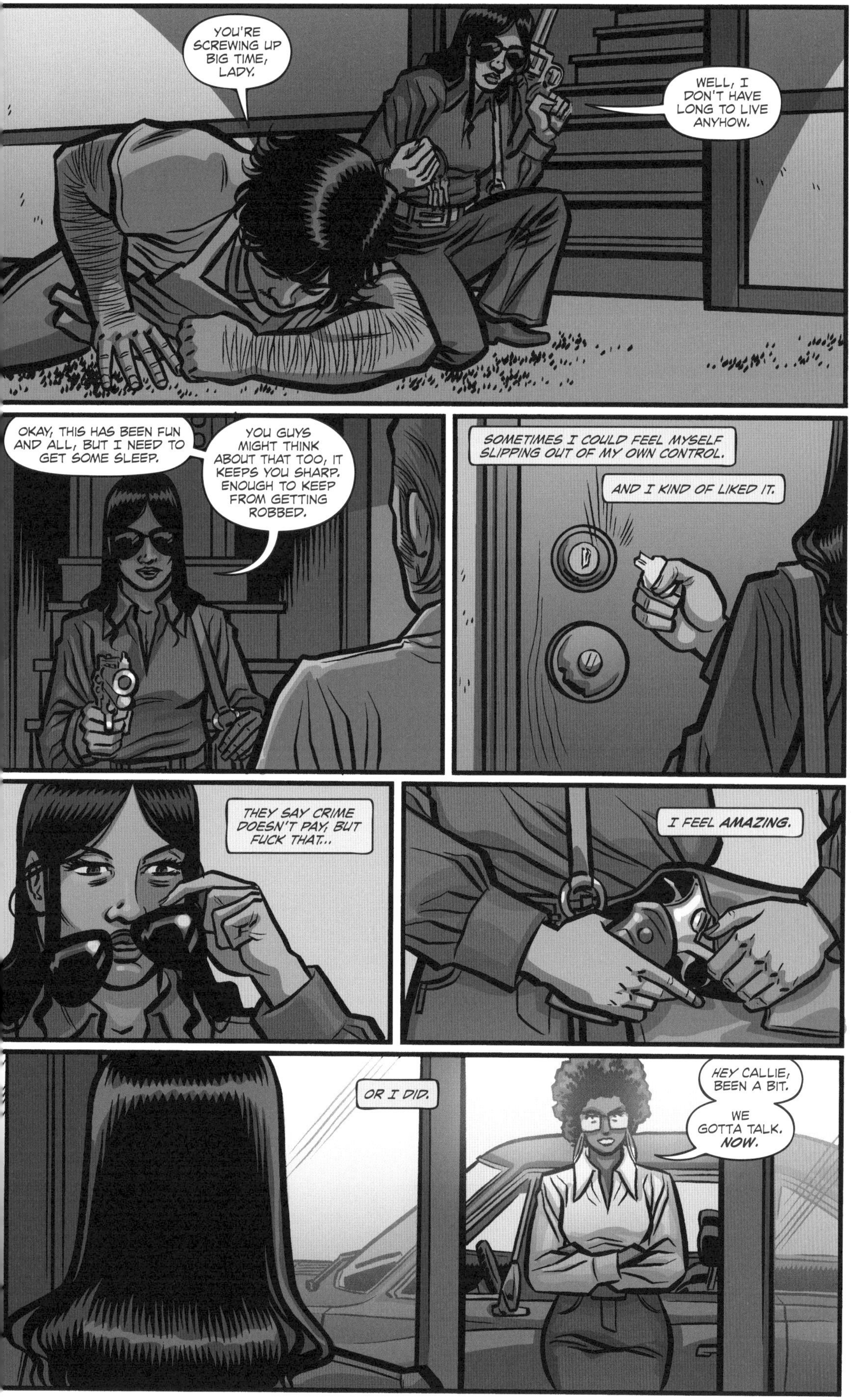
YOU'RE SCREWING UP BIG TIME, LADY.
WELL, I DON'T HAVE LONG TO LIVE ANYHOW.
OKAY, THIS HAS BEEN FUN AND ALL, BUT I NEED TO GET SOME SLEEP.
YOU GUYS MIGHT THINK ABOUT THAT TOO, IT KEEPS YOU SHARP. ENOUGH TO KEEP FROM GETTING ROBBED.
SOMETIMES I COULD FEEL MYSELF SLIPPING OUT OF MY OWN CONTROL.
AND I KIND OF LIKED IT.
THEY SAY CRIME DOESN'T PAY, BUT FUCK THAT...
I FEEL AMAZING.
OR I DID.
HEY CALLIE, BEEN A BIT.
WE GOTTA TALK. NOW.

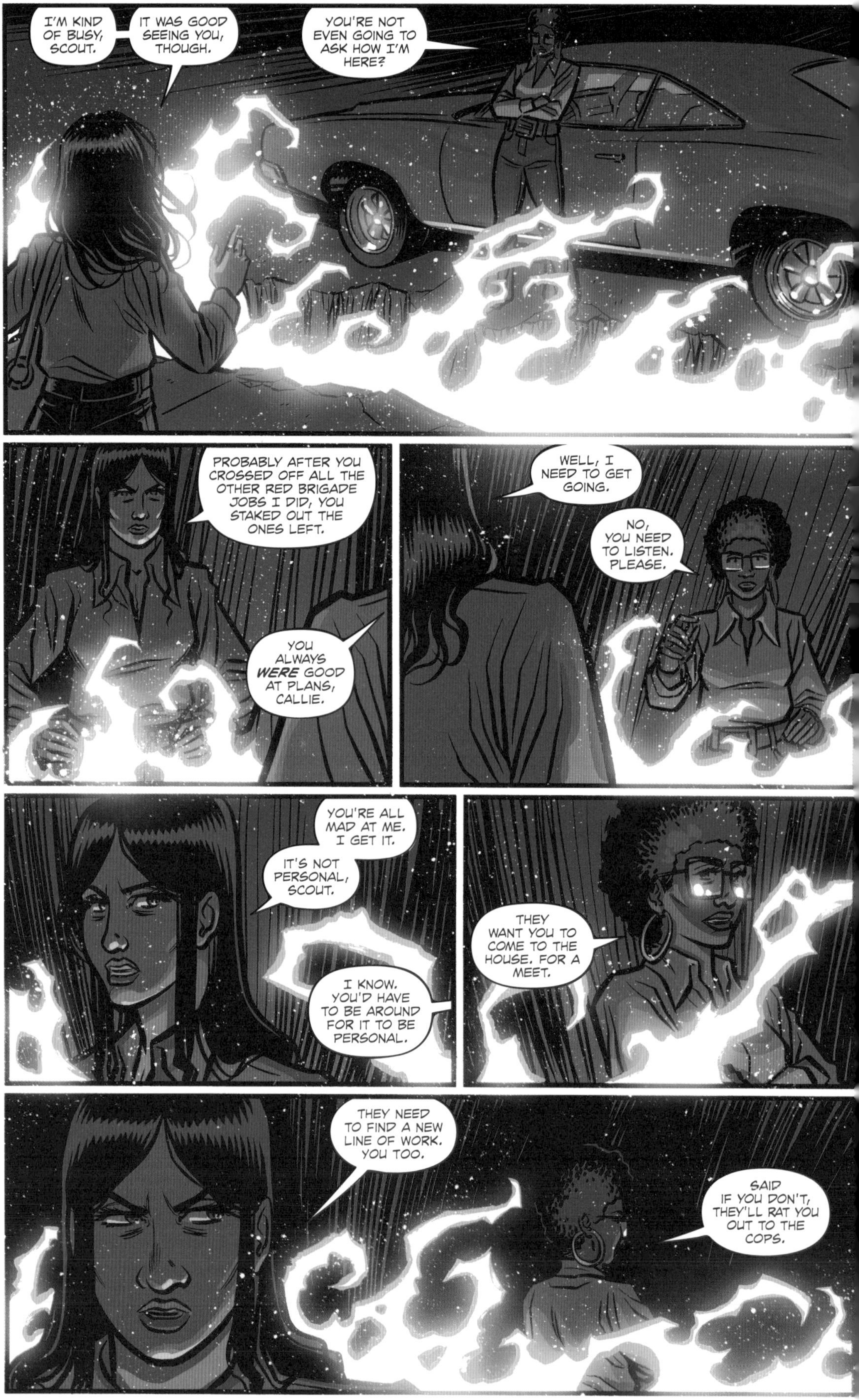
I'M KIND OF BUSY, SCOUT.
IT WAS GOOD SEEING YOU, THOUGH.
YOU'RE NOT EVEN GOING TO ASK HOW I'M HERE?
PROBABLY AFTER YOU CROSSED OFF ALL THE OTHER RED BRIGADE JOBS I DID, YOU STAKED OUT THE ONES LEFT.
YOU ALWAYS *WERE* GOOD AT PLANS, CALLIE.
WELL, I NEED TO GET GOING.
NO, YOU NEED TO LISTEN. PLEASE.
YOU'RE ALL MAD AT ME. I GET IT.
IT'S NOT PERSONAL, SCOUT.
I KNOW. YOU'D HAVE TO BE AROUND FOR IT TO BE PERSONAL.
THEY WANT YOU TO COME TO THE HOUSE. FOR A MEET.
THEY NEED TO FIND A NEW LINE OF WORK. YOU TOO.
SAID IF YOU DON'T, THEY'LL RAT YOU OUT TO THE COPS.

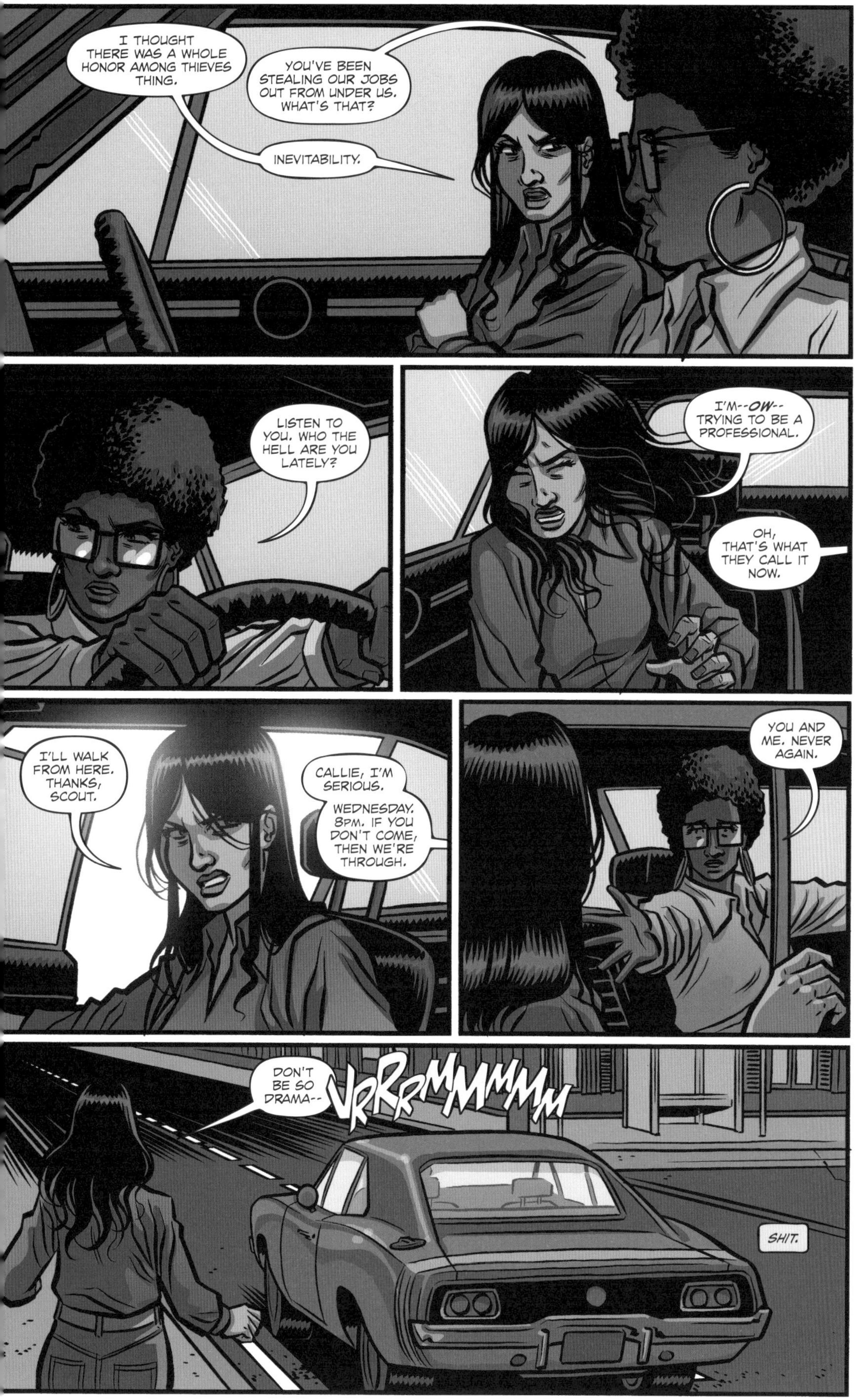
I THOUGHT THERE WAS A WHOLE HONOR AMONG THIEVES THING.
YOU'VE BEEN STEALING OUR JOBS OUT FROM UNDER US. WHAT'S THAT?
INEVITABILITY.
LISTEN TO YOU. WHO THE HELL ARE YOU LATELY?
I'M--OW--TRYING TO BE A PROFESSIONAL.
OH, THAT'S WHAT THEY CALL IT NOW.
I'LL WALK FROM HERE. THANKS, SCOUT.
CALLIE, I'M SERIOUS.
WEDNESDAY. 8PM. IF YOU DON'T COME, THEN WE'RE THROUGH.
YOU AND ME. NEVER AGAIN.
DON'T BE SO DRAMA--
VRRRMMMMM
SHIT.

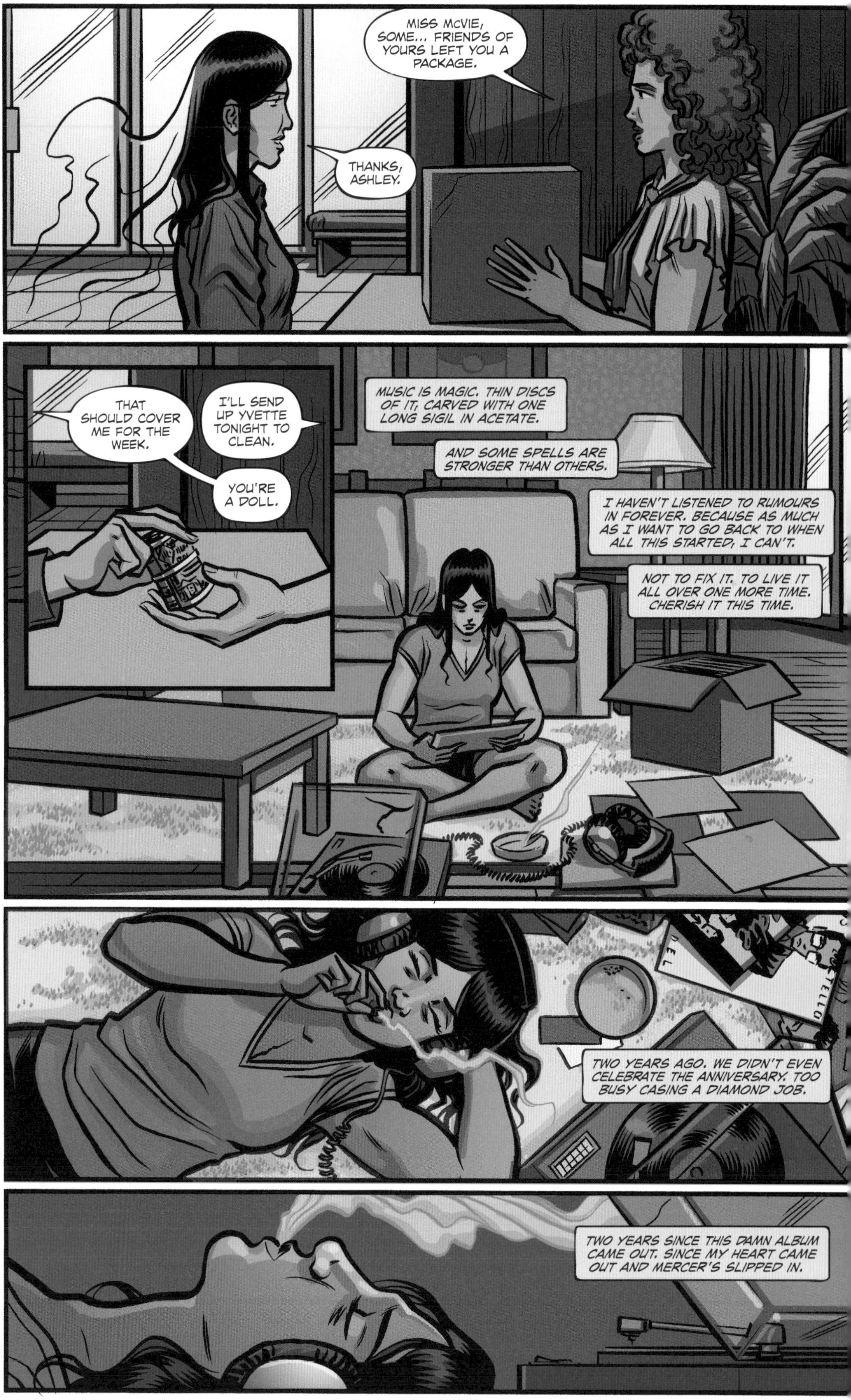
MISS McVIE, SOME... FRIENDS OF YOURS LEFT YOU A PACKAGE.
THANKS, ASHLEY.
THAT SHOULD COVER ME FOR THE WEEK.
I'LL SEND UP YVETTE TONIGHT TO CLEAN.
YOU'RE A DOLL.
MUSIC IS MAGIC. THIN DISCS OF IT, CARVED WITH ONE LONG SIGIL IN ACETATE.
AND SOME SPELLS ARE STRONGER THAN OTHERS.
I HAVEN'T LISTENED TO RUMOURS IN FOREVER. BECAUSE AS MUCH AS I WANT TO GO BACK TO WHEN ALL THIS STARTED, I CAN'T.
NOT TO FIX IT. TO LIVE IT ALL OVER ONE MORE TIME. CHERISH IT THIS TIME.
TWO YEARS AGO. WE DIDN'T EVEN CELEBRATE THE ANNIVERSARY. TOO BUSY CASING A DIAMOND JOB.
TWO YEARS SINCE THIS DAMN ALBUM CAME OUT. SINCE MY HEART CAME OUT AND MERCER'S SLIPPED IN.

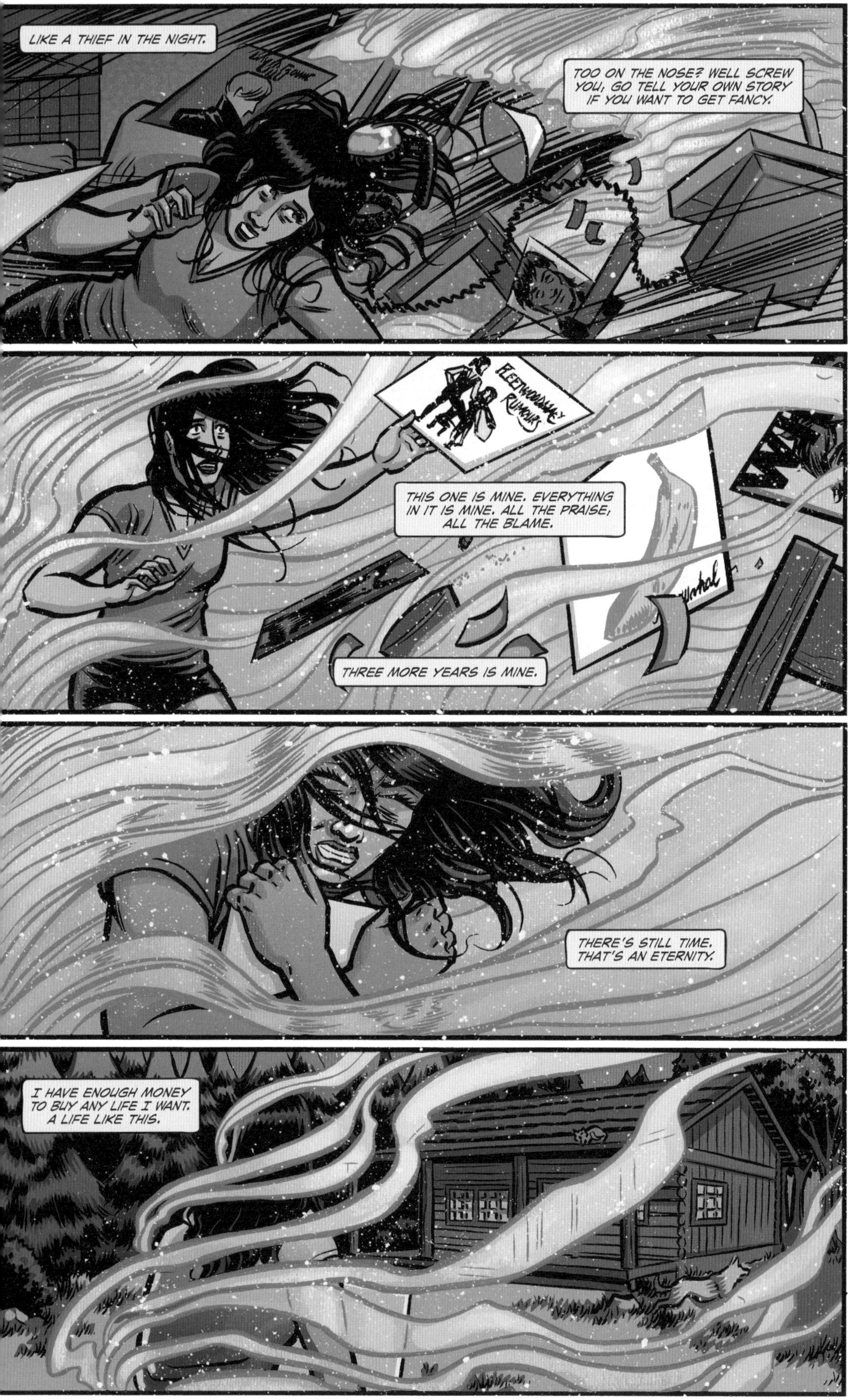
LIKE A THIEF IN THE NIGHT.
TOO ON THE NOSE? WELL SCREW YOU, GO TELL YOUR OWN STORY IF YOU WANT TO GET FANCY.
FLEETWOOD MAC RUMOURS
THIS ONE IS MINE. EVERYTHING IN IT IS MINE. ALL THE PRAISE, ALL THE BLAME.
Warhol
THREE MORE YEARS IS MINE.
THERE'S STILL TIME. THAT'S AN ETERNITY.
I HAVE ENOUGH MONEY TO BUY ANY LIFE I WANT. A LIFE LIKE THIS.

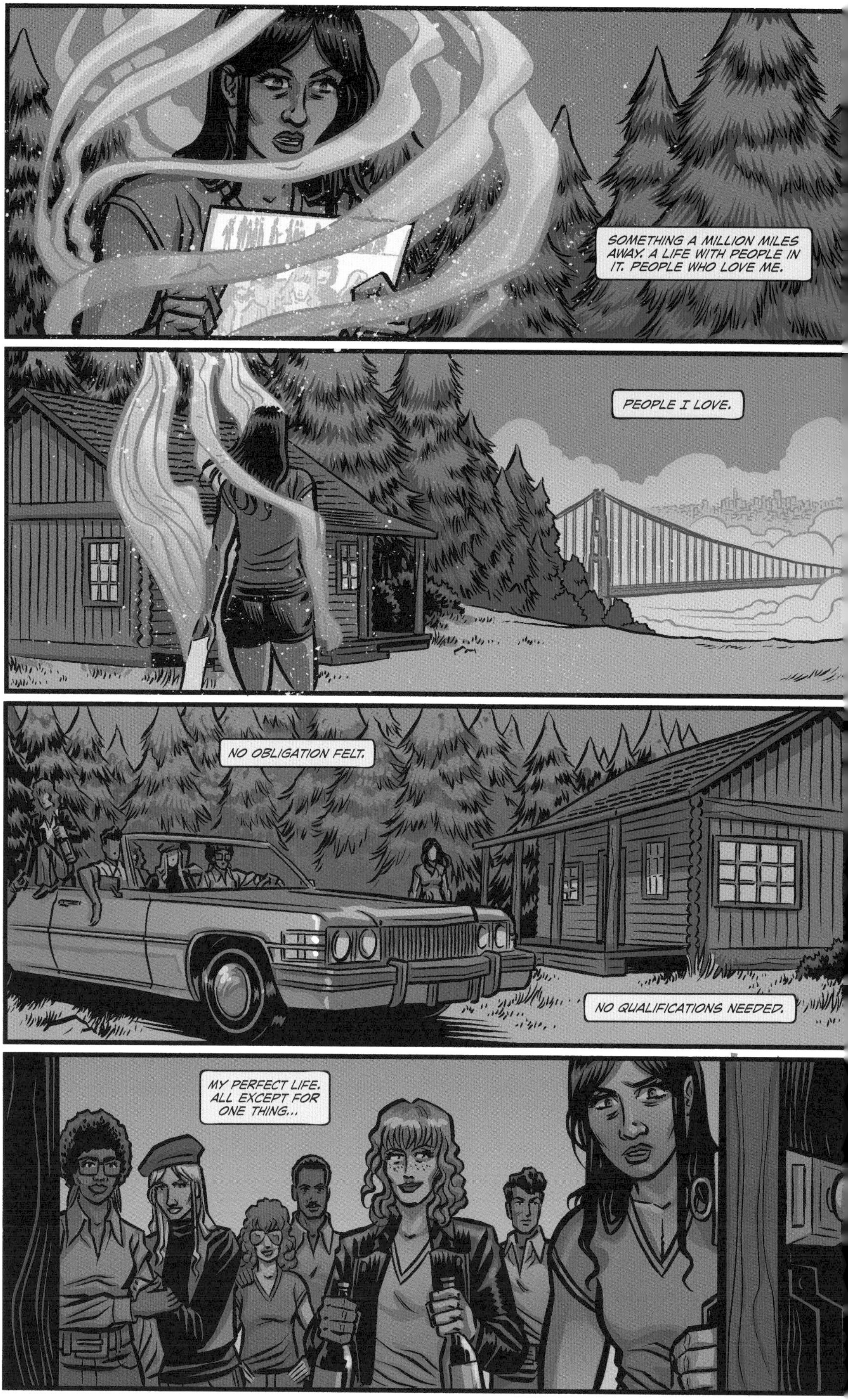
SOMETHING A MILLION MILES AWAY. A LIFE WITH PEOPLE IN IT. PEOPLE WHO LOVE ME.
PEOPLE I LOVE.
NO OBLIGATION FELT.
NO QUALIFICATIONS NEEDED.
MY PERFECT LIFE. ALL EXCEPT FOR ONE THING...

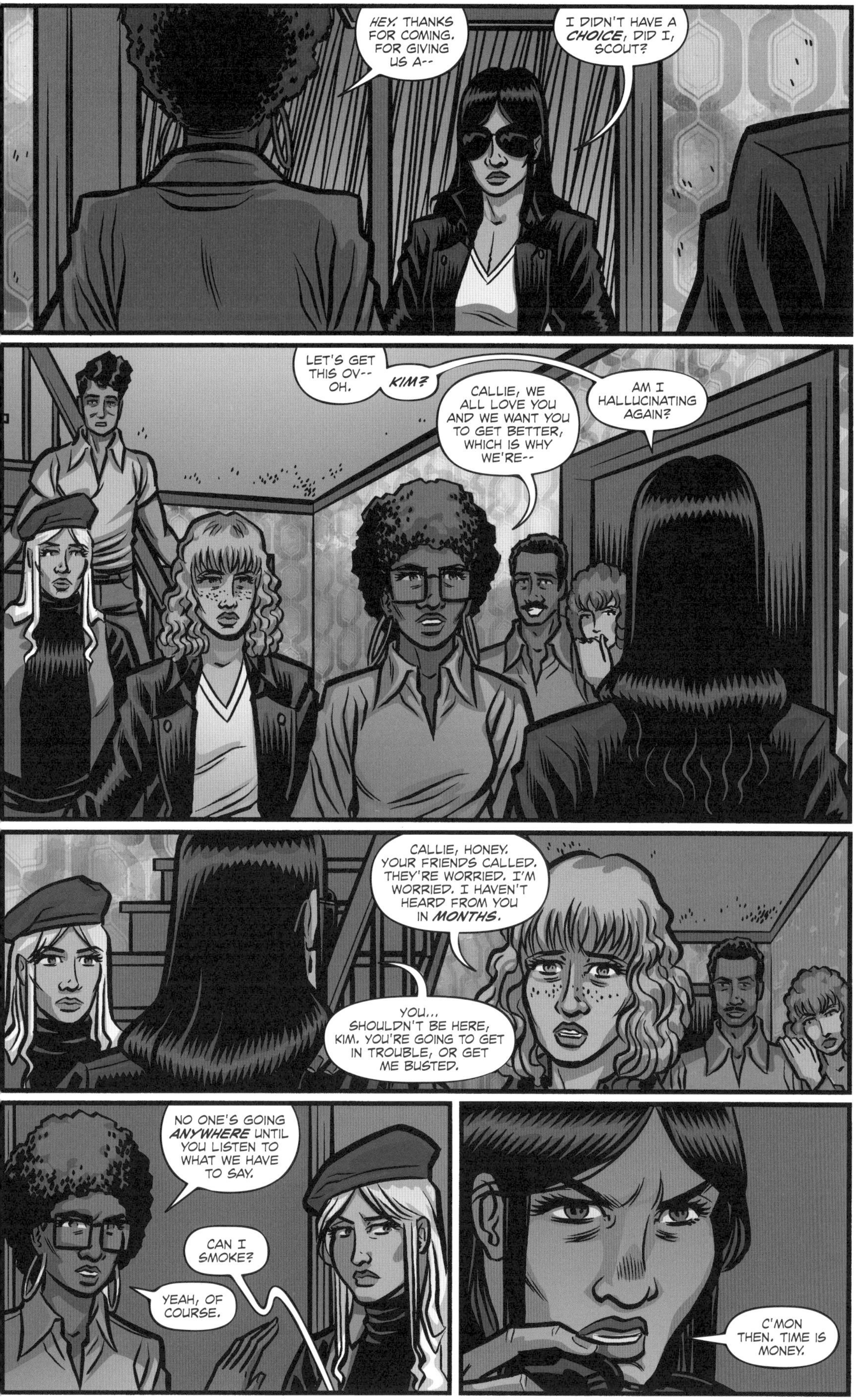
HEY. THANKS FOR COMING. FOR GIVING US A--
I DIDN'T HAVE A CHOICE, DID I, SCOUT?
LET'S GET THIS OV-- OH. KIM?
AM I HALLUCINATING AGAIN?
CALLIE, WE ALL LOVE YOU AND WE WANT YOU TO GET BETTER, WHICH IS WHY WE'RE--
CALLIE, HONEY. YOUR FRIENDS CALLED. THEY'RE WORRIED. I'M WORRIED. I HAVEN'T HEARD FROM YOU IN MONTHS.
YOU... SHOULDN'T BE HERE, KIM. YOU'RE GOING TO GET IN TROUBLE, OR GET ME BUSTED.
NO ONE'S GOING ANYWHERE UNTIL YOU LISTEN TO WHAT WE HAVE TO SAY.
CAN I SMOKE?
YEAH, OF COURSE.
C'MON THEN. TIME IS MONEY.

YOU VANISHED ON US, CALLIE. WE HAVEN'T SEEN YOU OR HEARD FROM YOU EXCEPT--

WHEN YOU STEAL OUR FUCKIN' JOBS OUT FROM UNDER US!

LET'S CALM DOWN. WE'RE NOT HERE TO ATTACK CALLIE. WE'RE HERE TO TELL HER HOW HER ACTIONS AFFECT US.

THEY *SUCK*. I MEAN, DRESS IT UP ALL YOU WANT. IT *SUCKS* BEING YOUR FRIEND, CALLIE.

YOU LIE ABOUT EVERYTHING UNTIL YOU'RE ALL OVER THE NEWS AND I CAN'T HELP BUT KNOW.

THEN YOU KEEP CALLING WHILE YOU'RE ON THE RUN LIKE THIS IS A FUN GAME. UNTIL YOU JUST STOP WITHOUT WARNING.

SEE, HIS IS WHAT UST SAID W OULDN'T E OING

WHEN ARE VE GONNA TAL BOUT WHAT SH OWES US?

CALM DOWN, MURPH. ALLIE'S PRETTY REASONABLE

HY AR YOU GUYS ALKING ABOU MONEY? THAT'S OT WHAT THI ABOU

SCOUT THEY HAVE A RIGHT TO E MAD

I'M GONNA TALK NOW.

WHAT'S THE FUCKING ENDGAME HERE?

OR IS THE PLAN TO BEAT ME INTO SUBMISSION WITH ALL YOUR FEELINGS?

I COULD BLAME THAT BIT ON MERCER, BUT HE HADN'T EVEN SHOWN UP YET.

SORRY. OVERSLE--WOW. TENSE.

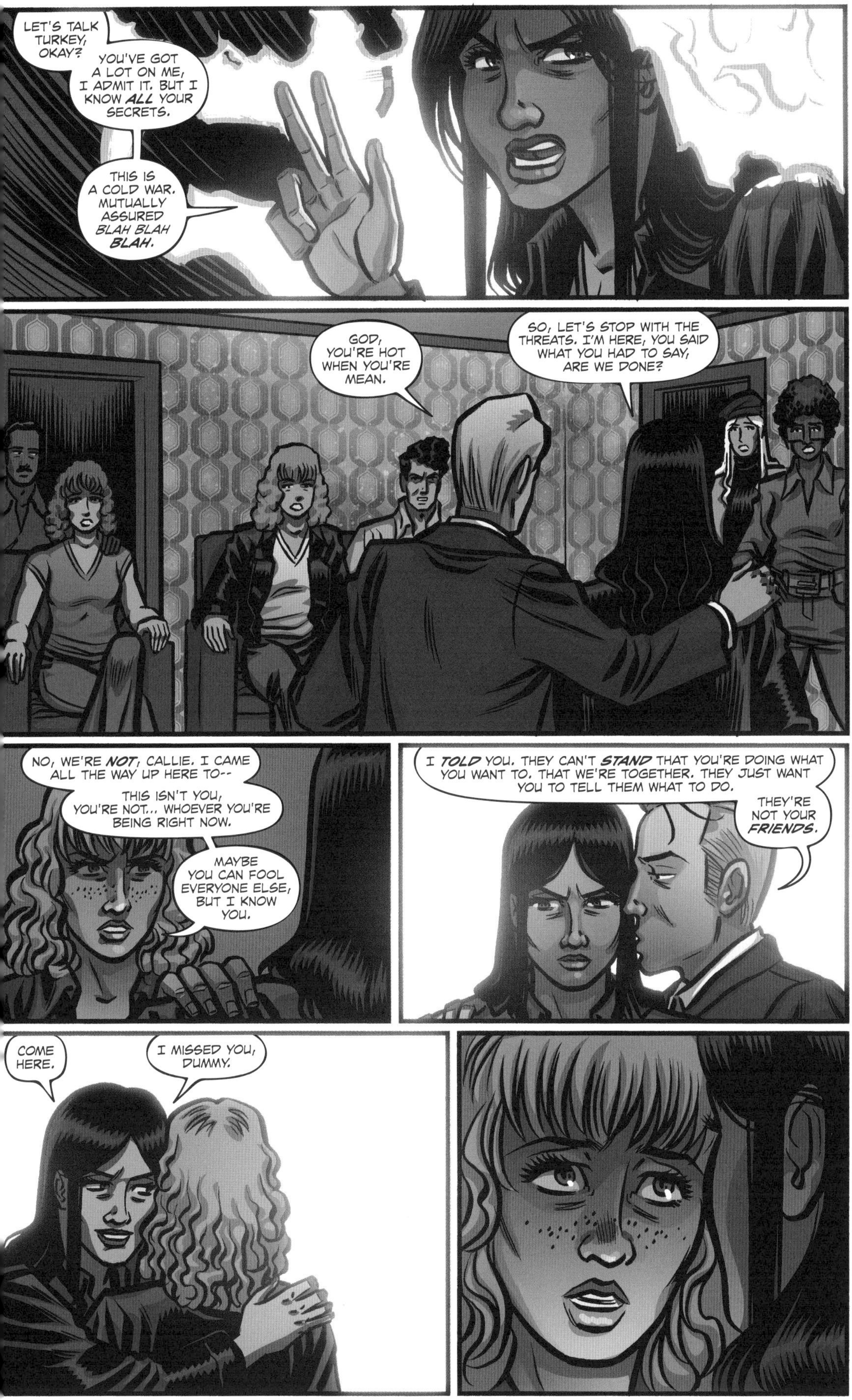
LET'S TALK TURKEY, OKAY?
YOU'VE GOT A LOT ON ME, I ADMIT IT. BUT I KNOW ALL YOUR SECRETS.
THIS IS A COLD WAR. MUTUALLY ASSURED BLAH BLAH BLAH.
GOD, YOU'RE HOT WHEN YOU'RE MEAN.
SO, LET'S STOP WITH THE THREATS. I'M HERE, YOU SAID WHAT YOU HAD TO SAY, ARE WE DONE?
NO, WE'RE NOT, CALLIE. I CAME ALL THE WAY UP HERE TO--
THIS ISN'T YOU, YOU'RE NOT... WHOEVER YOU'RE BEING RIGHT NOW.
MAYBE YOU CAN FOOL EVERYONE ELSE, BUT I KNOW YOU.
I TOLD YOU. THEY CAN'T STAND THAT YOU'RE DOING WHAT YOU WANT TO. THAT WE'RE TOGETHER. THEY JUST WANT YOU TO TELL THEM WHAT TO DO.
THEY'RE NOT YOUR FRIENDS.
COME HERE.
I MISSED YOU, DUMMY.

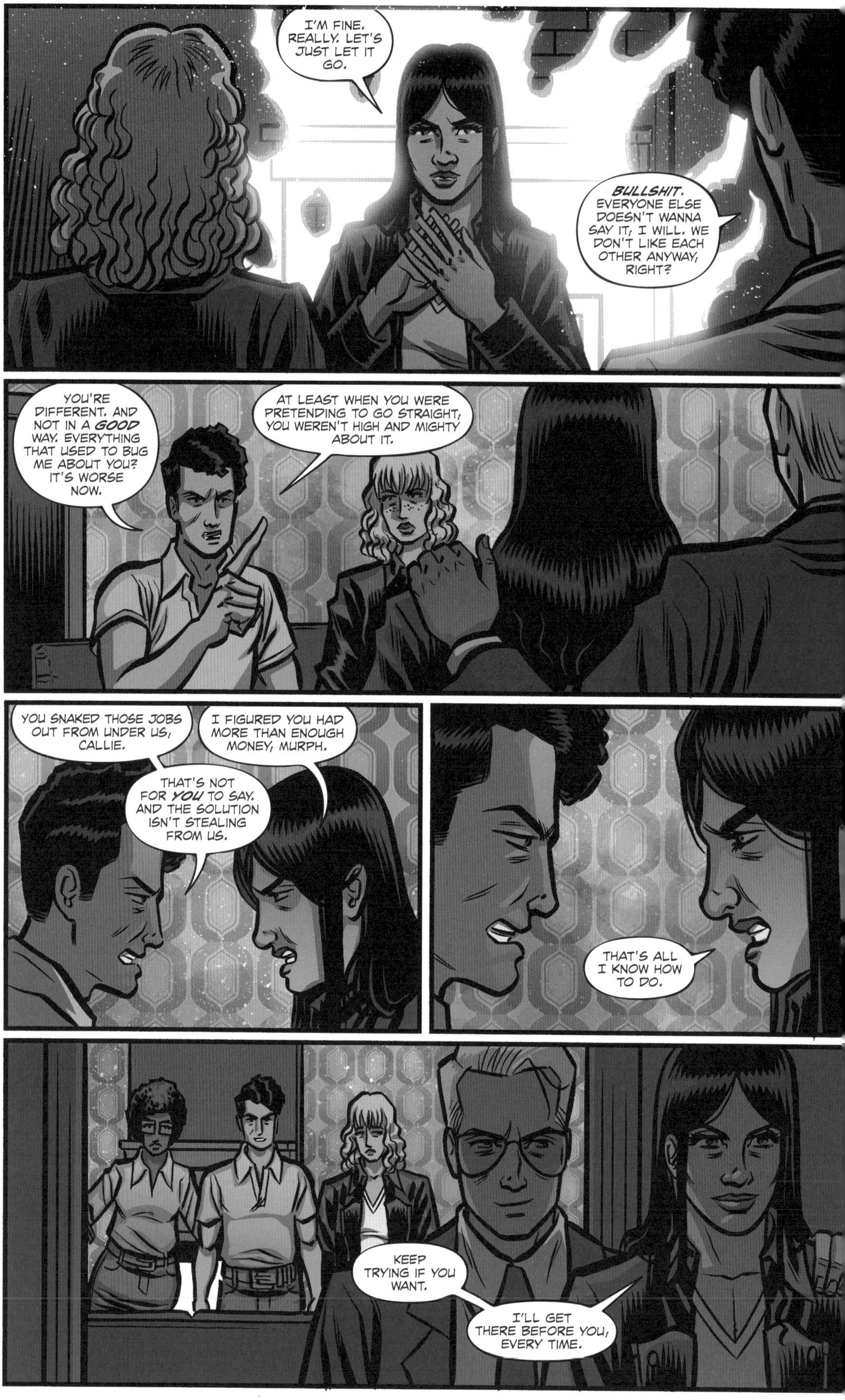
I'M FINE. REALLY. LET'S JUST LET IT GO.
BULLSHIT. EVERYONE ELSE DOESN'T WANNA SAY IT, I WILL. WE DON'T LIKE EACH OTHER ANYWAY, RIGHT?
YOU'RE DIFFERENT. AND NOT IN A GOOD WAY. EVERYTHING THAT USED TO BUG ME ABOUT YOU? IT'S WORSE NOW.
AT LEAST WHEN YOU WERE PRETENDING TO GO STRAIGHT, YOU WEREN'T HIGH AND MIGHTY ABOUT IT.
YOU SNAKED THOSE JOBS OUT FROM UNDER US, CALLIE.
I FIGURED YOU HAD MORE THAN ENOUGH MONEY, MURPH.
THAT'S NOT FOR YOU TO SAY. AND THE SOLUTION ISN'T STEALING FROM US.
THAT'S ALL I KNOW HOW TO DO.
KEEP TRYING IF YOU WANT.
I'LL GET THERE BEFORE YOU, EVERY TIME.

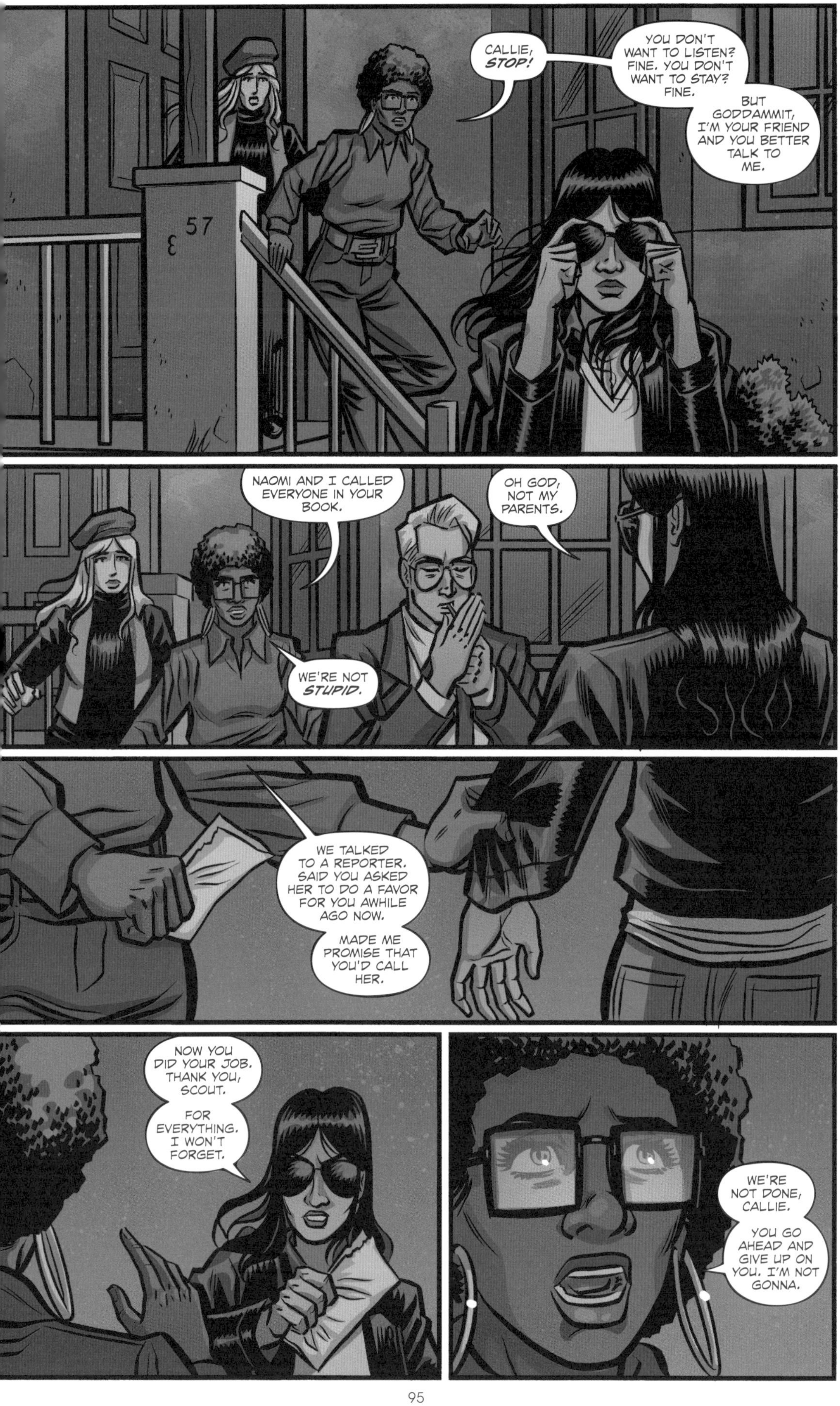
CALLIE, STOP!
YOU DON'T WANT TO LISTEN? FINE. YOU DON'T WANT TO STAY? FINE.
BUT GODDAMMIT, I'M YOUR FRIEND AND YOU BETTER TALK TO ME.
57
NAOMI AND I CALLED EVERYONE IN YOUR BOOK.
OH GOD, NOT MY PARENTS.
WE'RE NOT STUPID.
WE TALKED TO A REPORTER. SAID YOU ASKED HER TO DO A FAVOR FOR YOU AWHILE AGO NOW.
MADE ME PROMISE THAT YOU'D CALL HER.
NOW YOU DID YOUR JOB. THANK YOU, SCOUT.
FOR EVERYTHING. I WON'T FORGET.
WE'RE NOT DONE, CALLIE.
YOU GO AHEAD AND GIVE UP ON YOU. I'M NOT GONNA.

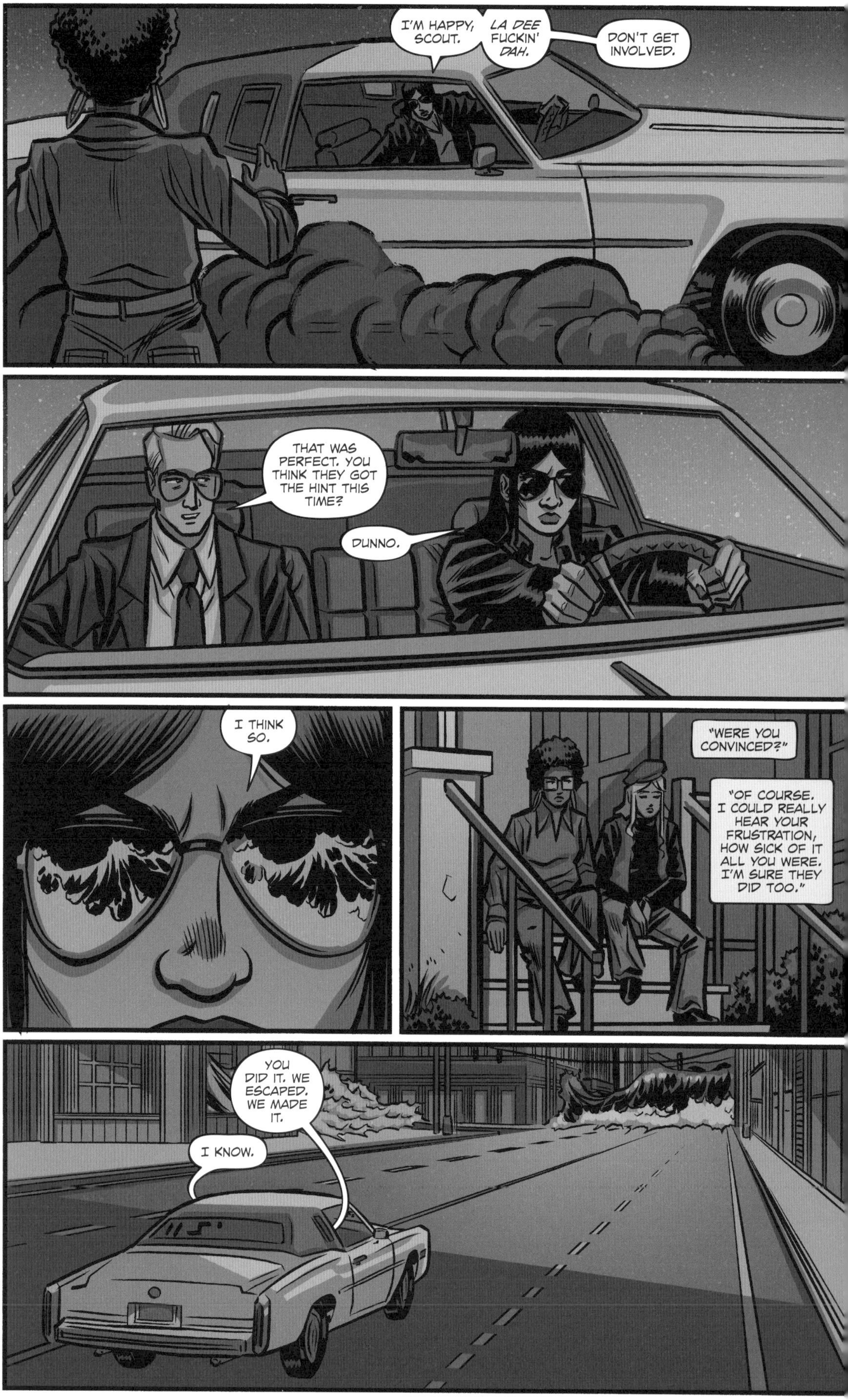
I'M HAPPY, SCOUT.
LA DEE FUCKIN' DAH.
DON'T GET INVOLVED.
THAT WAS PERFECT. YOU THINK THEY GOT THE HINT THIS TIME?
DUNNO.
I THINK SO.
"WERE YOU CONVINCED?"
"OF COURSE. I COULD REALLY HEAR YOUR FRUSTRATION, HOW SICK OF IT ALL YOU WERE. I'M SURE THEY DID TOO."
YOU DID IT. WE ESCAPED. WE MADE IT.
I KNOW.

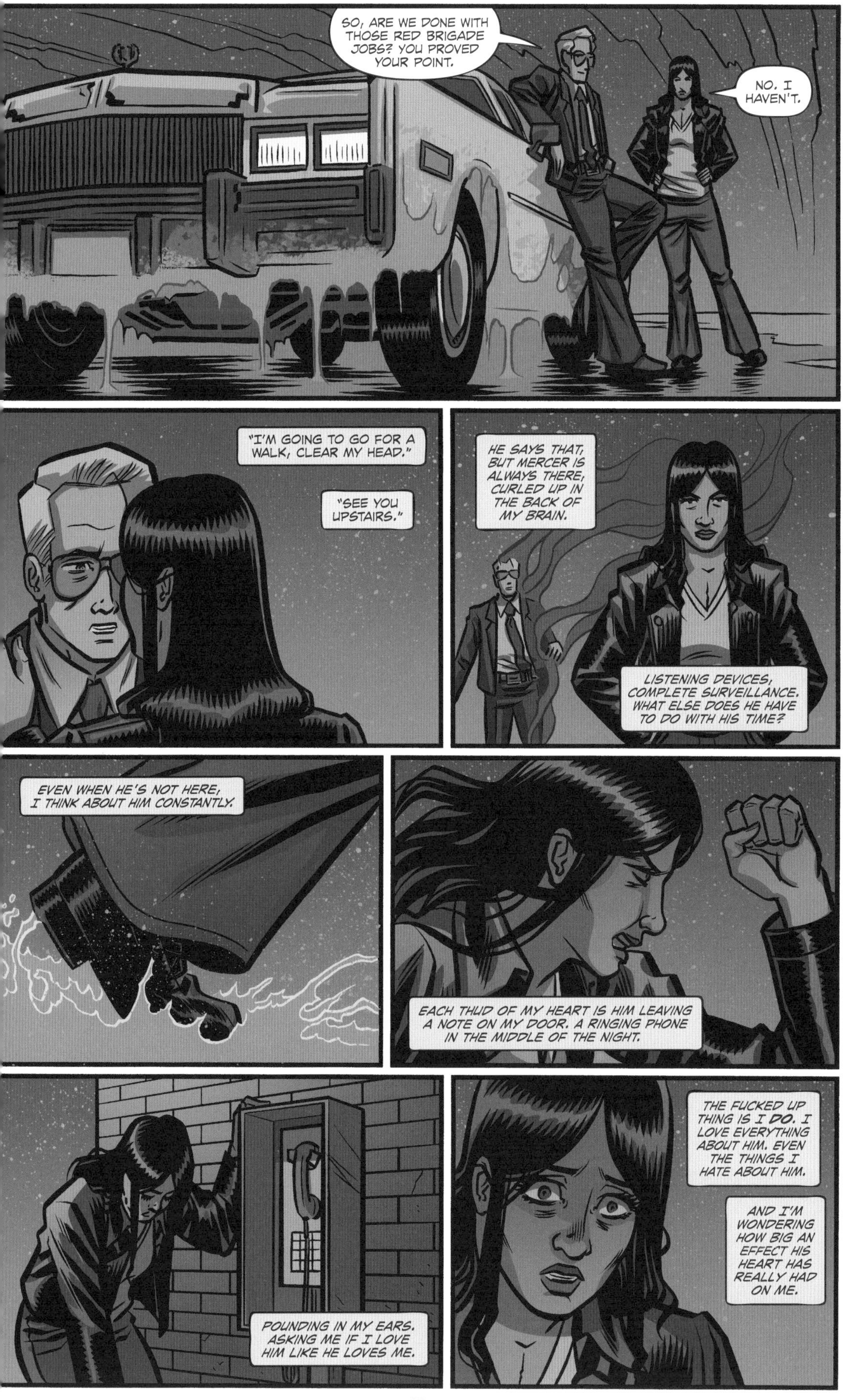
SO, ARE WE DONE WITH THOSE RED BRIGADE JOBS? YOU PROVED YOUR POINT.
NO. I HAVEN'T.
"I'M GOING TO GO FOR A WALK, CLEAR MY HEAD."
"SEE YOU UPSTAIRS."
HE SAYS THAT, BUT MERCER IS ALWAYS THERE, CURLED UP IN THE BACK OF MY BRAIN.
LISTENING DEVICES, COMPLETE SURVEILLANCE. WHAT ELSE DOES HE HAVE TO DO WITH HIS TIME?
EVEN WHEN HE'S NOT HERE, I THINK ABOUT HIM CONSTANTLY.
EACH THUD OF MY HEART IS HIM LEAVING A NOTE ON MY DOOR. A RINGING PHONE IN THE MIDDLE OF THE NIGHT.
POUNDING IN MY EARS. ASKING ME IF I LOVE HIM LIKE HE LOVES ME.
THE FUCKED UP THING IS I DO. I LOVE EVERYTHING ABOUT HIM. EVEN THE THINGS I HATE ABOUT HIM.
AND I'M WONDERING HOW BIG AN EFFECT HIS HEART HAS REALLY HAD ON ME.

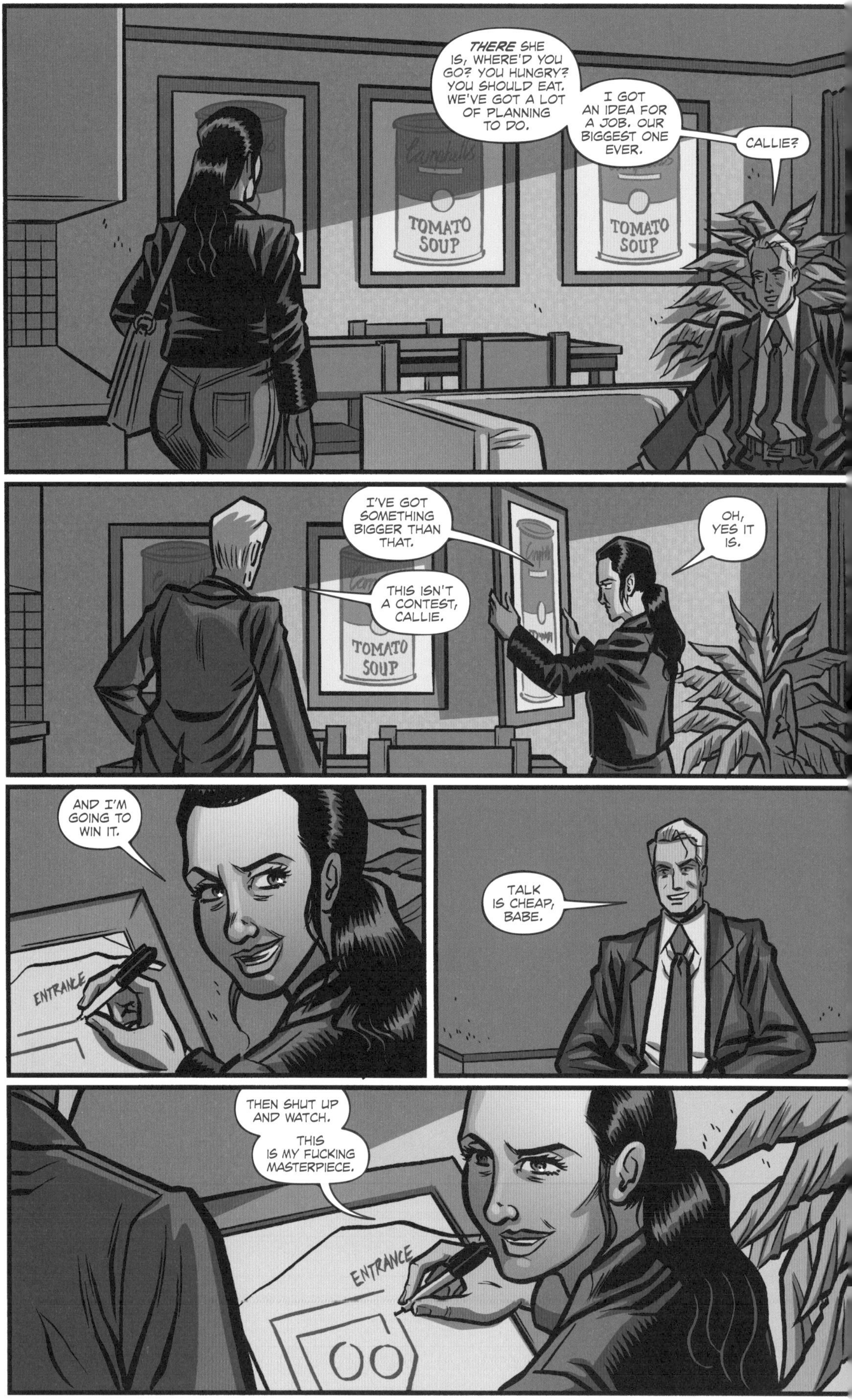
THERE SHE IS, WHERE'D YOU GO? YOU HUNGRY? YOU SHOULD EAT. WE'VE GOT A LOT OF PLANNING TO DO.
I GOT AN IDEA FOR A JOB. OUR BIGGEST ONE EVER.
CALLIE?
TOMATO SOUP
TOMATO SOUP
I'VE GOT SOMETHING BIGGER THAN THAT.
THIS ISN'T A CONTEST, CALLIE.
OH, YES IT IS.
TOMATO SOUP
AND I'M GOING TO WIN IT.
ENTRANCE
TALK IS CHEAP, BABE.
THEN SHUT UP AND WATCH.
THIS IS MY FUCKING MASTERPIECE.
ENTRANCE

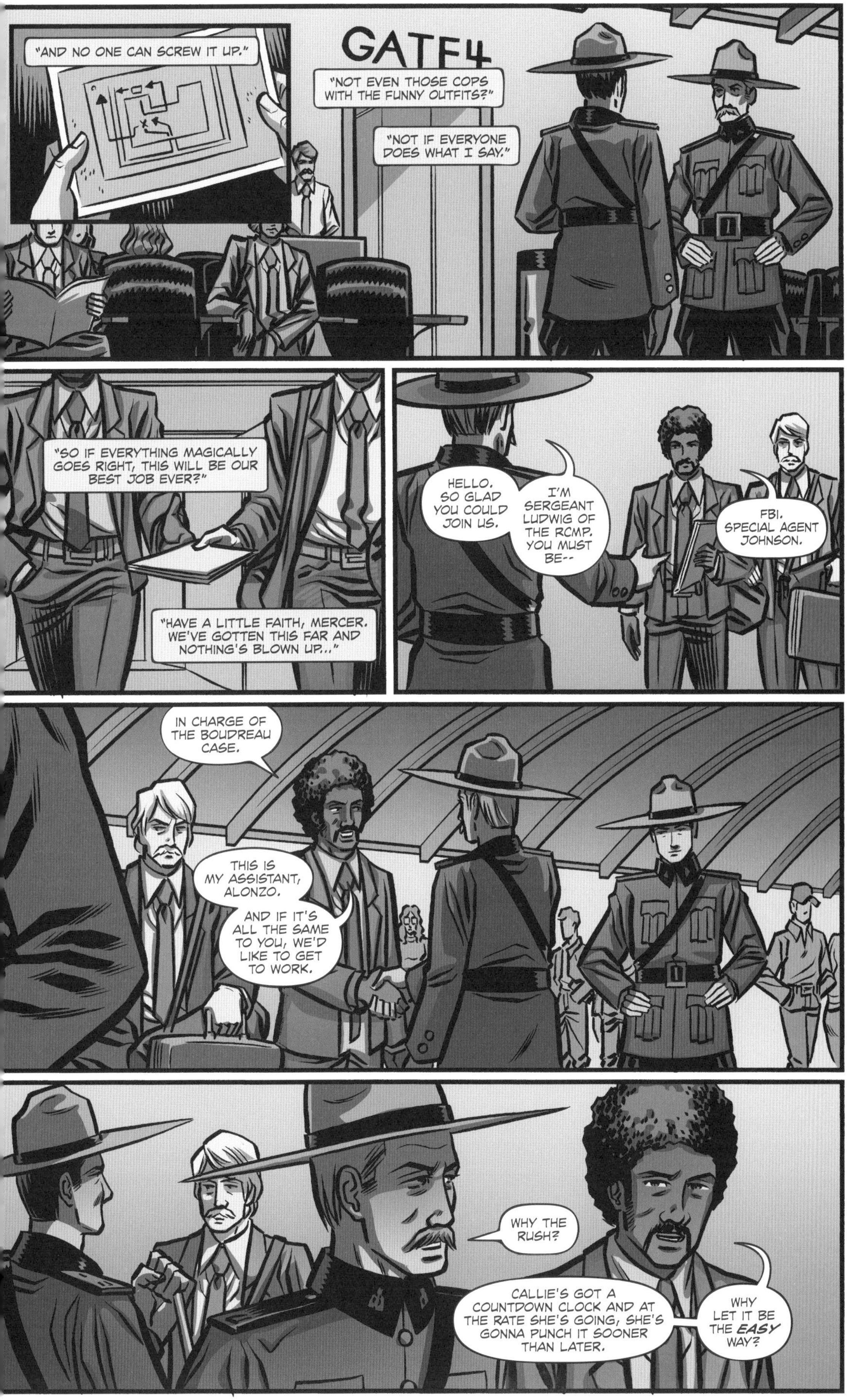
"AND NO ONE CAN SCREW IT UP."
GATE 4
"NOT EVEN THOSE COPS WITH THE FUNNY OUTFITS?"
"NOT IF EVERYONE DOES WHAT I SAY."
"SO IF EVERYTHING MAGICALLY GOES RIGHT, THIS WILL BE OUR BEST JOB EVER?"
"HAVE A LITTLE FAITH, MERCER. WE'VE GOTTEN THIS FAR AND NOTHING'S BLOWN UP..."
HELLO. SO GLAD YOU COULD JOIN US.
I'M SERGEANT LUDWIG OF THE RCMP. YOU MUST BE--
FBI. SPECIAL AGENT JOHNSON.
IN CHARGE OF THE BOUDREAU CASE.
THIS IS MY ASSISTANT, ALONZO.
AND IF IT'S ALL THE SAME TO YOU, WE'D LIKE TO GET TO WORK.
WHY THE RUSH?
CALLIE'S GOT A COUNTDOWN CLOCK AND AT THE RATE SHE'S GOING, SHE'S GONNA PUNCH IT SOONER THAN LATER.
WHY LET IT BE THE *EASY* WAY?

CHAPTER 5

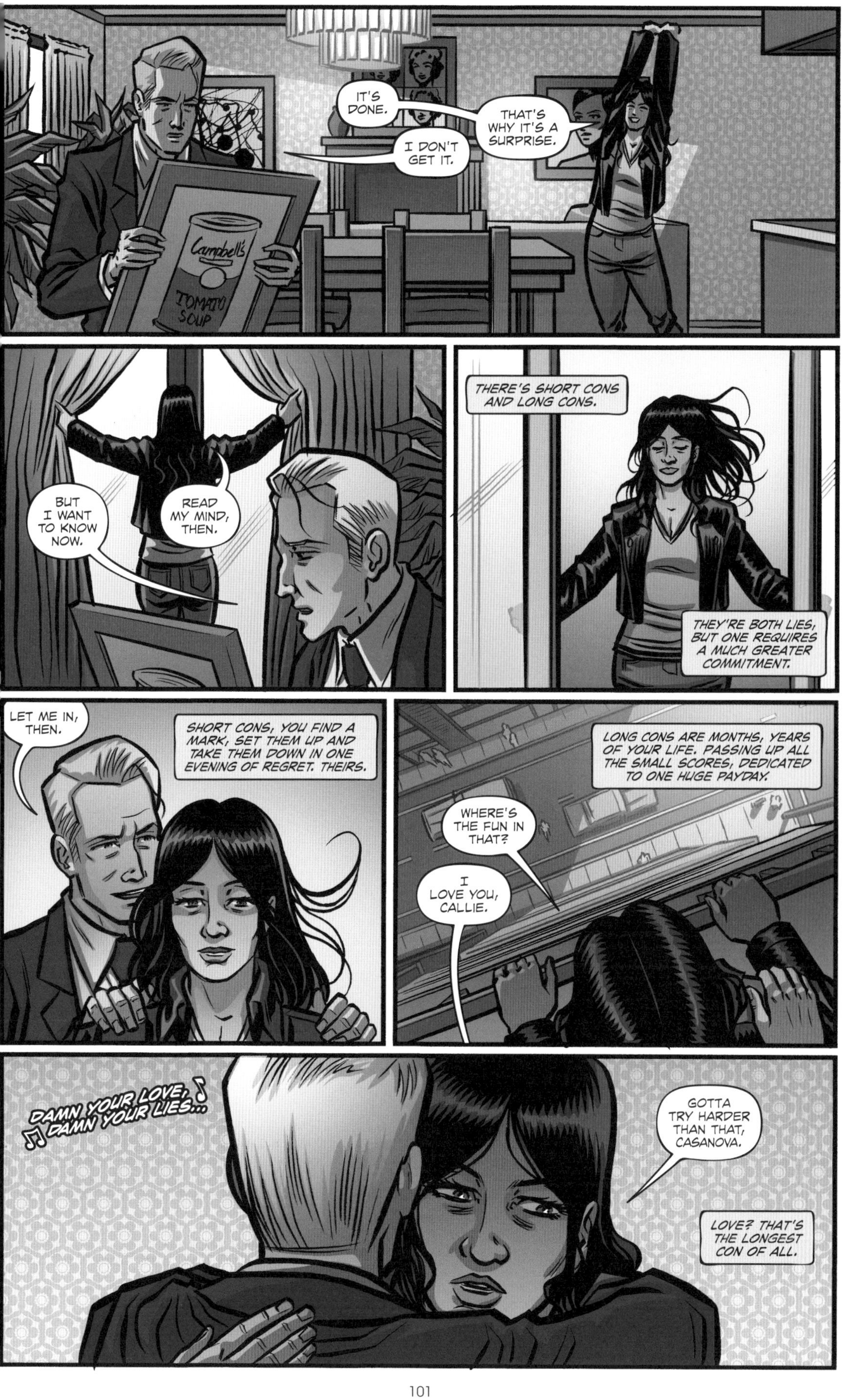
IT'S DONE.
I DON'T GET IT.
THAT'S WHY IT'S A SURPRISE.
Campbell's
TOMATO SOUP
BUT I WANT TO KNOW NOW.
READ MY MIND, THEN.
THERE'S SHORT CONS AND LONG CONS.
THEY'RE BOTH LIES, BUT ONE REQUIRES A MUCH GREATER COMMITMENT.
LET ME IN, THEN.
SHORT CONS, YOU FIND A MARK, SET THEM UP AND TAKE THEM DOWN IN ONE EVENING OF REGRET. THEIRS.
LONG CONS ARE MONTHS, YEARS OF YOUR LIFE. PASSING UP ALL THE SMALL SCORES, DEDICATED TO ONE HUGE PAYDAY.
WHERE'S THE FUN IN THAT?
I LOVE YOU, CALLIE.
DAMN YOUR LOVE, DAMN YOUR LIES...
GOTTA TRY HARDER THAN THAT, CASANOVA.
LOVE? THAT'S THE LONGEST CON OF ALL.

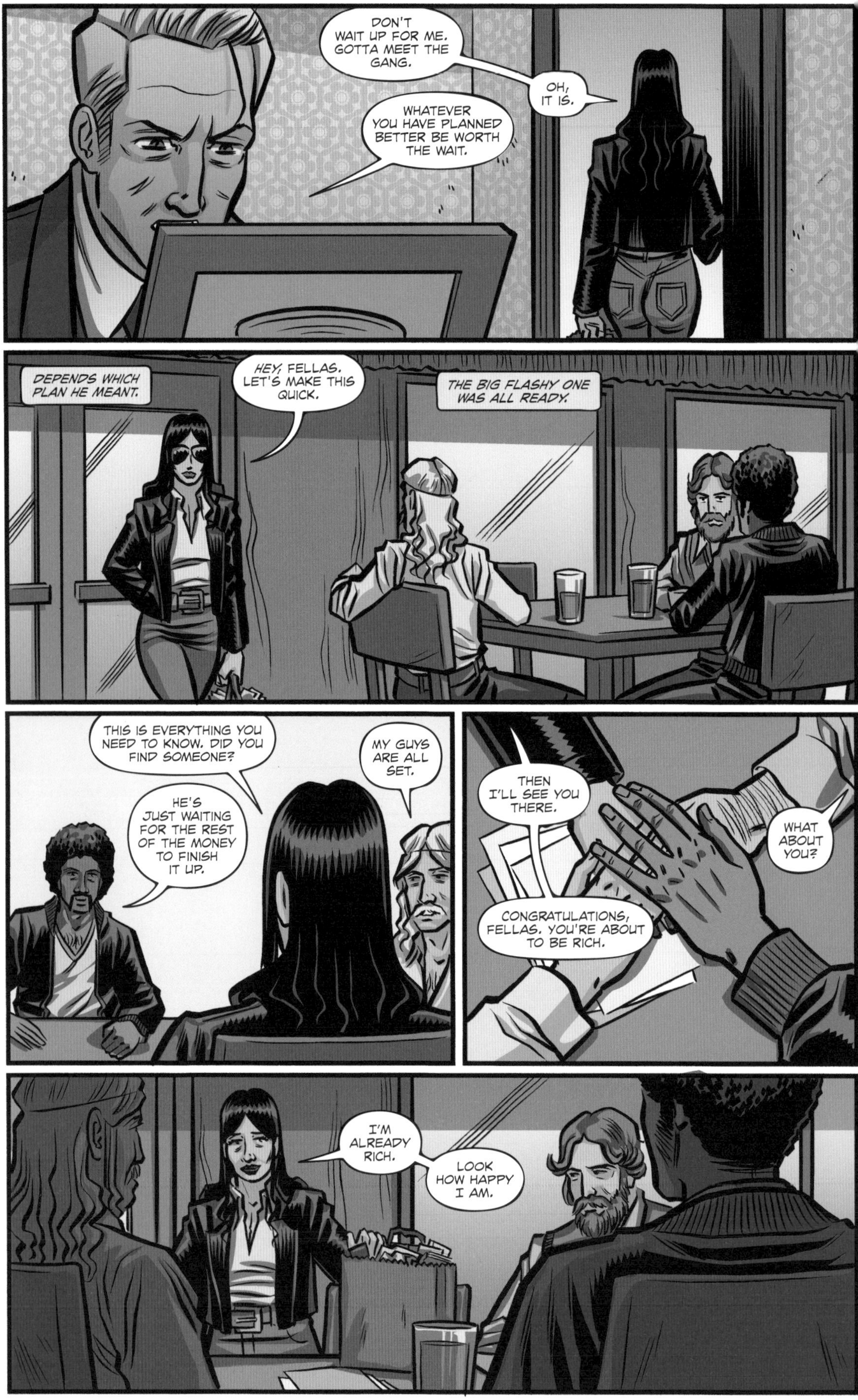

DON'T WAIT UP FOR ME. GOTTA MEET THE GANG.
WHATEVER YOU HAVE PLANNED BETTER BE WORTH THE WAIT.
OH, IT IS.
DEPENDS WHICH PLAN HE MEANT.
HEY, FELLAS. LET'S MAKE THIS QUICK.
THE BIG FLASHY ONE WAS ALL READY.
THIS IS EVERYTHING YOU NEED TO KNOW. DID YOU FIND SOMEONE?
HE'S JUST WAITING FOR THE REST OF THE MONEY TO FINISH IT UP.
MY GUYS ARE ALL SET.
THEN I'LL SEE YOU THERE.
WHAT ABOUT YOU?
CONGRATULATIONS, FELLAS. YOU'RE ABOUT TO BE RICH.
I'M ALREADY RICH.
LOOK HOW HAPPY I AM.

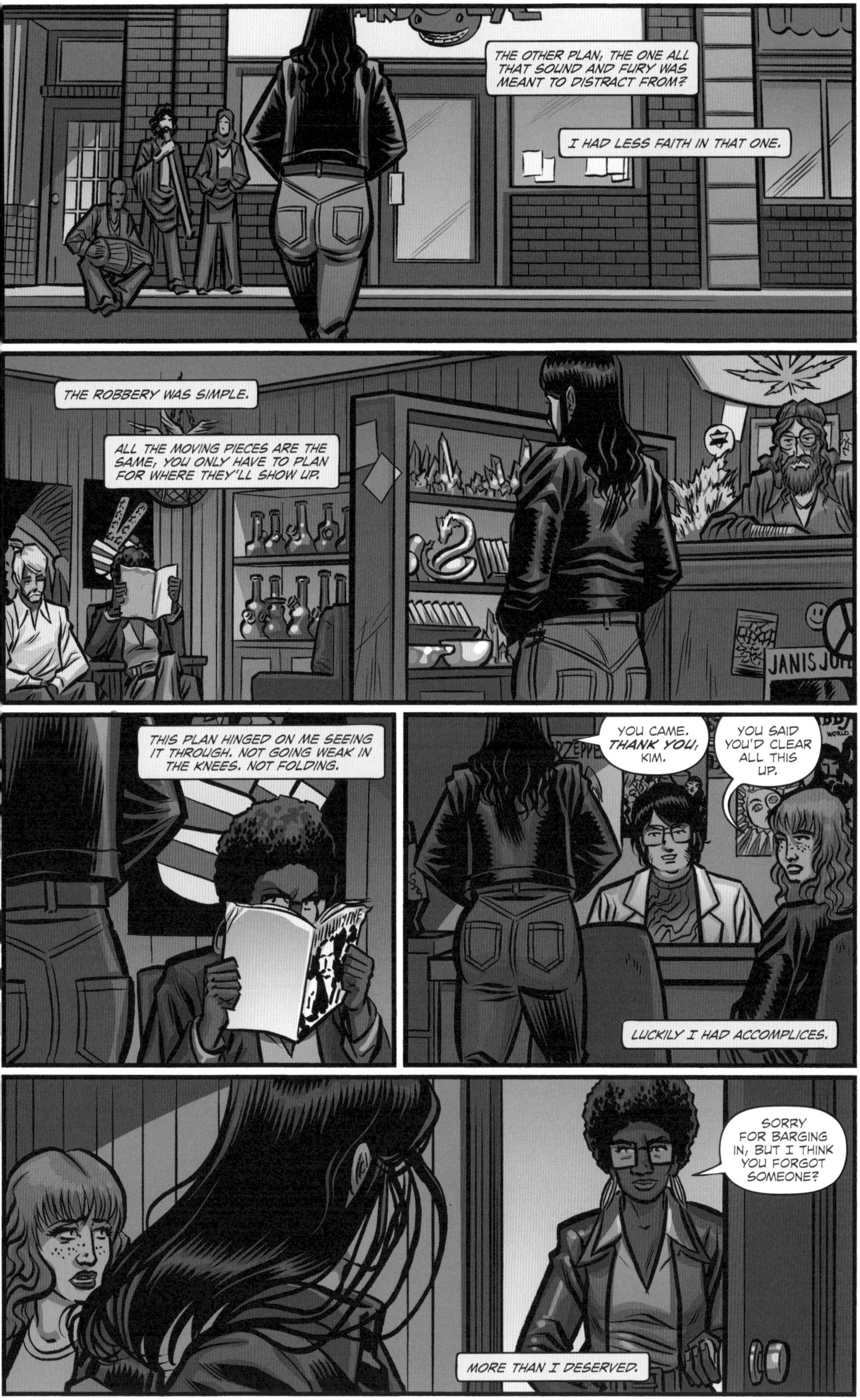
THE OTHER PLAN, THE ONE ALL THAT SOUND AND FURY WAS MEANT TO DISTRACT FROM?
I HAD LESS FAITH IN THAT ONE.
THE ROBBERY WAS SIMPLE.
ALL THE MOVING PIECES ARE THE SAME; YOU ONLY HAVE TO PLAN FOR WHERE THEY'LL SHOW UP.
THIS PLAN HINGED ON ME SEEING IT THROUGH. NOT GOING WEAK IN THE KNEES. NOT FOLDING.
YOU CAME. **THANK YOU,** KIM.
YOU SAID YOU'D CLEAR ALL THIS UP.
LUCKILY I HAD ACCOMPLICES.
SORRY FOR BARGING IN, BUT I THINK YOU FORGOT SOMEONE?
MORE THAN I DESERVED.

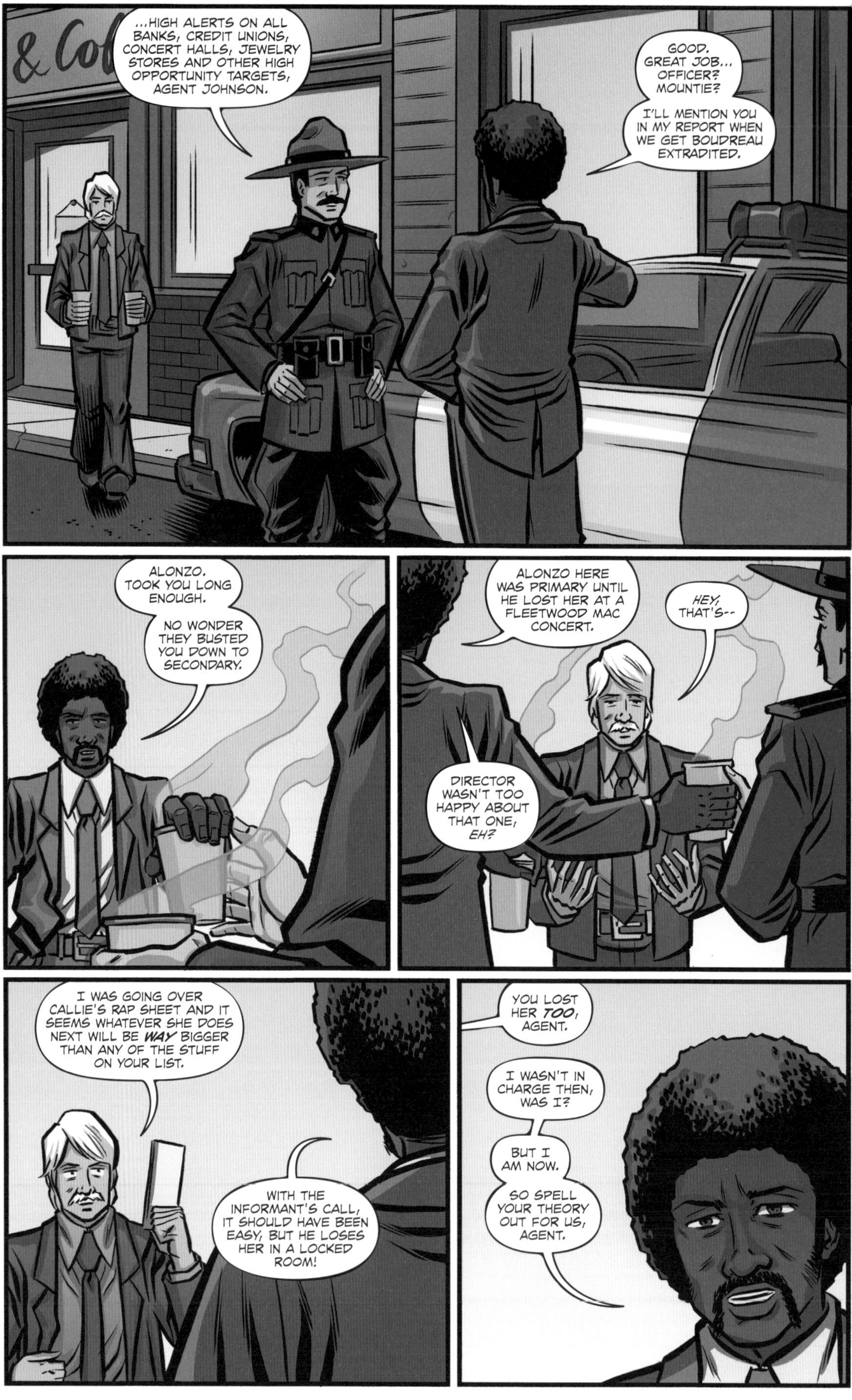
...HIGH ALERTS ON ALL BANKS, CREDIT UNIONS, CONCERT HALLS, JEWELRY STORES AND OTHER HIGH OPPORTUNITY TARGETS, AGENT JOHNSON.
GOOD. GREAT JOB... OFFICER? MOUNTIE?
I'LL MENTION YOU IN MY REPORT WHEN WE GET BOUDREAU EXTRADITED.
ALONZO. TOOK YOU LONG ENOUGH.
NO WONDER THEY BUSTED YOU DOWN TO SECONDARY.
ALONZO HERE WAS PRIMARY UNTIL HE LOST HER AT A FLEETWOOD MAC CONCERT.
HEY, THAT'S--
DIRECTOR WASN'T TOO HAPPY ABOUT THAT ONE, *EH?*
I WAS GOING OVER CALLIE'S RAP SHEET AND IT SEEMS WHATEVER SHE DOES NEXT WILL BE ***WAY*** BIGGER THAN ANY OF THE STUFF ON YOUR LIST.
WITH THE INFORMANT'S CALL, IT SHOULD HAVE BEEN EASY, BUT HE LOSES HER IN A LOCKED ROOM!
YOU LOST HER ***TOO***, AGENT.
I WASN'T IN CHARGE THEN, WAS I?
BUT I AM NOW.
SO SPELL YOUR THEORY OUT FOR US, AGENT.

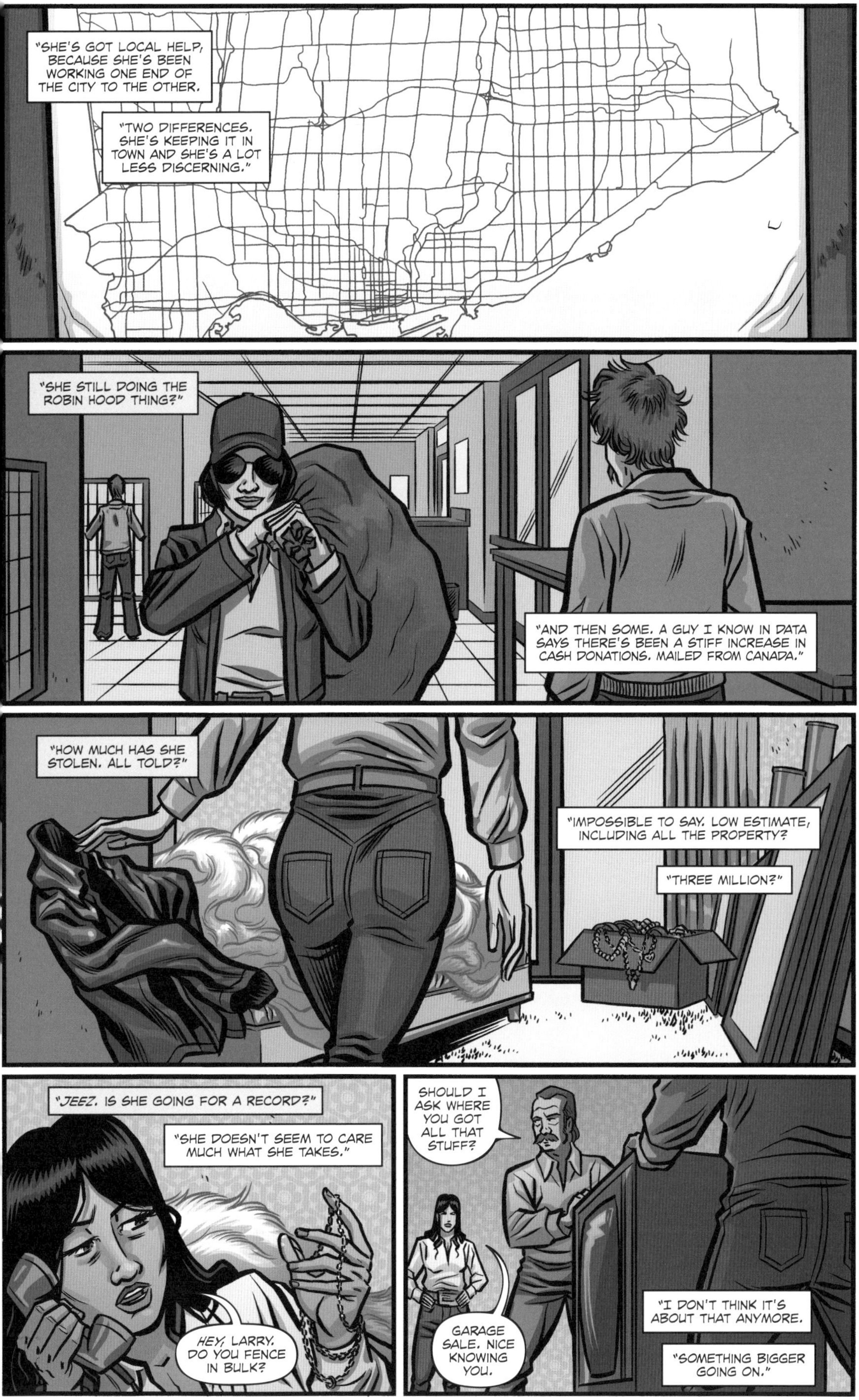
"SHE'S GOT LOCAL HELP, BECAUSE SHE'S BEEN WORKING ONE END OF THE CITY TO THE OTHER.
"TWO DIFFERENCES. SHE'S KEEPING IT IN TOWN AND SHE'S A LOT LESS DISCERNING."
"SHE STILL DOING THE ROBIN HOOD THING?"
"AND THEN SOME. A GUY I KNOW IN DATA SAYS THERE'S BEEN A STIFF INCREASE IN CASH DONATIONS. MAILED FROM CANADA."
"HOW MUCH HAS SHE STOLEN, ALL TOLD?"
"IMPOSSIBLE TO SAY. LOW ESTIMATE, INCLUDING ALL THE PROPERTY?
"THREE MILLION?"
"JEEZ. IS SHE GOING FOR A RECORD?"
"SHE DOESN'T SEEM TO CARE MUCH WHAT SHE TAKES."
HEY, LARRY. DO YOU FENCE IN BULK?
SHOULD I ASK WHERE YOU GOT ALL THAT STUFF?
GARAGE SALE. NICE KNOWING YOU.
"I DON'T THINK IT'S ABOUT THAT ANYMORE.
"SOMETHING BIGGER GOING ON."

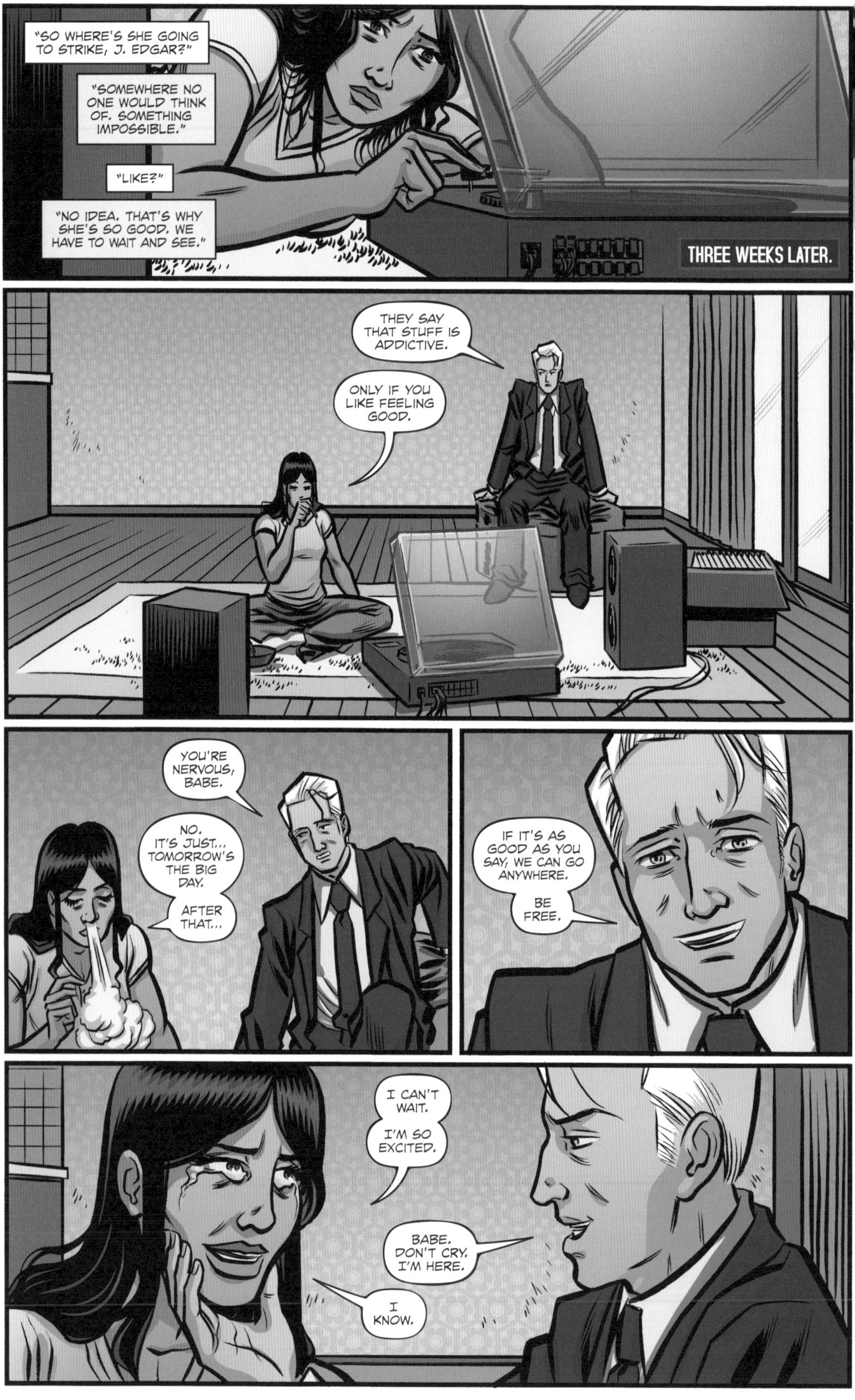
"SO WHERE'S SHE GOING TO STRIKE, J. EDGAR?"
"SOMEWHERE NO ONE WOULD THINK OF. SOMETHING IMPOSSIBLE."
"LIKE?"
"NO IDEA. THAT'S WHY SHE'S SO GOOD. WE HAVE TO WAIT AND SEE."
THREE WEEKS LATER.
THEY SAY THAT STUFF IS ADDICTIVE.
ONLY IF YOU LIKE FEELING GOOD.
YOU'RE NERVOUS, BABE.
NO. IT'S JUST... TOMORROW'S THE BIG DAY.
AFTER THAT...
IF IT'S AS GOOD AS YOU SAY, WE CAN GO ANYWHERE.
BE FREE.
I CAN'T WAIT.
I'M SO EXCITED.
BABE. DON'T CRY. I'M HERE.
I KNOW.

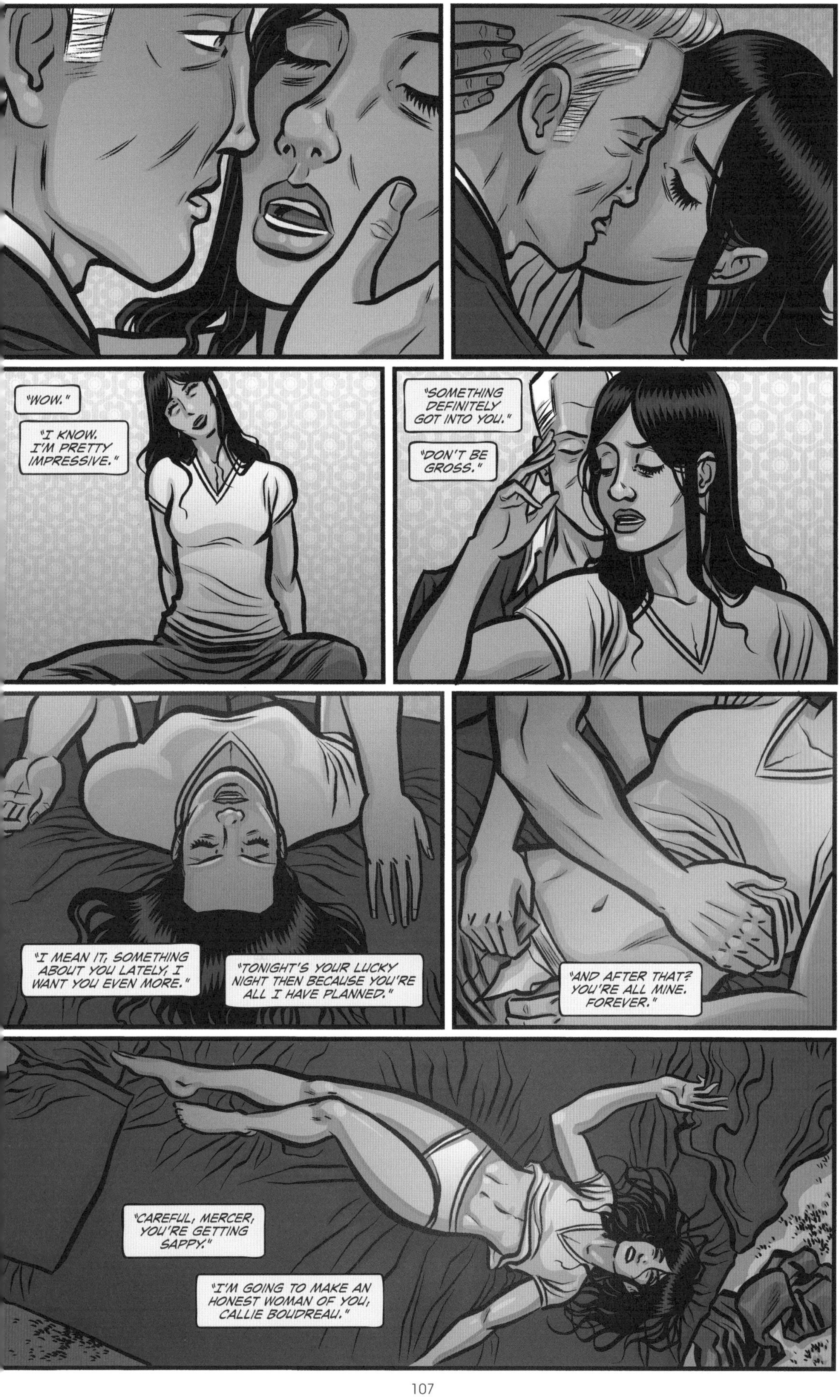
"WOW."
"I KNOW. I'M PRETTY IMPRESSIVE."
"SOMETHING DEFINITELY GOT INTO YOU."
"DON'T BE GROSS."
"I MEAN IT, SOMETHING ABOUT YOU LATELY, I WANT YOU EVEN MORE."
"TONIGHT'S YOUR LUCKY NIGHT THEN BECAUSE YOU'RE ALL I HAVE PLANNED."
"AND AFTER THAT? YOU'RE ALL MINE. FOREVER."
"CAREFUL, MERCER, YOU'RE GETTING SAPPY."
"I'M GOING TO MAKE AN HONEST WOMAN OF YOU, CALLIE BOUDREAU."

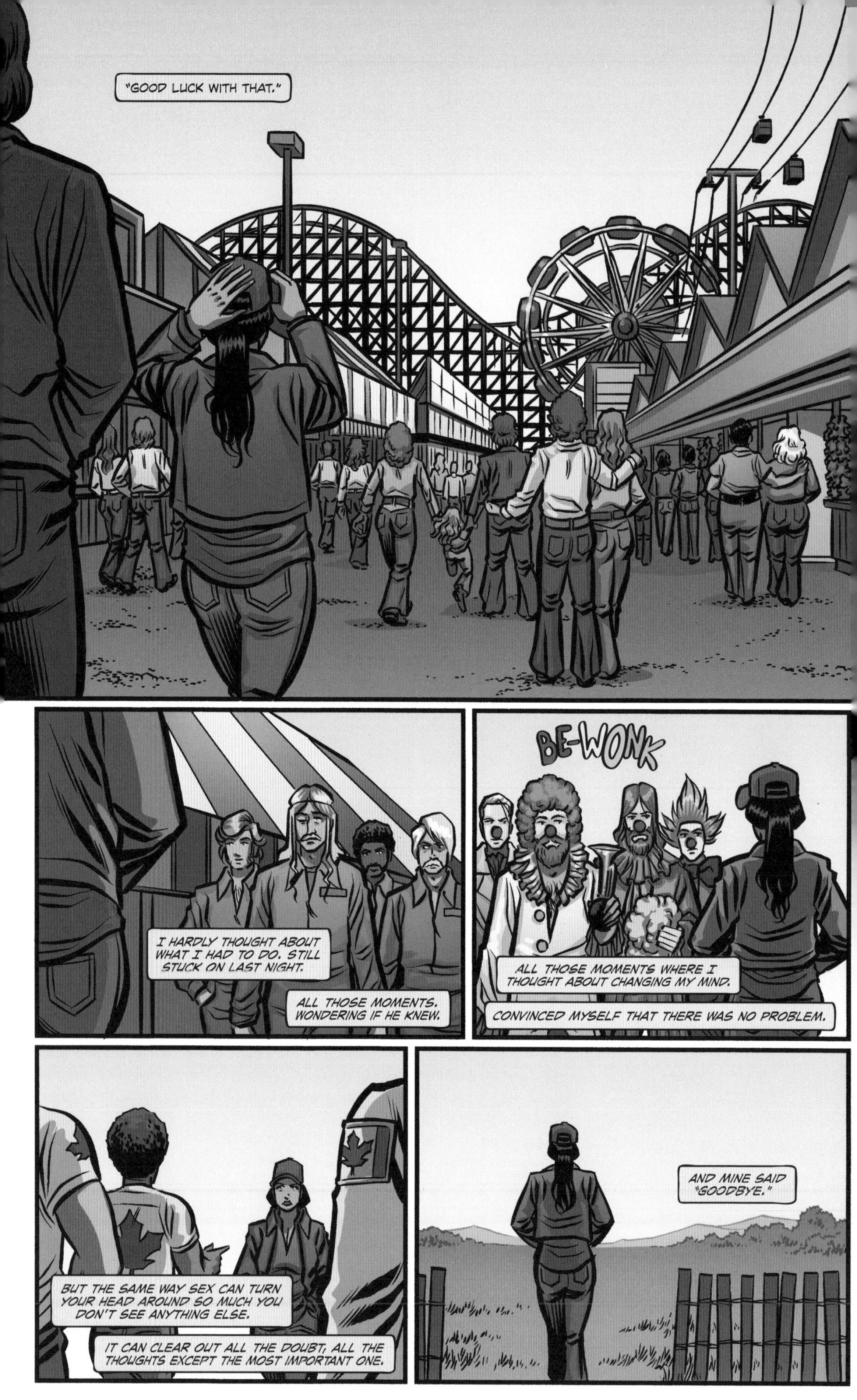
"GOOD LUCK WITH THAT."
I HARDLY THOUGHT ABOUT WHAT I HAD TO DO. STILL STUCK ON LAST NIGHT.
ALL THOSE MOMENTS. WONDERING IF HE KNEW.
BE-WONK
ALL THOSE MOMENTS WHERE I THOUGHT ABOUT CHANGING MY MIND.
CONVINCED MYSELF THAT THERE WAS NO PROBLEM.
BUT THE SAME WAY SEX CAN TURN YOUR HEAD AROUND SO MUCH YOU DON'T SEE ANYTHING ELSE.
IT CAN CLEAR OUT ALL THE DOUBT, ALL THE THOUGHTS EXCEPT THE MOST IMPORTANT ONE.
AND MINE SAID "GOODBYE."

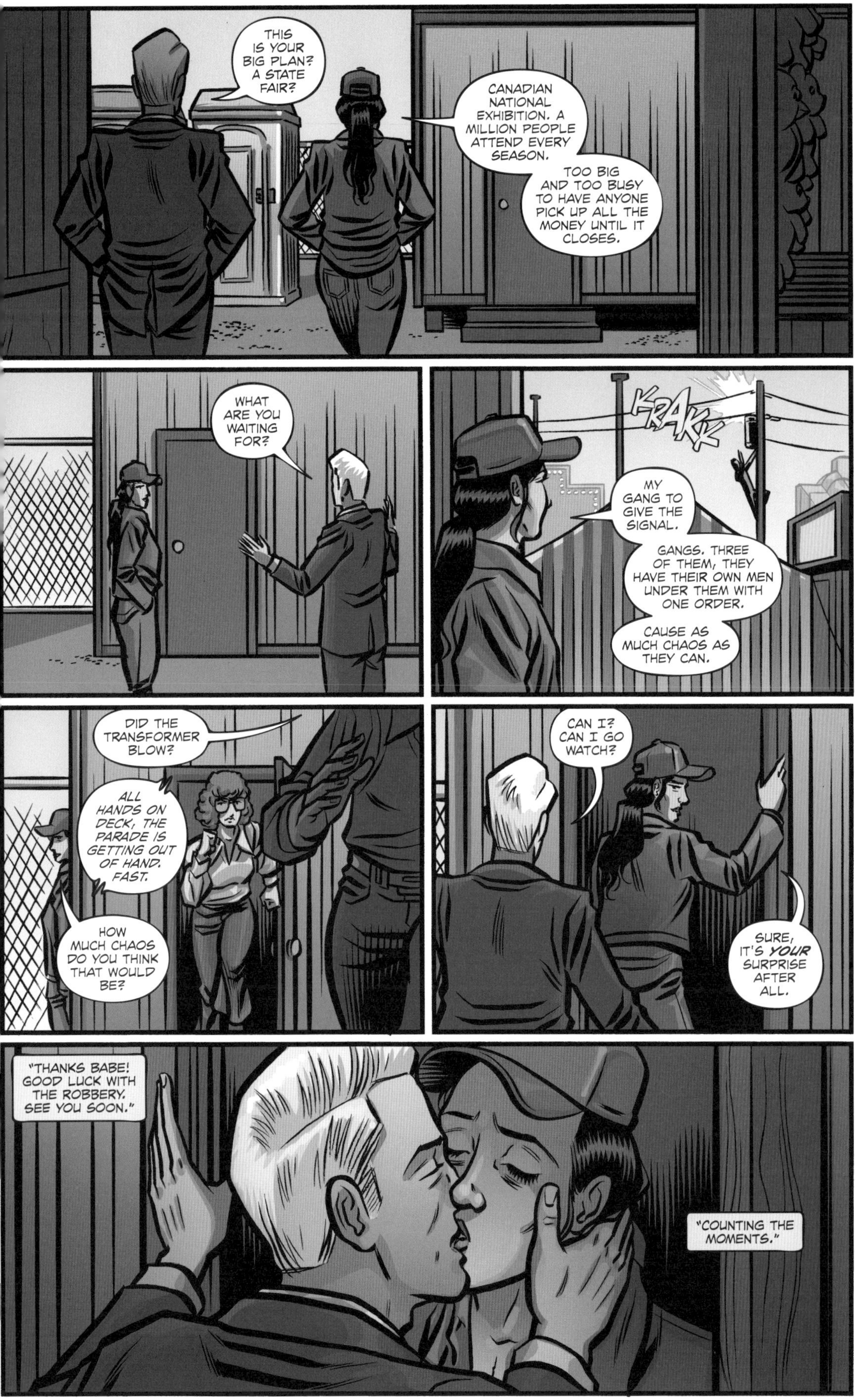
THIS IS YOUR BIG PLAN? A STATE FAIR?
CANADIAN NATIONAL EXHIBITION. A MILLION PEOPLE ATTEND EVERY SEASON.
TOO BIG AND TOO BUSY TO HAVE ANYONE PICK UP ALL THE MONEY UNTIL IT CLOSES.
WHAT ARE YOU WAITING FOR?
KRAKK
MY GANG TO GIVE THE SIGNAL.
GANGS. THREE OF THEM, THEY HAVE THEIR OWN MEN UNDER THEM WITH ONE ORDER.
CAUSE AS MUCH CHAOS AS THEY CAN.
DID THE TRANSFORMER BLOW?
ALL HANDS ON DECK, THE PARADE IS GETTING OUT OF HAND. FAST.
HOW MUCH CHAOS DO YOU THINK THAT WOULD BE?
CAN I? CAN I GO WATCH?
SURE, IT'S YOUR SURPRISE AFTER ALL.
"THANKS BABE! GOOD LUCK WITH THE ROBBERY. SEE YOU SOON."
"COUNTING THE MOMENTS."

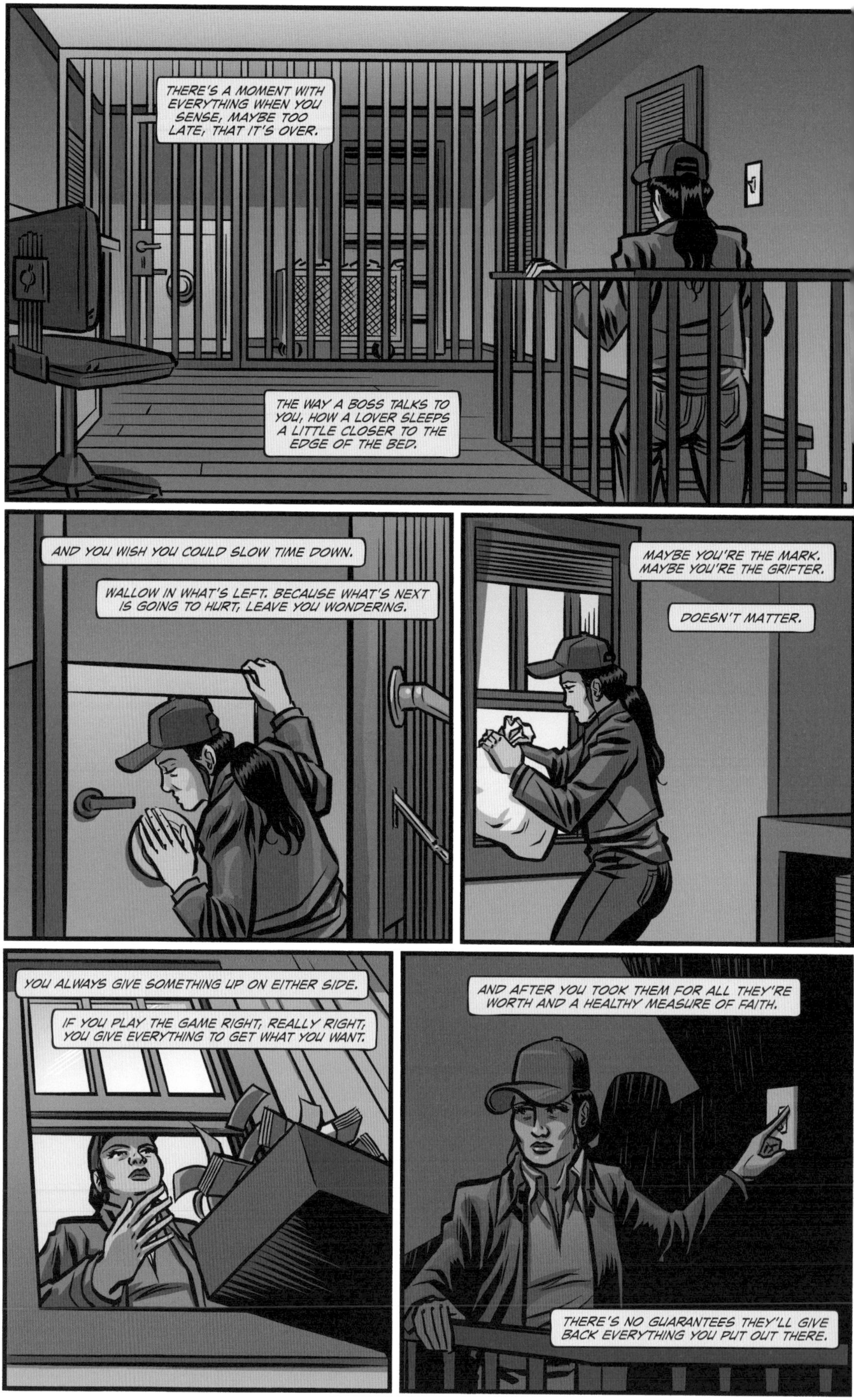
THERE'S A MOMENT WITH EVERYTHING WHEN YOU SENSE, MAYBE TOO LATE, THAT IT'S OVER.
THE WAY A BOSS TALKS TO YOU, HOW A LOVER SLEEPS A LITTLE CLOSER TO THE EDGE OF THE BED.
AND YOU WISH YOU COULD SLOW TIME DOWN.
WALLOW IN WHAT'S LEFT. BECAUSE WHAT'S NEXT IS GOING TO HURT, LEAVE YOU WONDERING.
MAYBE YOU'RE THE MARK. MAYBE YOU'RE THE GRIFTER.
DOESN'T MATTER.
YOU ALWAYS GIVE SOMETHING UP ON EITHER SIDE.
IF YOU PLAY THE GAME RIGHT, REALLY RIGHT, YOU GIVE EVERYTHING TO GET WHAT YOU WANT.
AND AFTER YOU TOOK THEM FOR ALL THEY'RE WORTH AND A HEALTHY MEASURE OF FAITH.
THERE'S NO GUARANTEES THEY'LL GIVE BACK EVERYTHING YOU PUT OUT THERE.

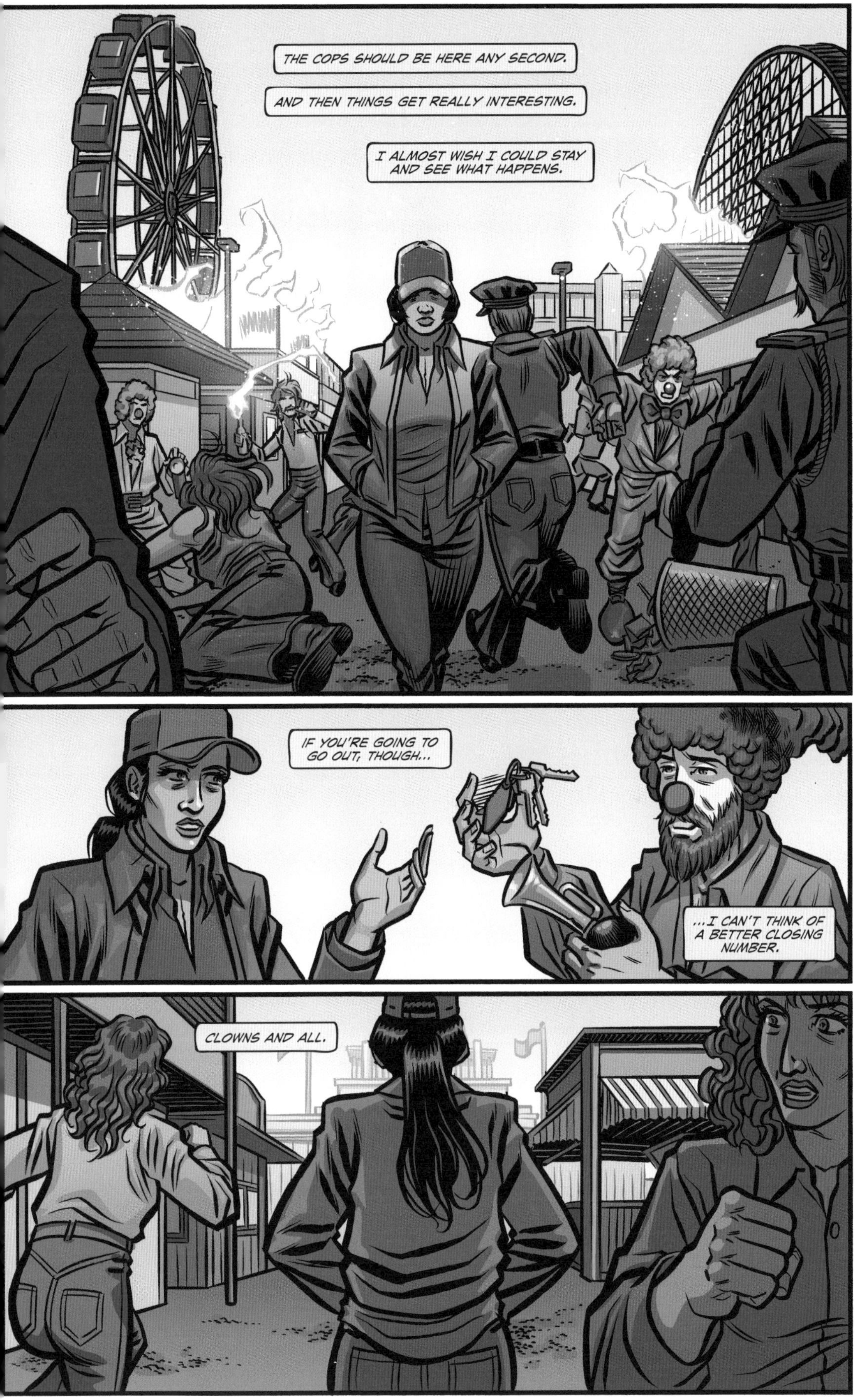
THE COPS SHOULD BE HERE ANY SECOND.
AND THEN THINGS GET REALLY INTERESTING.
I ALMOST WISH I COULD STAY AND SEE WHAT HAPPENS.
IF YOU'RE GOING TO GO OUT, THOUGH...
...I CAN'T THINK OF A BETTER CLOSING NUMBER.
CLOWNS AND ALL.

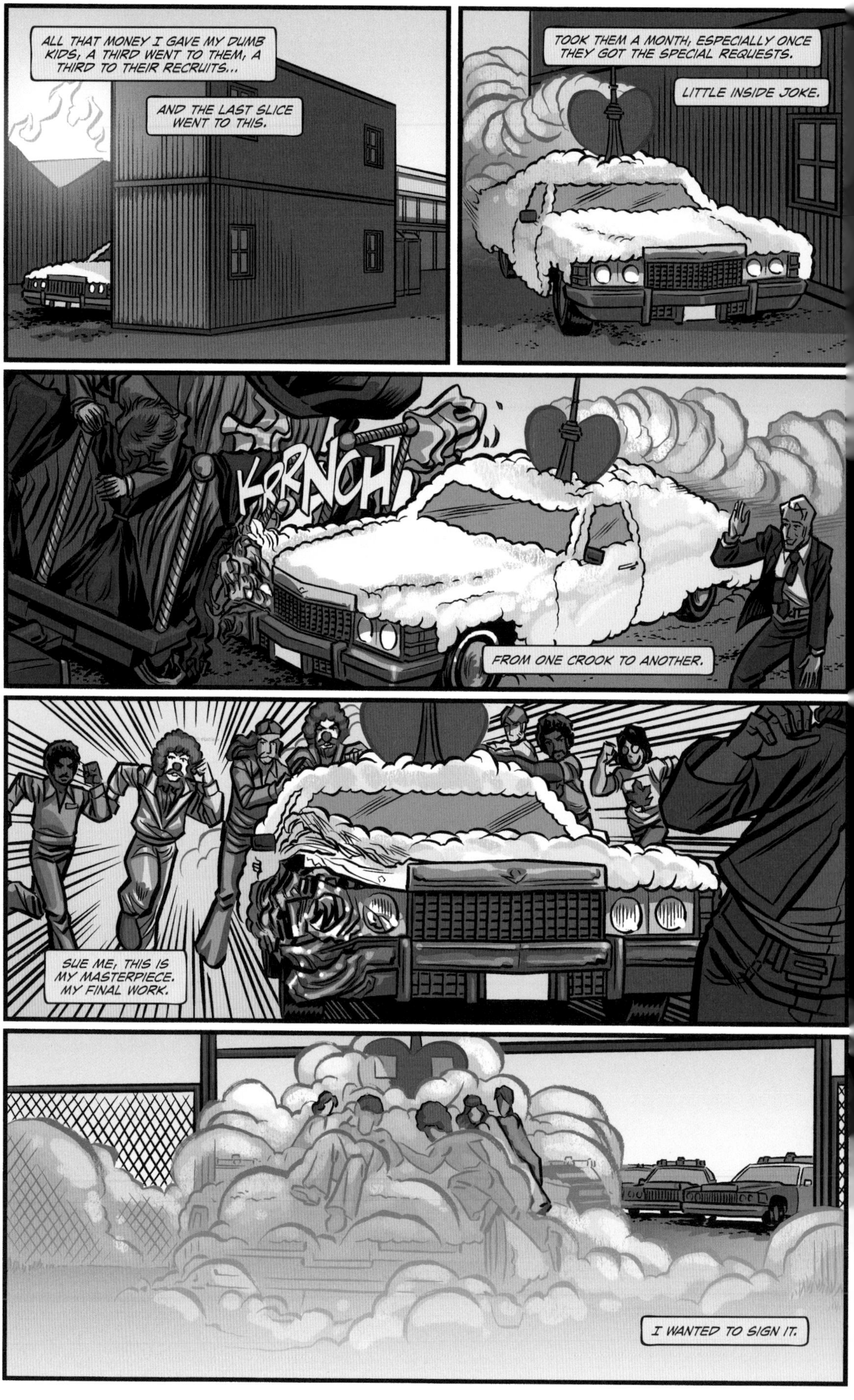
ALL THAT MONEY I GAVE MY DUMB KIDS, A THIRD WENT TO THEM, A THIRD TO THEIR RECRUITS...
AND THE LAST SLICE WENT TO THIS.
TOOK THEM A MONTH, ESPECIALLY ONCE THEY GOT THE SPECIAL REQUESTS.
LITTLE INSIDE JOKE.
KRRNCH!
FROM ONE CROOK TO ANOTHER.
SUE ME, THIS IS MY MASTERPIECE. MY FINAL WORK.
I WANTED TO SIGN IT.

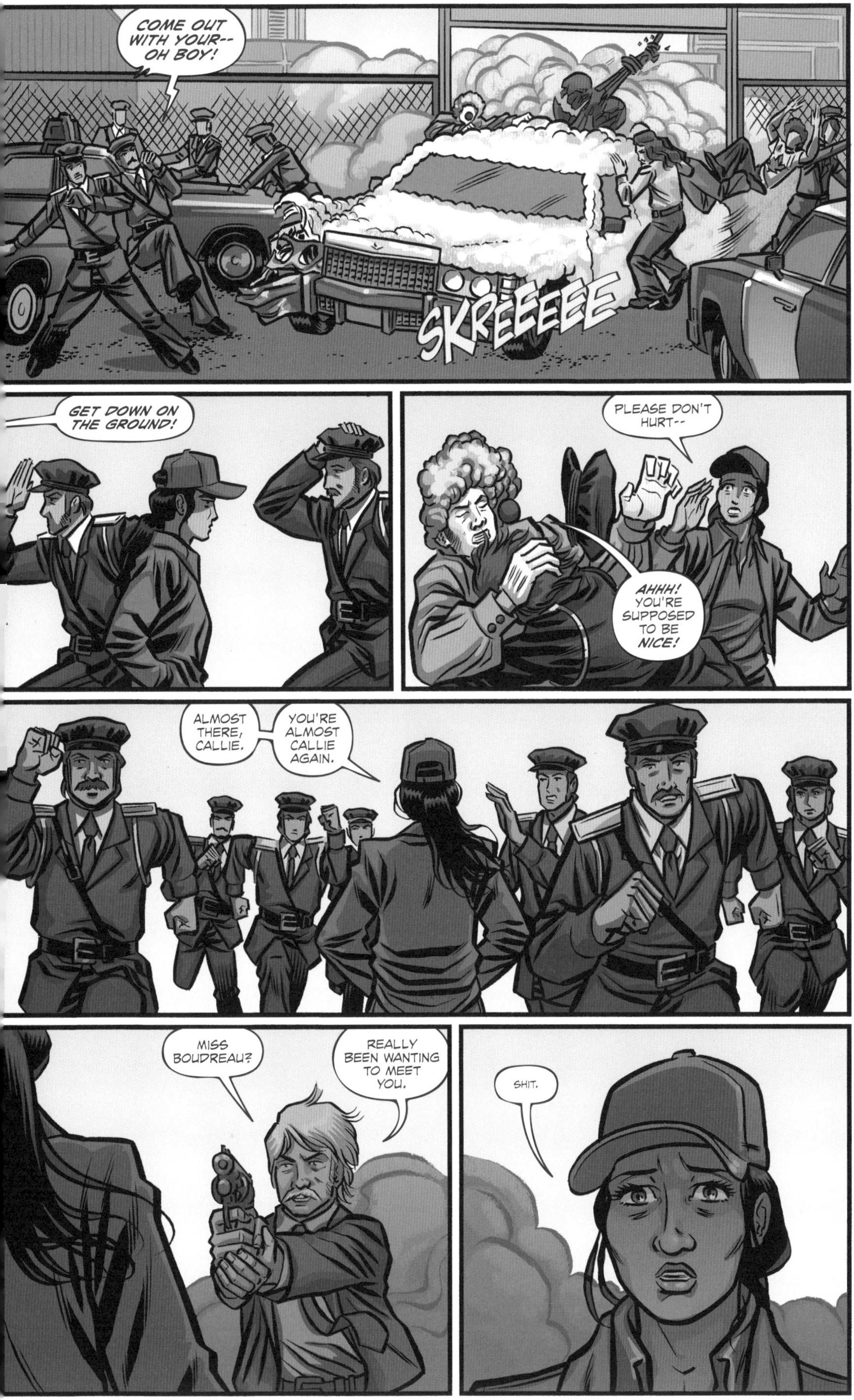
COME OUT WITH YOUR-- OH BOY!
SKREEEEEE
GET DOWN ON THE GROUND!
PLEASE DON'T HURT--
AHHH! YOU'RE SUPPOSED TO BE NICE!
ALMOST THERE, CALLIE.
YOU'RE ALMOST CALLIE AGAIN.
MISS BOUDREAU?
REALLY BEEN WANTING TO MEET YOU.
SHIT.

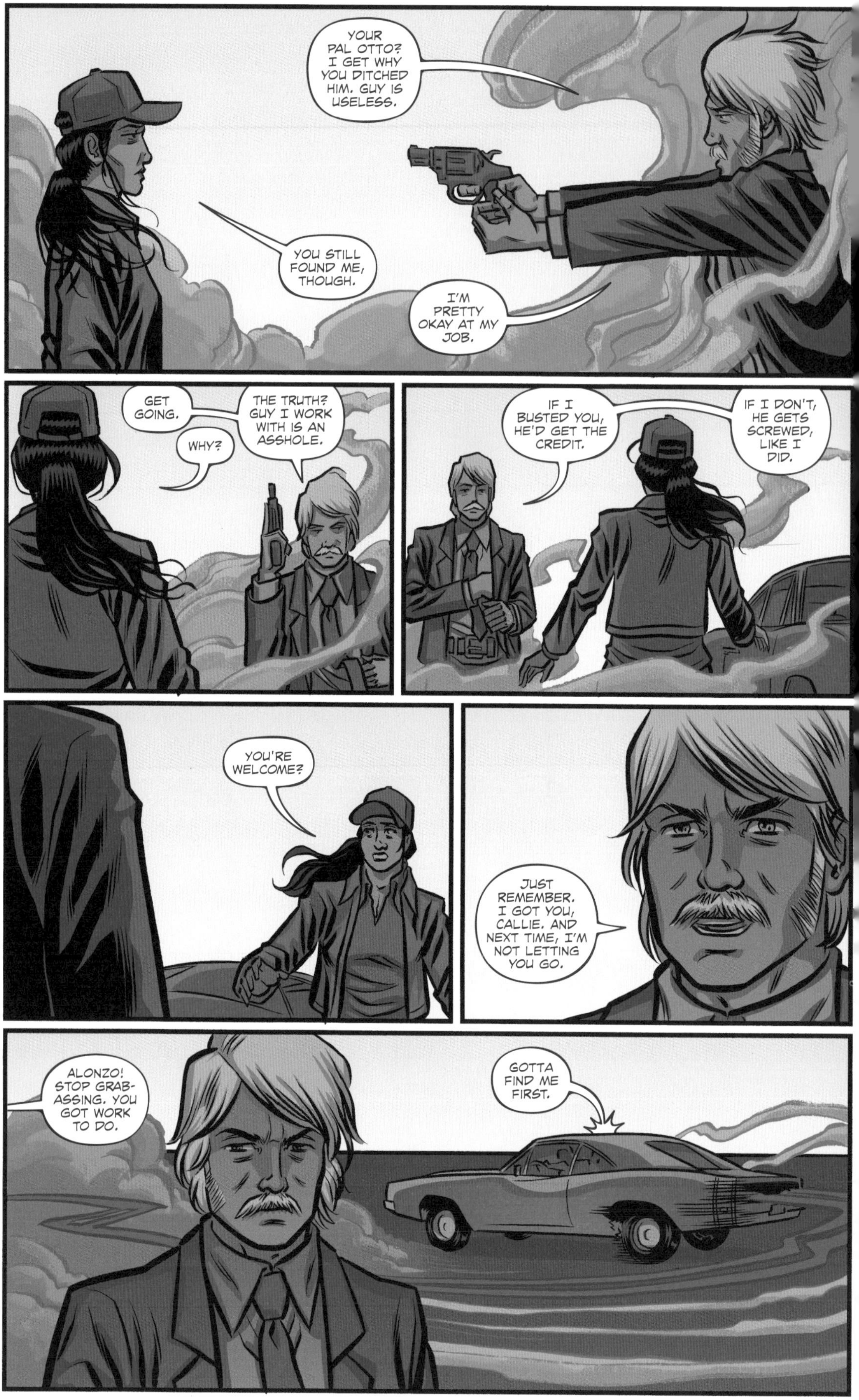
YOUR PAL OTTO? I GET WHY YOU DITCHED HIM. GUY IS USELESS.
YOU STILL FOUND ME, THOUGH.
I'M PRETTY OKAY AT MY JOB.
GET GOING.
WHY?
THE TRUTH? GUY I WORK WITH IS AN ASSHOLE.
IF I BUSTED YOU, HE'D GET THE CREDIT.
IF I DON'T, HE GETS SCREWED, LIKE I DID.
YOU'RE WELCOME?
JUST REMEMBER. I GOT YOU, CALLIE. AND NEXT TIME, I'M NOT LETTING YOU GO.
ALONZO! STOP GRAB-ASSING. YOU GOT WORK TO DO.
GOTTA FIND ME FIRST.

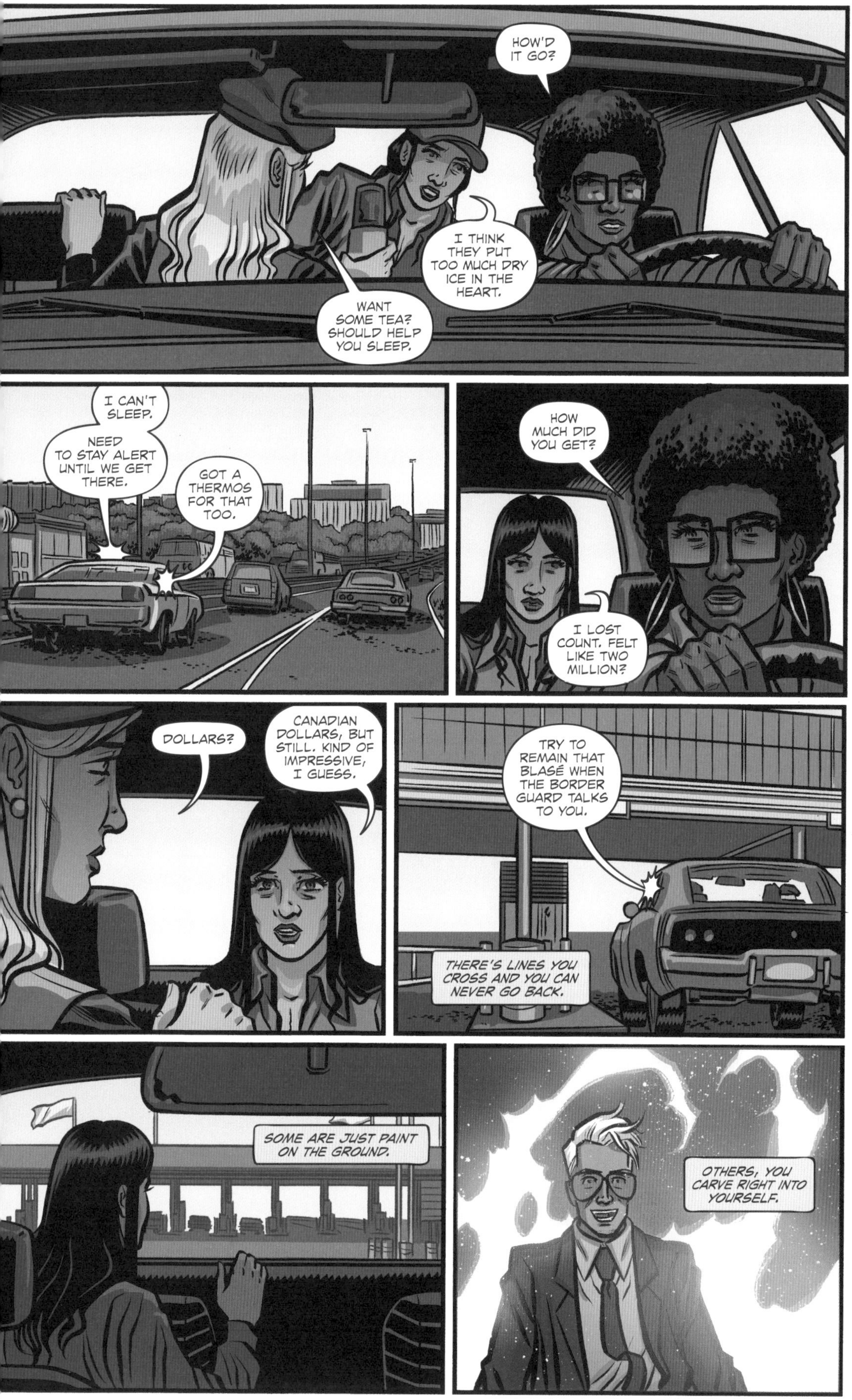
HOW'D IT GO?
I THINK THEY PUT TOO MUCH DRY ICE IN THE HEART.
WANT SOME TEA? SHOULD HELP YOU SLEEP.
I CAN'T SLEEP.
NEED TO STAY ALERT UNTIL WE GET THERE.
GOT A THERMOS FOR THAT TOO.
HOW MUCH DID YOU GET?
I LOST COUNT. FELT LIKE TWO MILLION?
DOLLARS?
CANADIAN DOLLARS, BUT STILL. KIND OF IMPRESSIVE, I GUESS.
TRY TO REMAIN THAT BLASÉ WHEN THE BORDER GUARD TALKS TO YOU.
THERE'S LINES YOU CROSS AND YOU CAN NEVER GO BACK.
SOME ARE JUST PAINT ON THE GROUND.
OTHERS, YOU CARVE RIGHT INTO YOURSELF.

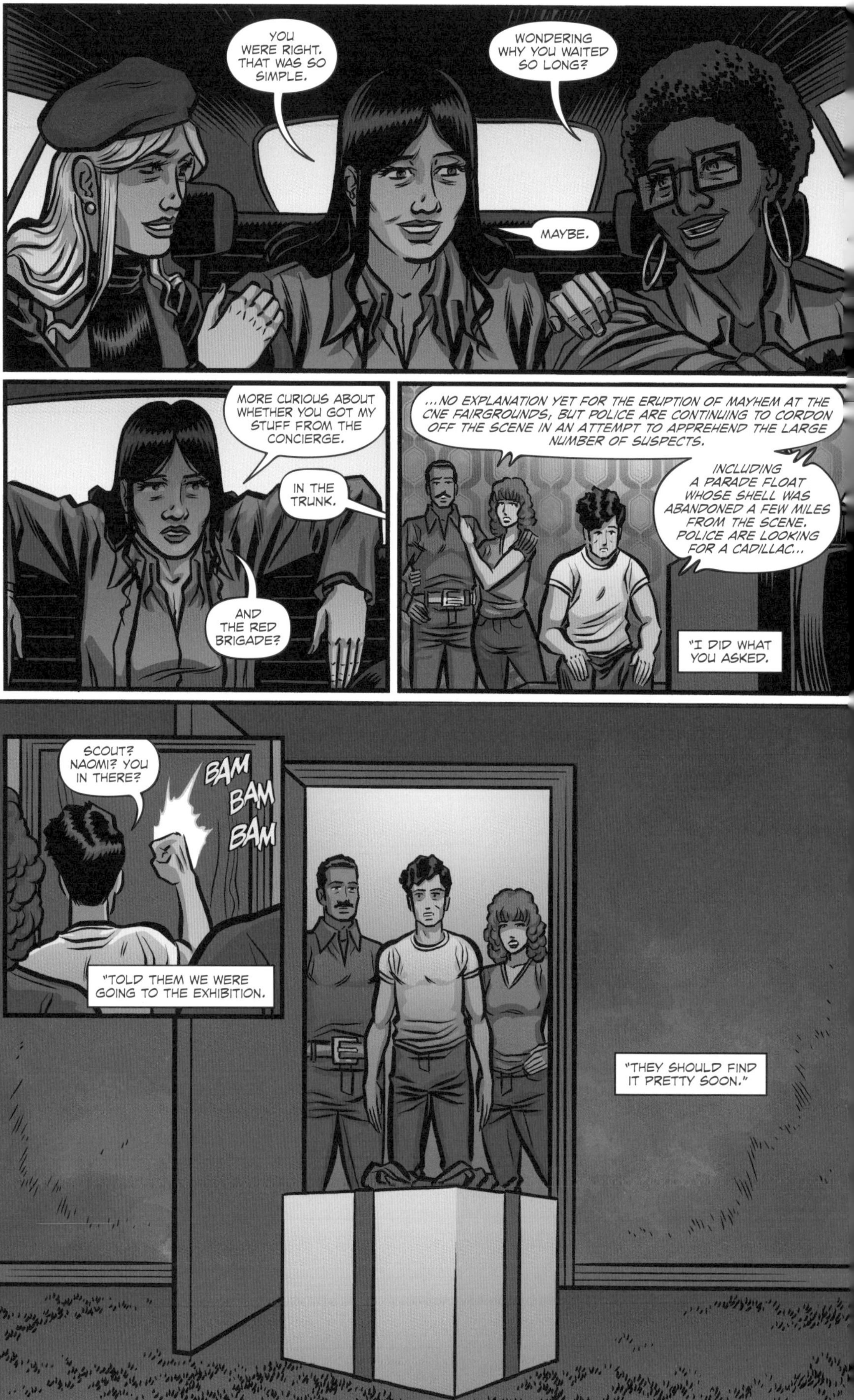
YOU WERE RIGHT. THAT WAS SO SIMPLE.
WONDERING WHY YOU WAITED SO LONG?
MAYBE.
MORE CURIOUS ABOUT WHETHER YOU GOT MY STUFF FROM THE CONCIERGE.
IN THE TRUNK.
AND THE RED BRIGADE?
...NO EXPLANATION YET FOR THE ERUPTION OF MAYHEM AT THE CNE FAIRGROUNDS, BUT POLICE ARE CONTINUING TO CORDON OFF THE SCENE IN AN ATTEMPT TO APPREHEND THE LARGE NUMBER OF SUSPECTS.
INCLUDING A PARADE FLOAT WHOSE SHELL WAS ABANDONED A FEW MILES FROM THE SCENE. POLICE ARE LOOKING FOR A CADILLAC...
"I DID WHAT YOU ASKED.
SCOUT? NAOMI? YOU IN THERE?
BAM BAM BAM
"TOLD THEM WE WERE GOING TO THE EXHIBITION.
"THEY SHOULD FIND IT PRETTY SOON."

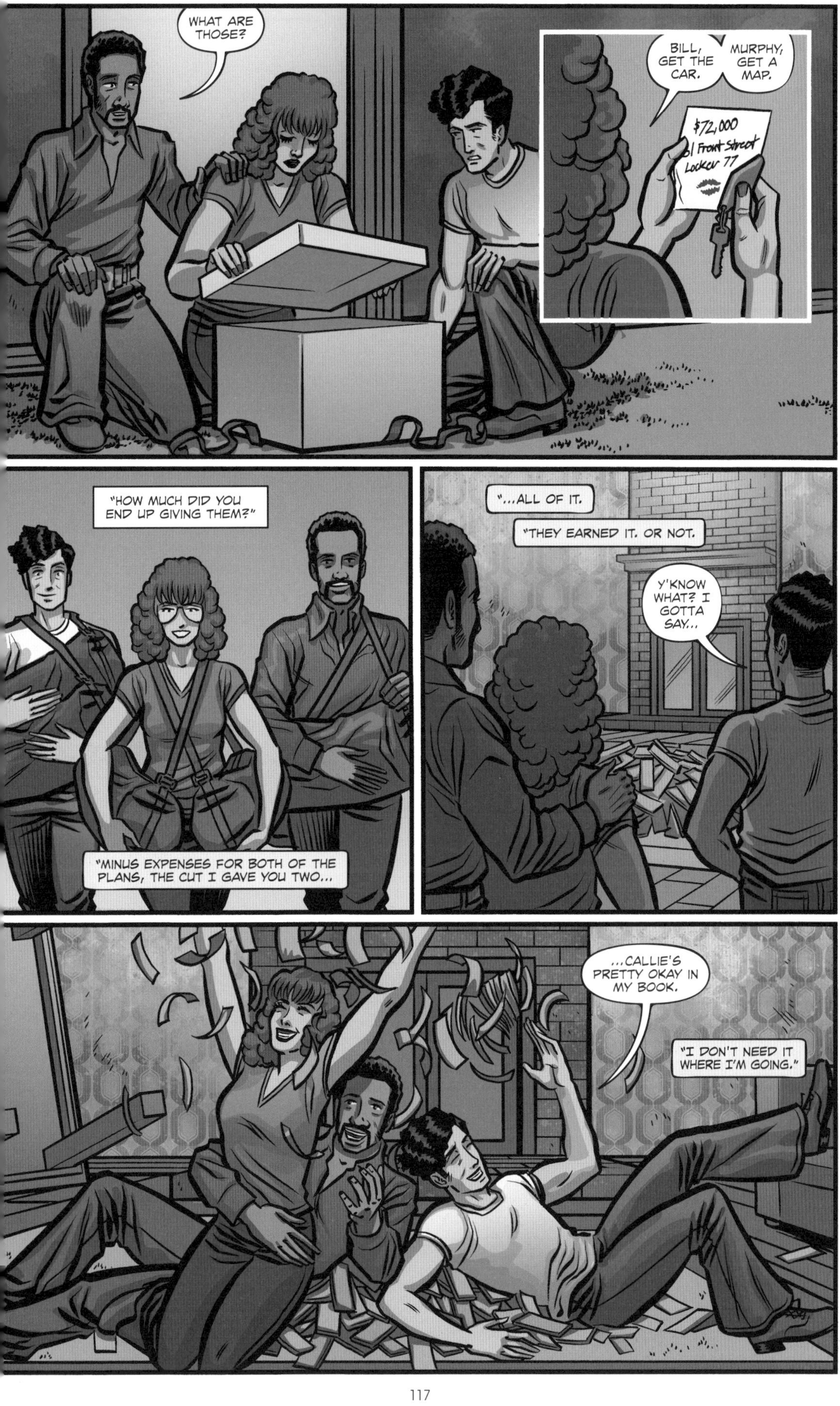
WHAT ARE THOSE?
BILL, GET THE CAR.
MURPHY, GET A MAP.
$72,000
Front Street
Locker 77
"HOW MUCH DID YOU END UP GIVING THEM?"
"MINUS EXPENSES FOR BOTH OF THE PLANS, THE CUT I GAVE YOU TWO...
"...ALL OF IT.
"THEY EARNED IT. OR NOT.
Y'KNOW WHAT? I GOTTA SAY...
...CALLIE'S PRETTY OKAY IN MY BOOK.
"I DON'T NEED IT WHERE I'M GOING."

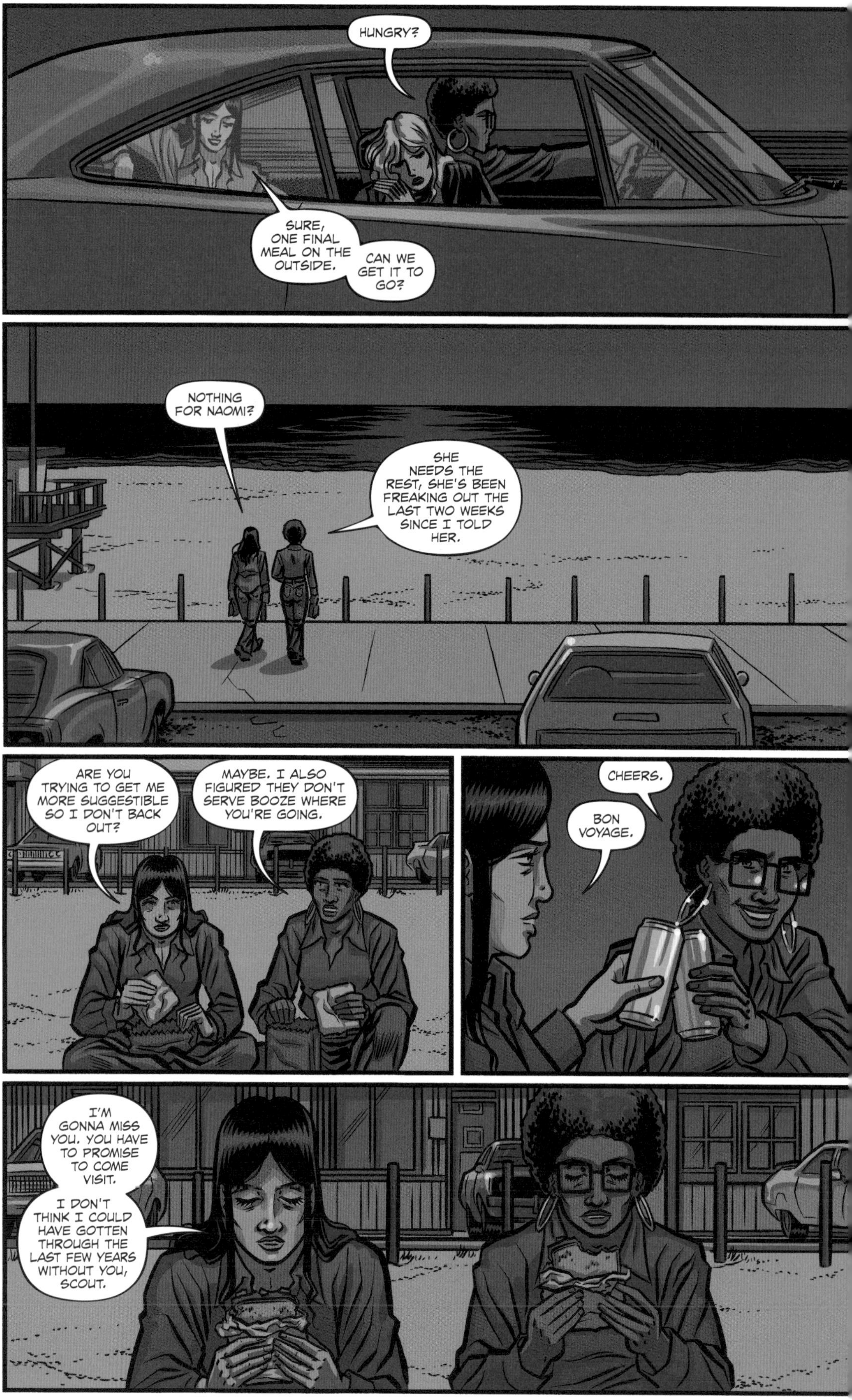
HUNGRY?
SURE, ONE FINAL MEAL ON THE OUTSIDE.
CAN WE GET IT TO GO?
NOTHING FOR NAOMI?
SHE NEEDS THE REST, SHE'S BEEN FREAKING OUT THE LAST TWO WEEKS SINCE I TOLD HER.
ARE YOU TRYING TO GET ME MORE SUGGESTIBLE SO I DON'T BACK OUT?
MAYBE. I ALSO FIGURED THEY DON'T SERVE BOOZE WHERE YOU'RE GOING.
CHEERS.
BON VOYAGE.
I'M GONNA MISS YOU. YOU HAVE TO PROMISE TO COME VISIT.
I DON'T THINK I COULD HAVE GOTTEN THROUGH THE LAST FEW YEARS WITHOUT YOU, SCOUT.

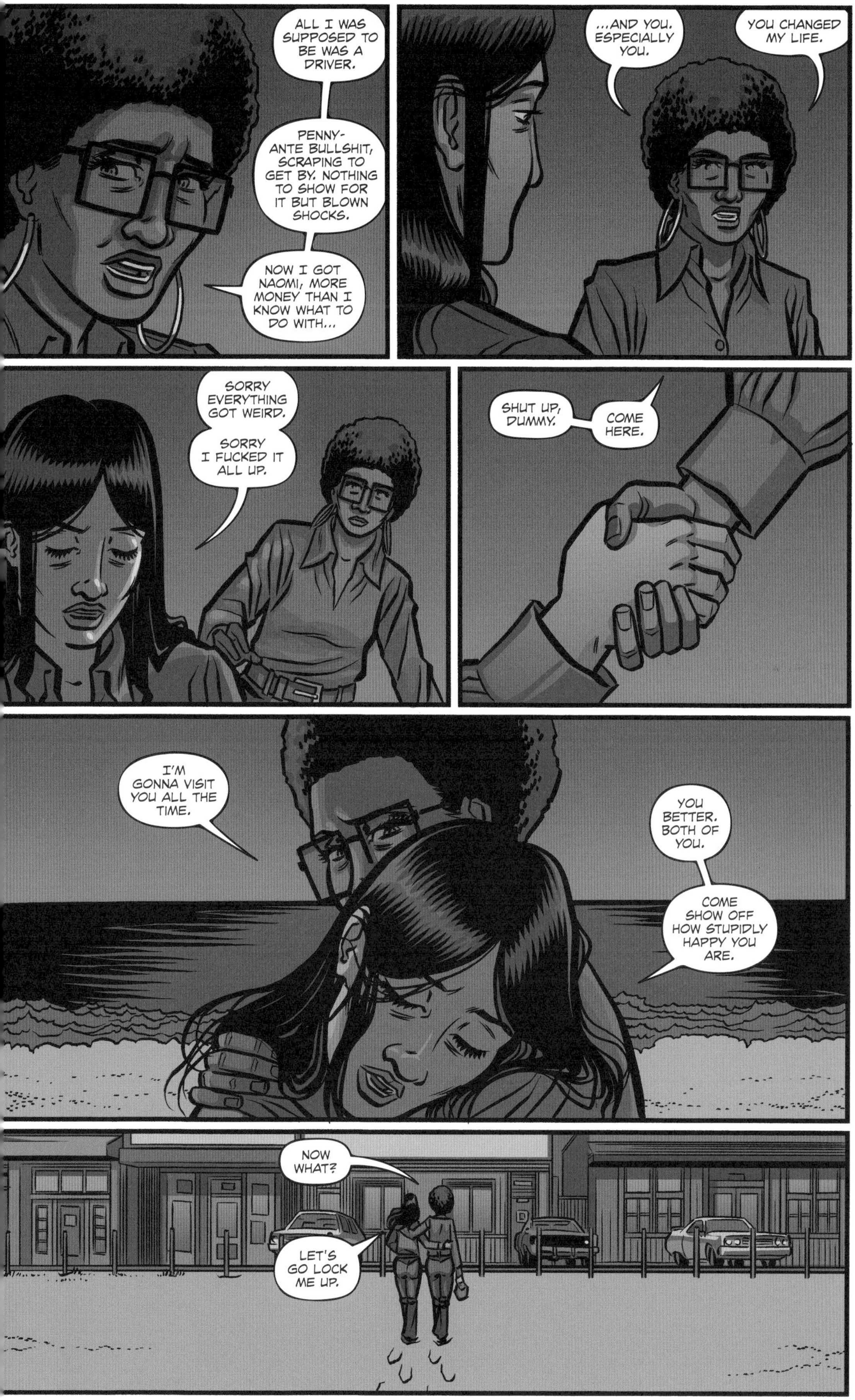
ALL I WAS SUPPOSED TO BE WAS A DRIVER.
PENNY-ANTE BULLSHIT, SCRAPING TO GET BY. NOTHING TO SHOW FOR IT BUT BLOWN SHOCKS.
NOW I GOT NAOMI, MORE MONEY THAN I KNOW WHAT TO DO WITH...
...AND YOU. ESPECIALLY YOU.
YOU CHANGED MY LIFE.
SORRY EVERYTHING GOT WEIRD.
SORRY I FUCKED IT ALL UP.
SHUT UP, DUMMY.
COME HERE.
I'M GONNA VISIT YOU ALL THE TIME.
YOU BETTER. BOTH OF YOU.
COME SHOW OFF HOW STUPIDLY HAPPY YOU ARE.
NOW WHAT?
LET'S GO LOCK ME UP.

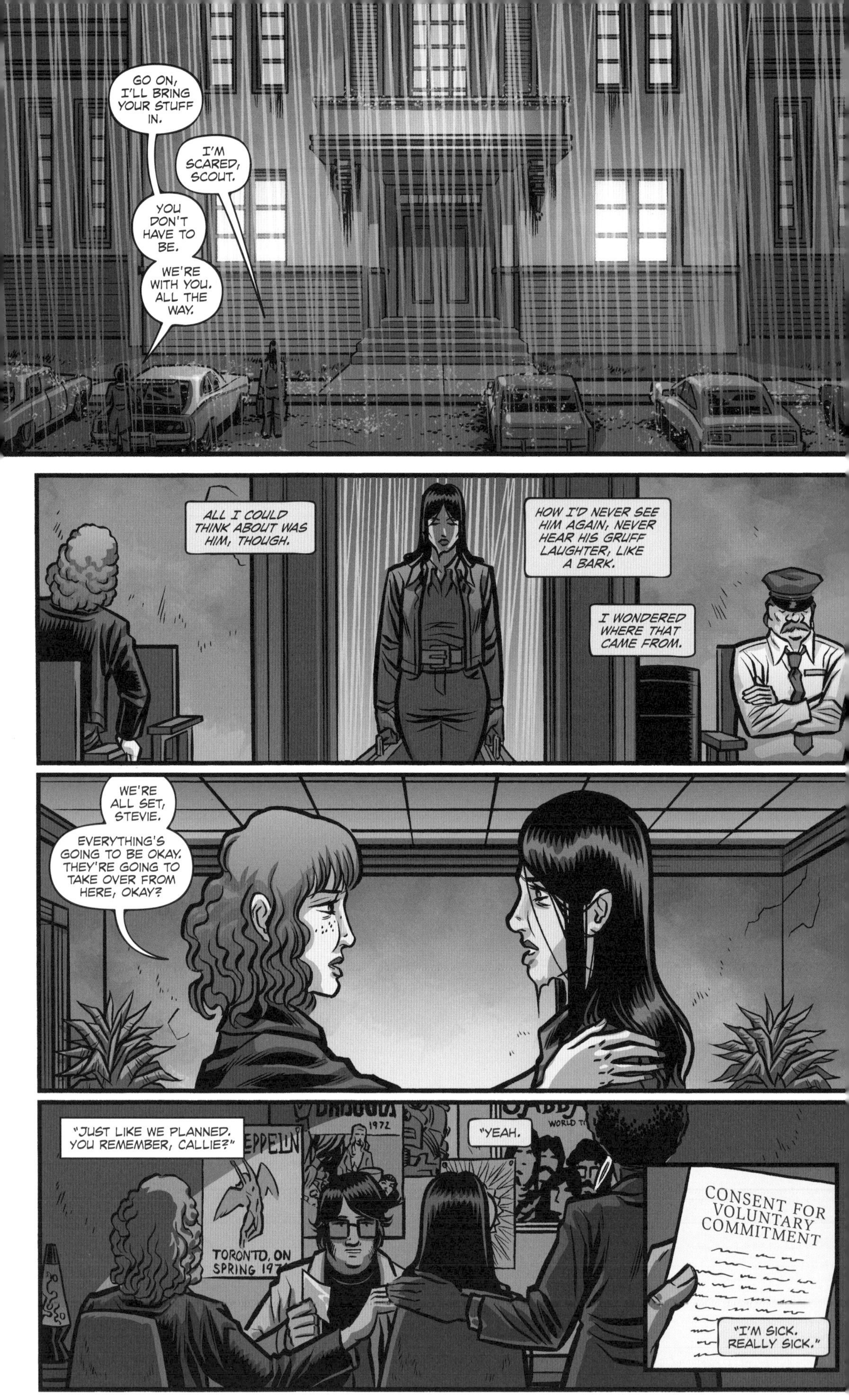
GO ON, I'LL BRING YOUR STUFF IN.
I'M SCARED, SCOUT.
YOU DON'T HAVE TO BE.
WE'RE WITH YOU. ALL THE WAY.
ALL I COULD THINK ABOUT WAS HIM, THOUGH.
HOW I'D NEVER SEE HIM AGAIN, NEVER HEAR HIS GRUFF LAUGHTER, LIKE A BARK.
I WONDERED WHERE THAT CAME FROM.
WE'RE ALL SET, STEVIE.
EVERYTHING'S GOING TO BE OKAY. THEY'RE GOING TO TAKE OVER FROM HERE, OKAY?
"JUST LIKE WE PLANNED. YOU REMEMBER, CALLIE?"
"YEAH.
TORONTO, ON
CONSENT FOR VOLUNTARY COMMITMENT
"I'M SICK. REALLY SICK."

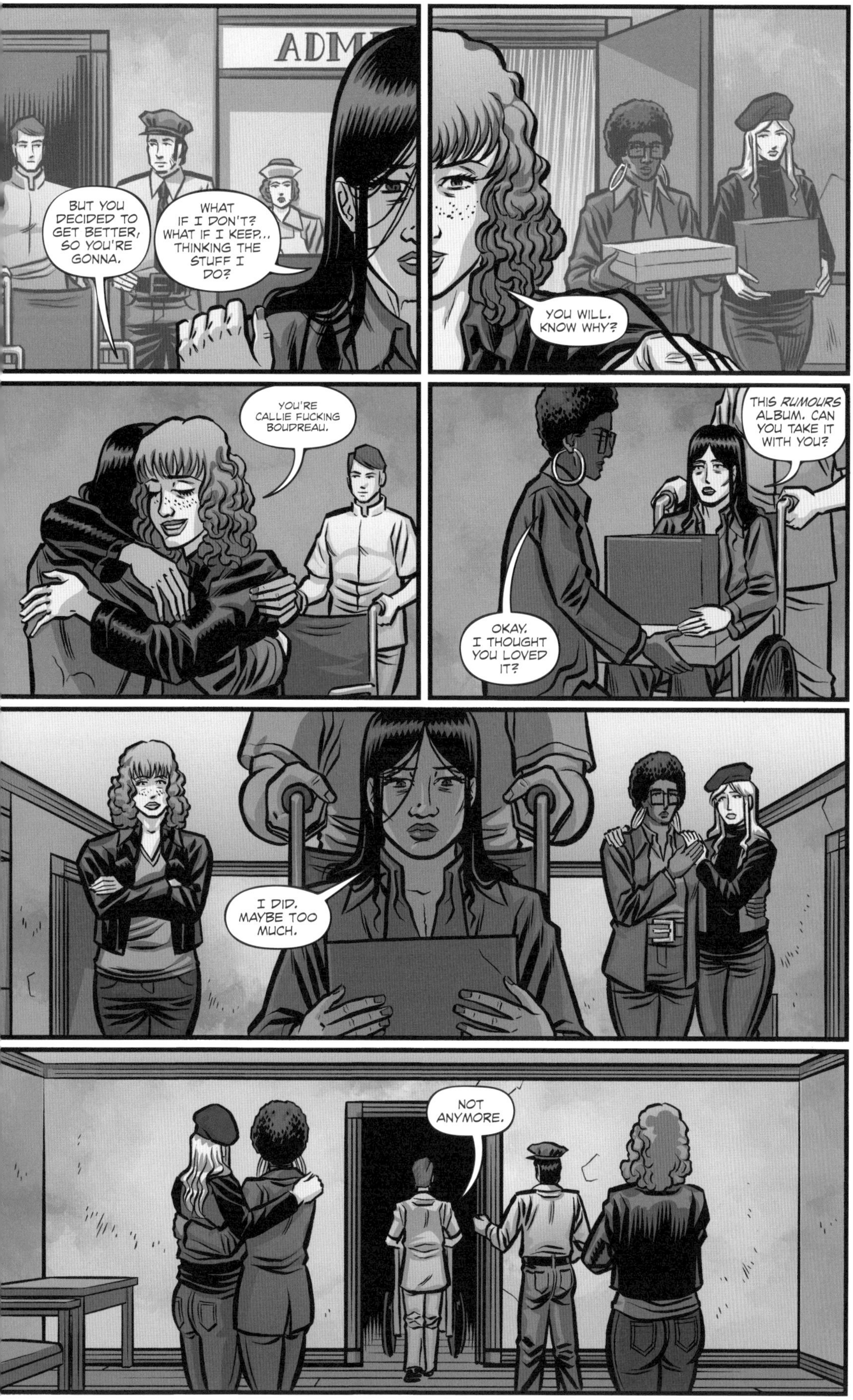
ADM
BUT YOU DECIDED TO GET BETTER, SO YOU'RE GONNA.
WHAT IF I DON'T? WHAT IF I KEEP... THINKING THE STUFF I DO?
YOU WILL. KNOW WHY?
YOU'RE CALLIE FUCKING BOUDREAU.
THIS *RUMOURS* ALBUM. CAN YOU TAKE IT WITH YOU?
OKAY. I THOUGHT YOU LOVED IT?
I DID. MAYBE TOO MUCH.
NOT ANYMORE.

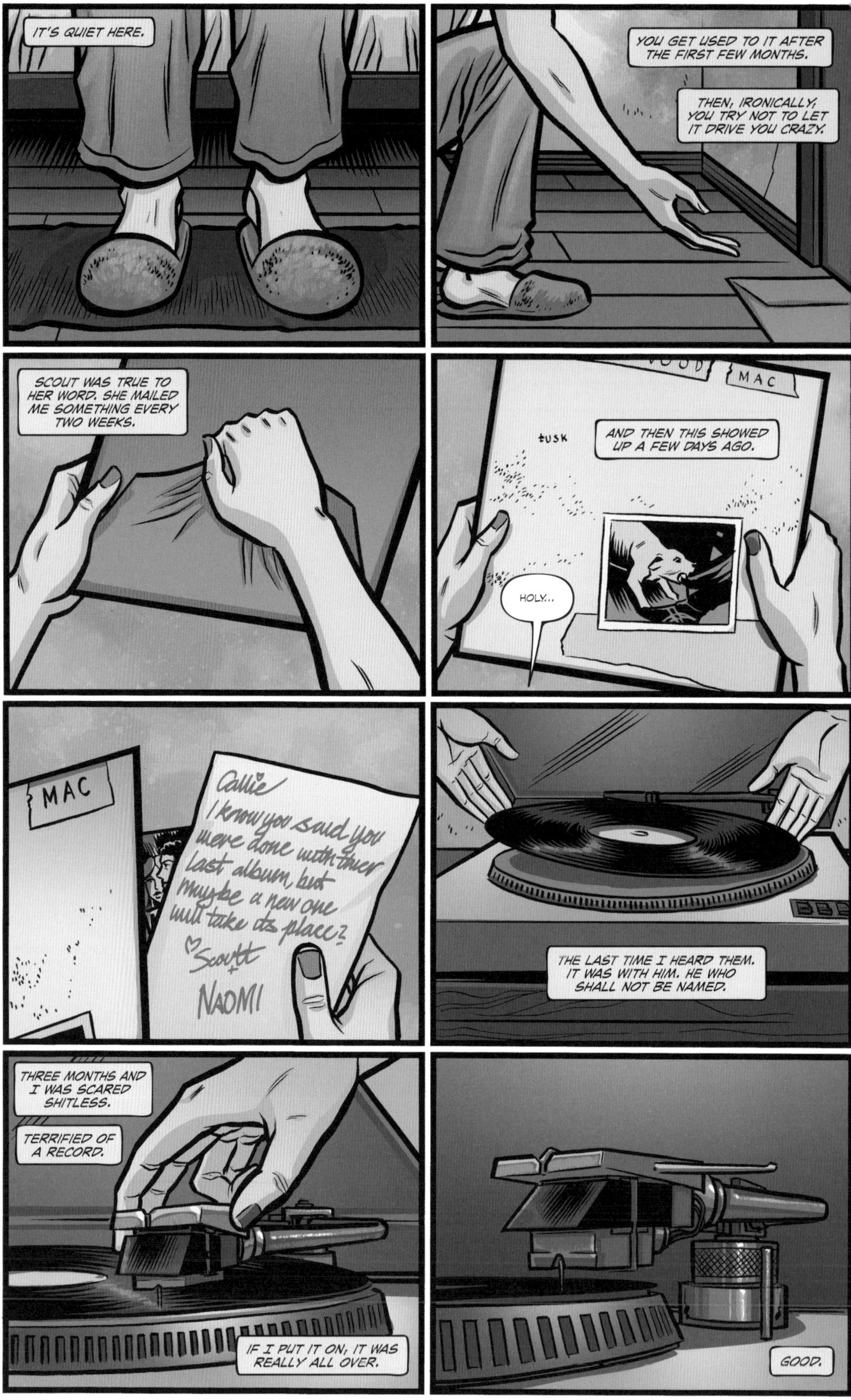
IT'S QUIET HERE.
YOU GET USED TO IT AFTER THE FIRST FEW MONTHS.
THEN, IRONICALLY, YOU TRY NOT TO LET IT DRIVE YOU CRAZY.
SCOUT WAS TRUE TO HER WORD. SHE MAILED ME SOMETHING EVERY TWO WEEKS.
MAC
TUSK
AND THEN THIS SHOWED UP A FEW DAYS AGO.
HOLY...
MAC
Callie
I know you said you were done with their last album, but maybe a new one will take its place?
Scout
+
NAOMI
THE LAST TIME I HEARD THEM. IT WAS WITH HIM. HE WHO SHALL NOT BE NAMED.
THREE MONTHS AND I WAS SCARED SHITLESS.
TERRIFIED OF A RECORD.
IF I PUT IT ON, IT WAS REALLY ALL OVER.
GOOD.

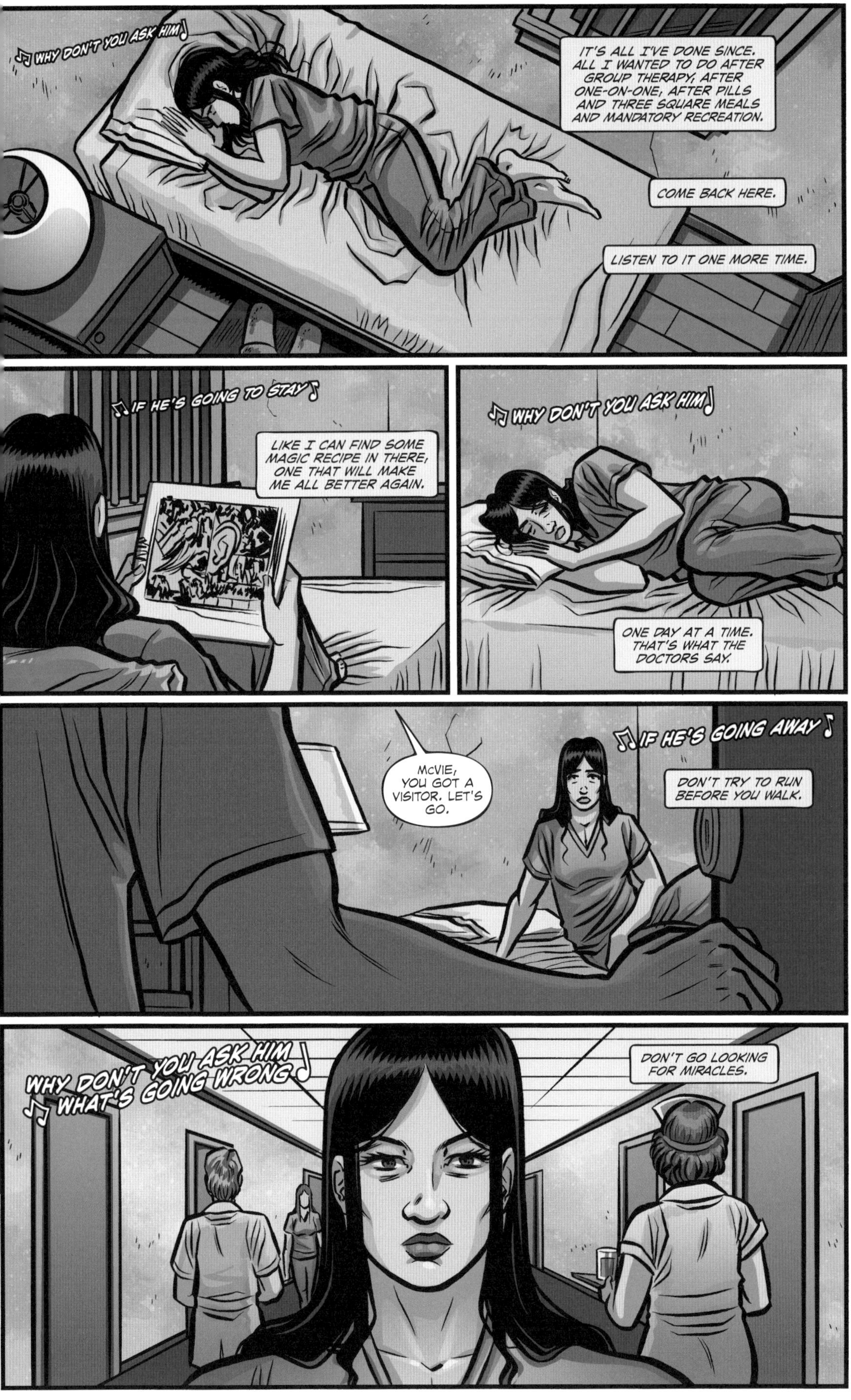
♫ WHY DON'T YOU ASK HIM ♪
IT'S ALL I'VE DONE SINCE. ALL I WANTED TO DO AFTER GROUP THERAPY, AFTER ONE-ON-ONE; AFTER PILLS AND THREE SQUARE MEALS AND MANDATORY RECREATION.
COME BACK HERE.
LISTEN TO IT ONE MORE TIME.
♫ IF HE'S GOING TO STAY ♪
LIKE I CAN FIND SOME MAGIC RECIPE IN THERE, ONE THAT WILL MAKE ME ALL BETTER AGAIN.
♫ WHY DON'T YOU ASK HIM ♪
ONE DAY AT A TIME. THAT'S WHAT THE DOCTORS SAY.
McVIE, YOU GOT A VISITOR. LET'S GO.
♫ IF HE'S GOING AWAY ♪
DON'T TRY TO RUN BEFORE YOU WALK.
WHY DON'T YOU ASK HIM ♪
♫ WHAT'S GOING WRONG ♪
DON'T GO LOOKING FOR MIRACLES.

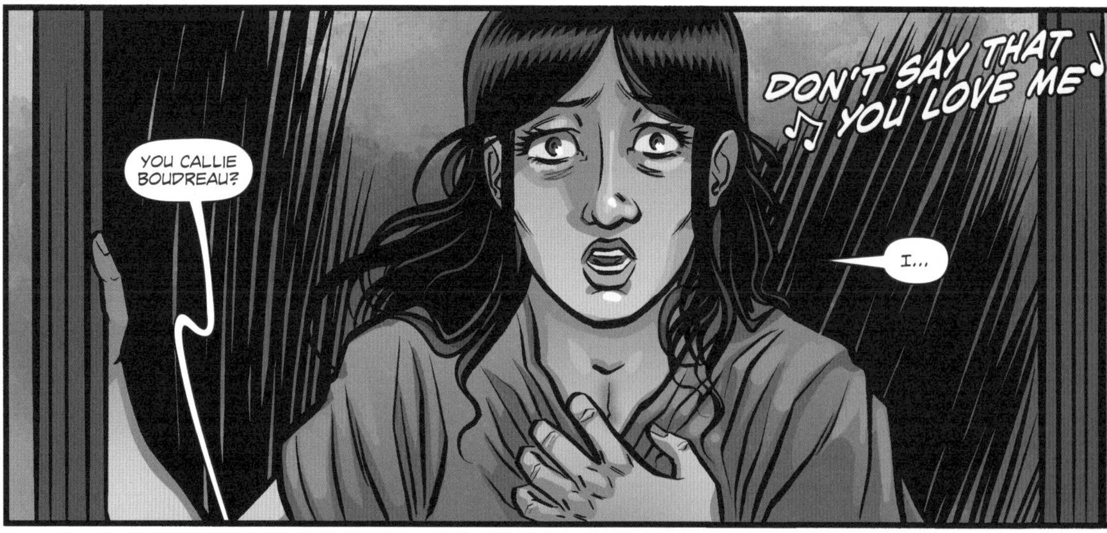
DON'T SAY THAT ♪ YOU LOVE ME ♫
YOU CALLIE BOUDREAU?
I...

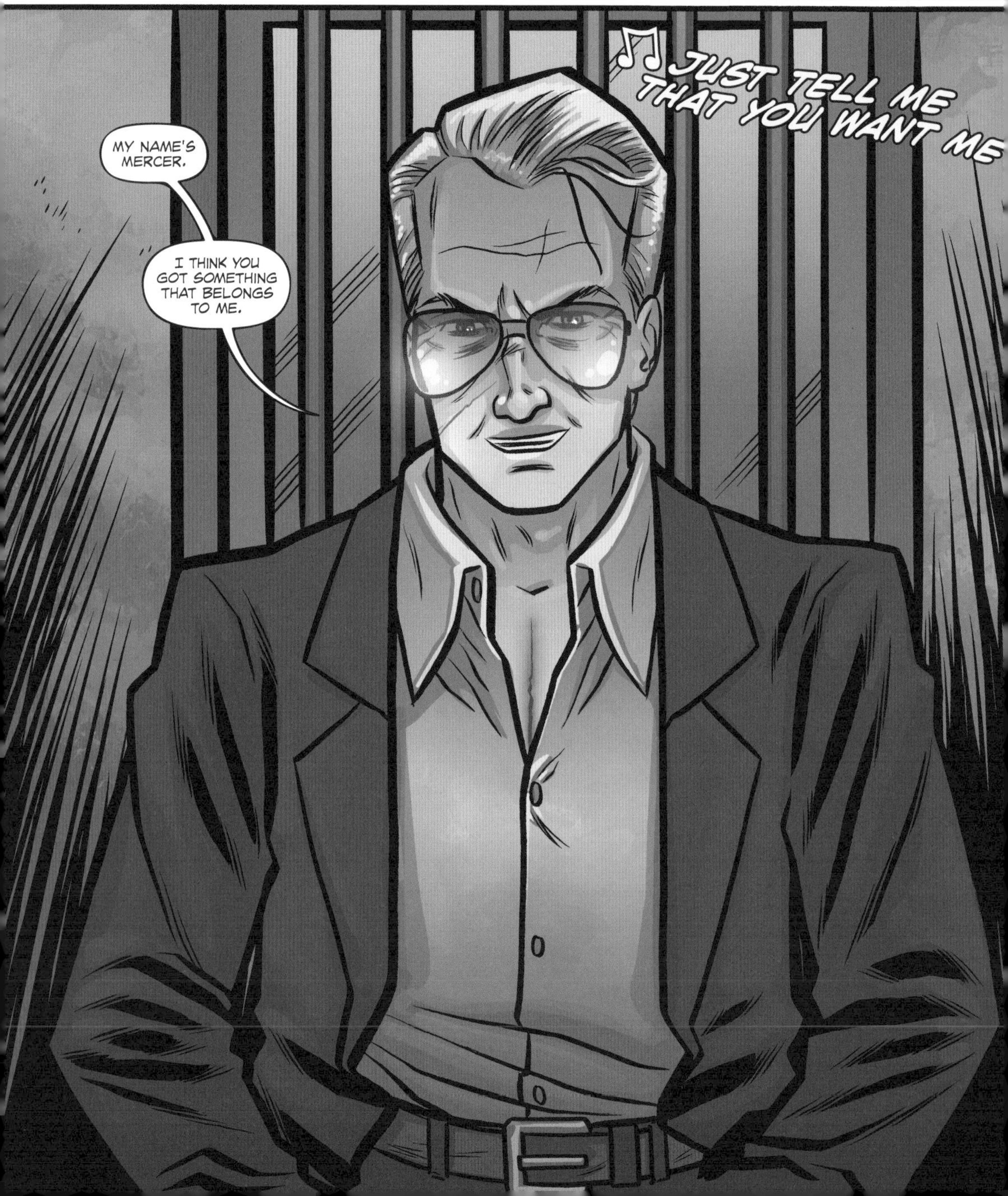
♫ JUST TELL ME THAT YOU WANT ME
MY NAME'S MERCER.
I THINK YOU GOT SOMETHING THAT BELONGS TO ME.

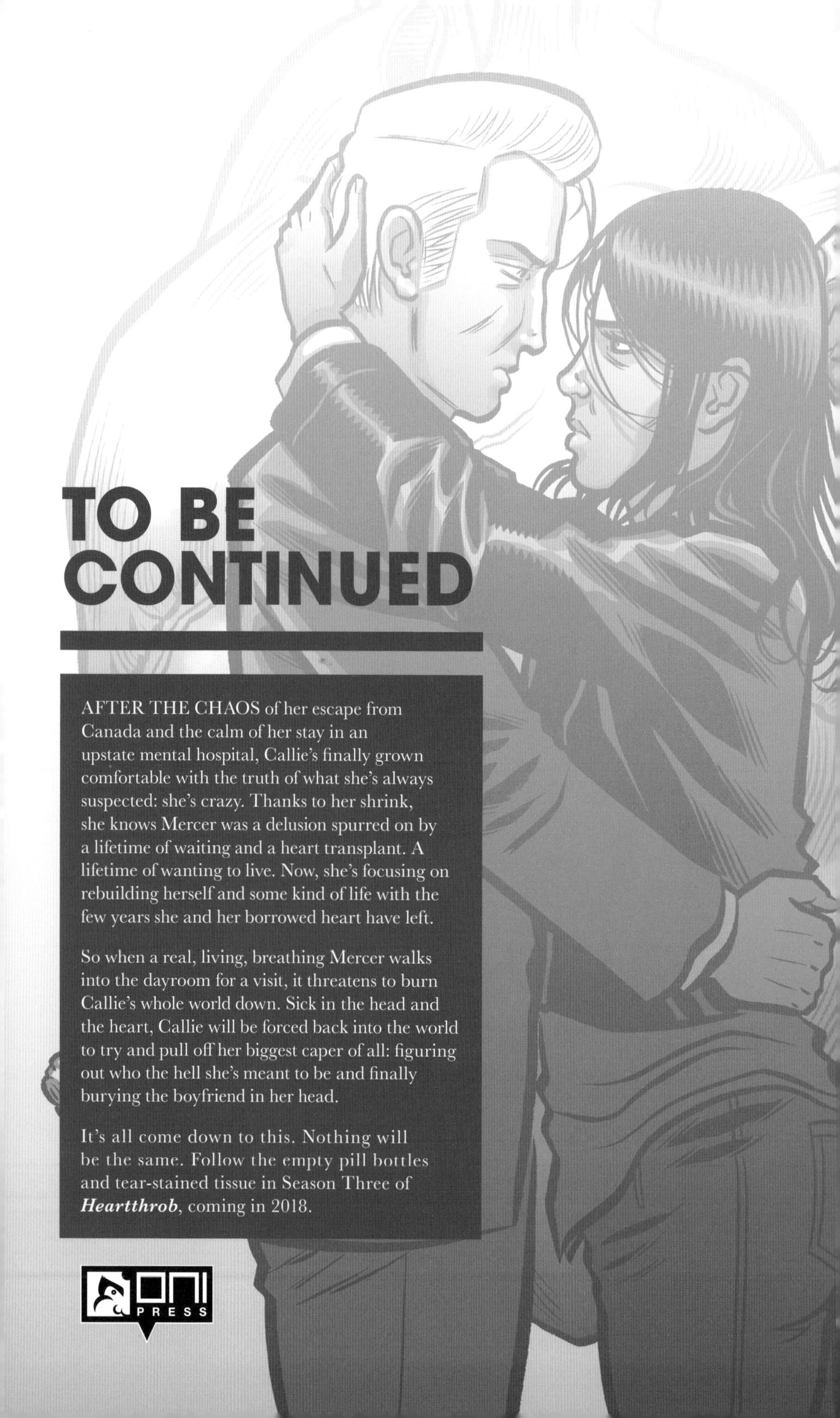

TO BE CONTINUED

AFTER THE CHAOS of her escape from Canada and the calm of her stay in an upstate mental hospital, Callie's finally grown comfortable with the truth of what she's always suspected: she's crazy. Thanks to her shrink, she knows Mercer was a delusion spurred on by a lifetime of waiting and a heart transplant. A lifetime of wanting to live. Now, she's focusing on rebuilding herself and some kind of life with the few years she and her borrowed heart have left.

So when a real, living, breathing Mercer walks into the dayroom for a visit, it threatens to burn Callie's whole world down. Sick in the head and the heart, Callie will be forced back into the world to try and pull off her biggest caper of all: figuring out who the hell she's meant to be and finally burying the boyfriend in her head.

It's all come down to this. Nothing will be the same. Follow the empty pill bottles and tear-stained tissue in Season Three of ***Heartthrob***, coming in 2018.

ONI PRESS

ABOUT THE CREATORS

WRITTEN BY
CHRISTOPHER SEBELA

Christopher Sebela is a two-time Eisner-losing writer living in Portland, Oregon. He's written original works like *High Crimes*, *We(l)come Back* and *Dead Letters* as well as books like *Escape From New York* and *Captain Marvel*. When he gets a dog, he's going to name it Tusk.

> christophersebela.com / @xtop

ILLUSTRATED BY
ROBERT WILSON IV

Robert Wilson IV is a comic artist and illustrator living in Dallas, TX. He is the artist and co-creator of *Knuckleheads* and *Like A Virus* as well as the artist for *Bitch Planet* #3. He is active in the poster community making tour and concert posters for bands such as The Mountain Goats, Ray LaMontagne, and The Sword. He already has a dog, though its name does not reference Fleetwood Mac.

> robertwilsoniv.com / @robertwilsoniv

COLORED BY
NICK FILARDI

Nick Filardi has colored for just about every major comic book publisher including DC, Marvel, Image and Dark Horse. He's currently also coloring *Cave Carson has a Cybernetic Eye* and *The Realm*. When he isn't buried in pages, you can find his digital likeness pulling up other artists with tips and tricks at twitch.tv/nickfil, making dad jokes at twitter.com/nickfil, and just spreading dope art at instagram.com/nick_filardi. He lives in Florida with his 3-legged dog and lovely fiancée.

> nickfilardi.tumblr.com / @nickfil

LETTERED BY
CRANK!

Hi! I go by crank! You might know my work from several recent Oni books like *The Sixth Gun*, *Brides of Helheim*, *Terrible Lizard*, *Rick and Morty*, etc. Maybe you've seen my letters in *Revival*, *HACK/slash*, *Spread*, or *God Hates Astronauts* (Image). Perhaps you've read *Lady Killer*, *Ghost Fleet*, or *Sundowners* (Dark Horse). Heck, you might even be reading the award-winning *Battlepug* (battlepug.com) right now! If you're weird you could have heard me online at crankcast.net where I talk with Mike Norton, Tim Seeley, Sean Dove and Jenny Frison weekly about things that are sometimes comics related. If you're super-obscure you've heard me play music with the Vladimirs or Sono Morti (sonomorti.bandcamp.com). Probably you don't know who I am at all. That's OK.

> @ccrank

DESIGNED BY
DYLAN TODD

Dylan Todd is a writer, art director and graphic designer. When he's not reading comics, making comics, writing about comics or designing stuff for comics, he can probably be found thinking about comics. He's the editor of the *2299* sci-fi comics anthology and, alongside Mathew Digges, is the co-creator of *The Creep Crew*, a comic about undead teen detectives.

> bigredrobot.net / @bigredrobot

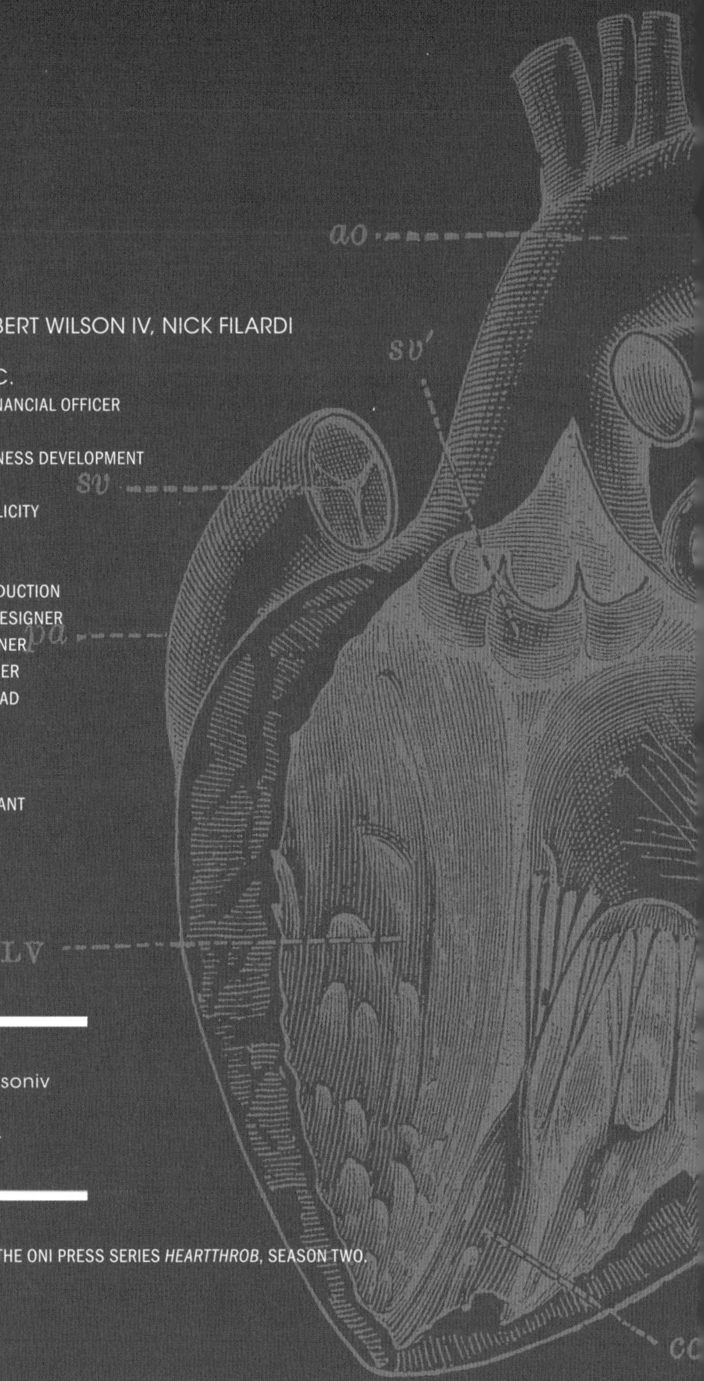
ao
sv'
sv
pa
LV
cc

HEARTTHROB

BY CHRISTOPHER SEBELA, ROBERT WILSON IV, NICK FILARDI

PUBLISHED BY ONI PRESS, INC.
Joe Nozemack FOUNDER & CHIEF FINANCIAL OFFICER
James Lucas Jones PUBLISHER
Charlie Chu V.P. OF CREATIVE & BUSINESS DEVELOPMENT
Brad Rooks DIRECTOR OF OPERATIONS
Melissa Meszaros DIRECTOR OF PUBLICITY
Margot Wood DIRECTOR OF SALES
Rachel Reed MARKETING MANAGER
Troy Look DIRECTOR OF DESIGN & PRODUCTION
Hilary Thompson SENIOR GRAPHIC DESIGNER
Kate Z. Stone JUNIOR GRAPHIC DESIGNER
Sonja Synak JUNIOR GRAPHIC DESIGNER
Angie Knowles DIGITAL PREPRESS LEAD
Ari Yarwood EXECUTIVE EDITOR
Robin Herrera SENIOR EDITOR
Desiree Wilson ASSOCIATE EDITOR
Alissa Sallah ADMINISTRATIVE ASSISTANT
Jung Lee LOGISTICS ASSOCIATE

onipress.com
facebook.com/onipress
twitter.com/onipress
onipress.tumblr.com
instagram.com/onipress

christophersebela.com / @xtop
robertwilsoniv.com / @robertwilsoniv
nickfilardi.tumblr.com / @nickfil
bigredrobot.net / @bigredrobot
@ccrank

THIS VOLUME COLLECTS ISSUES #1-5 OF THE ONI PRESS SERIES *HEARTTHROB*, SEASON TWO.

FIRST EDITION: JULY 2018

ISBN 978-1-62010-515-3
EISBN 978-1-62010-516-0

LIBRARY OF CONGRESS CONTROL NUMBER: 2016903942

1 3 5 7 9 10 8 6 4 2

PRINTED IN CHINA.

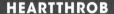